Cultural Production of Hallyu in the Digital Platform Era

Cultural Production of Hallyu in the Digital Platform Era

Industry Perspectives

Dal Yong Jin

UNIVERSITY OF MICHIGAN PRESS

Ann Arbor

Published in the United States of America by the
University of Michigan Press
First published August 2025

A CIP catalog record for this book is available from the British Library.

Library of Congress Cataloging-in-Publication data has been applied for.

ISBN 978-0-472-07756-4 (hardcover : alk. paper)
ISBN 978-0-472-05756-6 (paper : alk. paper)
ISBN 978-0-472-90512-6 (open access ebook)

DOI: https://doi.org/10.3998/mpub.14416305

The open-access publication of this book was supported by The Eugene B. Power Fund.

The University of Michigan Press's open access publishing program is made possible thanks to additional funding from the University of Michigan Office of the Provost and the generous support of contributing libraries.

Cover image: iStock.com / HoodieHoony

Authorized Representative: Easy Access System Europe, Mustamäe tee 50, 10621 Tallinn, Estonia, gpsr.requests@easproject.com

Contents

Digital materials related to this title can be found on the Fulcrum platform via the following citable URL: https://doi.org/10.3998/mpub.14416305

List of Tables

List of Figures

List of Figures

Preface

With the recent surge of Korean popular culture in the global cultural markets, many scholars in various fields, such as communication, sociology, film studies, Asian studies, political science, and anthropology, are interested in how Korea has advanced its cultural power. Several cultural forms, such as dramas, films, K-pop, digital games, and webtoons, are well-received in many parts of the globe, and *Squid Game*, *Parasite*, and BTS have become globally popular. The cultural wave of Hallyu illustrates how local cultural content and its production strategies have effectively been integrated with the ongoing transformation of global media environments.

In the early 21st century, cultural production in the Korean context has rapidly changed due to the advent of digital platforms, which asks scholars, students, policymakers, and industry personnel to contemplate the ways in which this new trend has shifted the major characteristics of local and/or global cultural production. The Korean Wave has been integrated into emerging media environments, and major digital platforms deeply shape the ways culture is produced and circulated. Therefore, it is essential to explore how digital platforms, including OTT (over-the-top) service platforms (e.g., Netflix) and social media platforms (e.g., YouTube), reshape Korean cultural industries and texts and their global audiences.

Given the increasing significance of digital platforms in shaping the recent phase of Korean media and culture production in the global context, comprehensive studies of the platformization of Hallyu are urgently needed. It is especially crucial to advance people's understanding of Korean popular culture and digital technologies related to digital platforms through an integrative and interdisciplinary approach. People need to understand the cultural production, circulation, and consumption of Korean media and culture in the digital platform-driven environment. By addressing the digitalization of Korean media and culture through platforms—a research area that remains under-examined in Korean studies—

the book explores how digital platforms, including OTT service platforms and social media platforms, reshape Korean cultural industries and texts and the reception of global audiences.

This book attempts to advance Korean studies through an integrative and interdisciplinary approach to Korean media and culture. It holistically explores the complex process of digital platformization of Korean media and culture, which informs the cultural production of Hallyu by analyzing industries, texts, and audiences. This book explores a new research area of Korean studies and Hallyu studies—the platformization of Korean media and culture, especially concerning industries, texts, and audiences. It aims to examine how digital platformization has reshaped the production, circulation, and consumption of Korean media and culture.

This book is part of the global lab project that the Academy of Korean Studies supports. I would like to express my sincere gratitude to the people who have worked hard to bring the project, including Professor Kyong Yoon at the University of British Columbia at Okanagan and Professor Benjamin Han at the University of Georgia. While this book analyzes cultural production from the industry perspective, these two scholars focus on texts and audiences, and these three book projects work together to provide comprehensive and systematic analyses of the Korean Wave phenomenon. It has always been grateful to have these wonderful colleagues who are academic friends to make our journey enjoyable and meaningful.

Finally, I want to acknowledge that this work was supported by the Laboratory Program for Korean Studies of the Ministry of Education of the Republic of Korea and the Korean Studies Promotion Service at the Academy of Korean Studies (AKS-2022-LAB-2230004). In addition, I want to acknowledge that there are three previously published journal articles for this book. The first one is "Critical Cultural Industries Studies: A New Approach to the Korean Wave in the Netflix Era." *International Journal of Communication* 17: 6896–6914. The second one is "Platformization of the Korean Wave: a critical perspective." *Communication Research and Practice*, 9(4), 408–427. And the third one is "Netflix's Effects on the Korean Wave: power relations between local cultural industries and global OTT platforms." *Asian Journal of Communication*, 33(5), 452–469. They have been updated and reinterpreted from the original versions.

1

Introduction

Korea has become one of the major forces in the realm of popular culture and digital culture over the past several decades. Starting in the early 1990s, Korea has developed its cultural industries and various popular cultures, and the country's cultural content has become globally popular. In the early stage of the Korean Wave (*Hallyu* in Korean), only a few East Asian countries, such as China, Japan, Singapore, and Taiwan, received and enjoyed Korean popular culture. However, in the early 2020s, many countries in both the Global North and the Global South enjoyed a multitude of Korean cultural products, including drama (e.g., *Squid Game 1*, 2021, *Squid Game 2*, 2024, and *Squid Game 3*, 2025), reality shows (e.g., *Culinary Class Wars*, 2024), film (Bong Joon-ho's *Parasite*, 2019), K-pop (e.g., Blackpink's Rosé's and Bruno Mars' *APT*, 2024), and webtoons and webtoon-based dramas and films (e.g., *Jeongnyeon: The Star Is Born*, 2024). Korea has also advanced various digital technologies and cultures, such as digital gaming and esports. The surge of digital technologies has become significant because they are parts of digital Hallyu and media convergence between popular culture and digital technologies.

Korea was the 10th largest economy in the world in the early 2020s, and Korea has also become a cultural powerhouse with the 7th largest cultural economy in terms of market share in the global cultural industries (PricewaterhouseCoopers, 2023). In February 2023, the Ministry of Culture, Sports and Tourism stated that Korea planned to become one of the world's top four cultural powers by boosting its content exports, such as television dramas and pop music. It set out a goal to achieve US$25 billion in cultural content exports by 2027. By entering the world's top four countries with the most cultural influence after the U.S., China, and Japan, the Korean government expects that the Korean cultural industries will have a positive influence on the national brand image and exports of other related industries (Kwak, 2023), meaning the Korean government attempts to utilize the Korean Wave as a source of soft power.

Due to the recent surge of Korean popular culture in the global cultural markets, numerous global media outlets and media scholars call the Korean Wave—referring to the rapid growth of local cultural industries and the popularity of cultural products in the global cultural markets—a miracle. As Irina Lyan (2023) points out, many global audiences designated the recent growth of Korean popular culture in the global scene as a cultural miracle, comparable to the country's economic miracle in the 1970s and 1980s. Jungsoo Kim (2016) also claimed that Hallyu became another miracle on the Han River in Seoul.[1] *Jakarta Globe*, an Indonesian newspaper, referred to Hallyu as "the revolution of 0.7%" since it was a miracle performed by Koreans who made up only 0.7% of the global population (Sim, 2016). When American President Obama visited Korea in 2012, he already seemed to have caught the Korean Wave. The term Hallyu in Korean popped up in the president's speech at the Hankuk University of Foreign Studies. "It's no wonder so many people around the world have caught the Korean Wave—hallyu," Obama stated (Hennessey, 2012).

In the global cultural markets, the Korean Wave is unique as it symbolizes the growth of non-Western culture. Although a few countries in the Global South developed their global penetration with popular culture, the process was mainly limited to a certain type of popular culture, such as Telenovelas in Mexico and Brazil, films in Hong Kong and India, and anime in Japan. These countries have also advanced a limited number of cultural forms in the global cultural markets. For example, Japanese anime has been globally popular; however, its television dramas and popular music (J-pop) were limited in their popularity to a few Asian countries instead of the global markets. Therefore, the Korean Wave has been arguably, and perhaps unequivocally, the first true non-Western cultural force, as Korea develops a variety of cultural content, including dramas, films, K-pop, digital games, and webtoons, to become globally popular beyond the regional boundary.

Due to the recent growth of its economic, technological, and cultural power, Korea can be categorized as the Global North, although it is

---

1. The Miracle on the Han River refers to the rapid economic growth in Korea, in which Korea transformed one of the poorest countries in the world at the end of the Korean War (1950–1953) into a strong economy comparable to that of a few Western European countries (OECD, 2021).

located in Asia. Unlike other terms like the West-East binary and the Third World, the notion of the Global South is relatively flexible, and it allows us to categorize Korea, "not only as the Global South but also as the Global North-in-South, if not the Global North" (Jin, 2022, p. 12). However, it is vital to consider that the idea of the Global South seeks to draw links across nations that "share a history of exclusion and oppression but also to highlight ways in which those histories are not necessarily confined to specific geographical boundaries" (Hofmeyr, 2007; Levander and Mignolo,2011; Prashad, 2014, cited in Iqani and Resende, 2019, p. 2). The Global South is also "the location where new visions of the future are emerging and where the global political and decolonial society is at work" (Levander and Mignolo, 2011, p. 3), which is not pessimistic in using the term the Global South. Therefore, it is not dicey to include Korea in the Global South, although it has overcome the Southern conditions in economy and technology. It is crucial to understand that the notion of the Global South and the Global North is not static; however, it is also important to acknowledge the significance of the historical and socio-cultural milieu surrounding popular culture and the Korean Wave.

The global acceptance of Korean cultural content, both in terms of popular and digital cultures, did not come all at once. In the early stage of the phenomenon, various dramas and films played a pivotal role, and in the middle stage, starting in the late 2000s, K-pop and digital culture became leading players. Since Bong Joon-ho's *Parasite* (2019) earned four Oscars in 2000, several cultural programs, such as *Minari* (2020) and *Past Lives* (2023)—directed by Korean American filmmakers—were also nominated in a few cultural festivals and earned several prestigious awards. Although they were not created in Korea, these recent achievements have certainly proven the growth of Korean popular culture and influence in the global cultural sphere.

Most of all, since the late 2010s, Korean cultural content has been globally popular due to the increasing role of digital platforms, both OTT (over-the-top, e.g., Netflix) and social media (e.g., YouTube) platforms. Here, OTT is a streaming platform that delivers audio-visual content through the Internet instead of using cable or network television channels (Amazon, n.d.), and it has substituted traditional broadcasting television channels and movie theaters. As can be seen in the cases of *Kingdom* (series, 2019), *Squid Game* (series, 2021), *The Glory* (series, 2022–2023), *Physical: 100* (reality show, 2023), *Jung_E* (movie, 2023), and *Culinary Class Wars* (reality show, 2024), Netflix has become a global producer and distributor of Korean cultural products, and therefore, many Korean cultural programs can be distributed simultaneously.

Because of the recent growth of digital platforms in the Korean Wave tradition, a few media scholars and agencies even call this "Platform Hallyu" (Korean Foundation for International Cultural Exchange, KOFICE, 2023). During the Korean Society for Journalism & Communication Studies conference held in Seoul, Korea, in October 2023, two papers (K. C. Kim, 2023; S. M. Lee, 2023) talked about the notion of Platform Hallyu by emphasizing the increasing role of platforms in the Korean Wave phenomenon. While their approaches provided different perspectives, both urged media scholars to map out the comprehensive studies of the platformization of Hallyu, given the increasing significance of digital platforms in shaping the recent phase of Korean cultural production in the global context, known as the Korean Wave.

Media studies and Korean studies, and more specifically Hallyu studies, have only partially addressed the complex processes of the platformization of Korean culture in the global mediascape, let alone the systematic studies of cultural production from industry perspectives. Therefore, the platformization of Korea's cultural production, referring to the process through which digital platforms shape the creation, circulation, and consumption of cultural content, has remained a blind spot in Korean studies and Hallyu studies. It is premature to claim that the contemporary Korean Wave is synonymous with the concept of Platform Hallyu; however, it is not dicey to argue that we are witnessing a platformized Hallyu phenomenon and that the Korean Wave and digital platforms are riding each other. Digital platforms have continued to expand their roles in cultural production, not only the circulation of cultural production, but also the production of cultural content, while Korean cultural creators heavily rely on digital platforms in both production and consumption.

This book investigates the cultural production of Korean media and culture in the digital platform-driven environment. The Korean Wave has been integrated into emerging media environments, and major digital platforms deeply shape the ways culture is produced and circulated. By addressing the digitalization of Korean popular culture[2] through platforms—a research area that remains under-examined—the book attempts to provide an understanding of how digital platforms reshape

2. In this book, the digitalization of popular culture implies the increasing role of digital platforms, both social media platforms and OTT platforms, in the entire process of cultural production, such as production, distribution, and consumption.

Korea's cultural industries. The book holistically addresses the complex process of digital platformization of Korean media and culture, which informs the cultural production of Hallyu. As the proliferation of digital platforms has seemingly enabled counter-flows of popular culture from different national markets, including Korea, this book on the relationship between Korean popular culture and digital platforms critically situates Korea at the center of global media scholarship, while decolonizing the West-East binary.

More specifically, it focuses on the cultural industries, which are some of the most significant areas of the platformization of the Korean Wave at global and local levels. This book explores how histories, industry structures, and politics interact in the platformization of the Korean Wave, although it does not exclude cultural texts—the ways in which platforms have facilitated the production of diverse and creative media genres using cultural diversity and tourism—and audiences—how the platformization of Hallyu has generated a user-driven participatory culture among global audiences. In other words, the book maps out the interplay of global and local cultural industries and their influence on cultural texts in cultural content like films and dramas in the digital platform era, which involves the extensive platformization of media environments. Addressing the increasing significance of digital platforms, it analyzes the transformative roles of digital platforms, which include OTT service platforms (e.g., Netflix, Viki, and V Live), video-sharing platforms (e.g., YouTube), and interactive social media platforms (e.g., TikTok and Instagram), in conjunction with the globalization of Korean media and culture.[3]

Furthermore, the book analyzes the complex processes of the transformation of Korean cultural industries by examining power relations between different stakeholders, including content producers, information technology sectors, the government, cultural intermediaries (e.g., distributors and critics), creative laborers, and audience groups, as well as between Korea-made platforms as part of the non-Western region and a few mega global platforms located in a handful of Western countries. It examines the development of supporting systems regarding the digital platformization of Hallyu, such as IP (intellectual property) policies and the expanding NFT (non-fungible token) market. In response to the

3. While these platforms are mainly created by American entrepreneurs, their major scopes are different. Social media platforms are mostly free, other than premium services, to share their own texts and videos, and therefore, the users share their feelings and emotions; however, OTT platforms are primarily controlled by platform owners as the customers cannot upload their own texts and images.

accelerated platformization of cultural production, Hallyu industries have called for a systematic infrastructure, including the intensification of IP rights for creators, and have been critical of global platforms' increasing control over local content (Jin, 2021a).

As Bouquillion, Ithurbide, and Mattelart (2024, p. 1) astutely discuss, "there is a paradox inherent in the emerging research field of digital platforms. Most major global digital platforms have more users in the Global South than in the Global North. . . . Yet the issues raised by digital platforms are usually studied from the perspective of North American or West European experiences, and much less frequently from the perspectives of the countries comprising the Global South." Therefore, the current research as the case study of the Korean Wave and local cultural production concerning the ever-increasing digital platforms will shed light on our current discussions on cultural industries, digital platforms, and media studies. This book is expected to advance Korean studies, cultural studies, and media studies through an integrative and interdisciplinary approach to Korean media and culture, which attracts many global scholars in the fields of Korean studies, Asian studies, media studies, sociology, cultural policy studies, and anthropology.

Theoretical Approaches: The Nexus of Cultural Production and Platformization

Korean popular culture has become globally widespread as exemplified by the continued success of various cultural genres such as dramas, films, K-pop, digital games, and webtoons. Korea has advanced its export of various cultural products in the past three decades, from US$188.9 million in 1998 to $11.6 billion in 2022 (Ministry of Culture and Tourism, 2006; Ministry of Culture, Sports and Tourism, 2022; Korea Creative Content Agency, 2023).[4] This global circulation of Korean cultural content signals unique and significant ways in which a once peripheral, local cultural form evolves as a new wave of a global cultural trend.

Hallyu vividly illustrates how local cultural content and its production strategies have effectively been integrated with the ongoing transformation of global cultural environments, which has been driven by major digital platforms. Different types of digital platforms—especially

---

4. This data includes the broadcasting, film, animation, character, music, manhwa, and game sectors.

subscription-based platforms, video-streaming, and social media platforms—have redefined local cultural production and global circulation of local content. The platformization of cultural production has markedly influenced the Korean cultural industries and their content. Digital platforms have made a significant impact on the global cultural landscape in the 21st century and, more recently, during the COVID-19 and the post-pandemic eras. In order to understand the growth of the Korean Wave, one may need to understand two different theoretical perspectives which are connected—cultural production and platformization—in the digital platform era.

To begin with, the discourse of cultural production, which goes back to the 1970s, has been mainly established in national contexts in a few Western countries, such as the United States, the United Kingdom, and Canada. There are two major approaches to cultural production. One is derived "from sociology, especially cultural sociology and organizational sociology in their U.S. versions," and the other approach, known as the political economy of culture approach, is derived "primarily from critical and Marxian versions of social science in Europe" (Hesmondhalgh & Saha, 2013, p. 181). As discussed elsewhere, the political economy of media and culture examines the power relationship in cultural production between cultural industries corporations and governments (Flew, 2012b; Yoon & Kang, 2017), while cultural studies researchers also argue for attention to everyday or ordinary production practices and focus on the cultural practices, beliefs, and discourses of media producers (Caldwell, 2008) (see also chapter 2). "Due to the evolution of cultural production in different fields at the same time, scholars have offered different approaches and ideas" (Jin, 2021b, p. 1812).

Regardless of its origin and direction, cultural production is used "as a shorthand term to refer to industrialized or semi-industrialized symbol making and circulation in modern societies" (Hesmondhalgh & Saha, 2013, p. 181). The notion of cultural production has changed. As cultural production used to "emphasize the creation of cultural meaning, various elements have been deeply involved in the production of culture" (Jin, 2021b, p. 1813). Bourdieu (1983; 1993) especially pointed out that the field of cultural production situates artistic works within the social conditions of their production, circulation, and consumption. He emphasized that people needed to examine not only cultural creators (e.g., writers and producers) but also cultural institutions involved in making cultural products what they are. In other words, he always emphasized the significance of the analysis of the structure of the cultural field itself as well as its position within the broader social structures of power. Peterson and Anand (2004) later argued that there were mainly six areas that were closely combined to produce cultural content, namely technology, laws and regulations, industry structure, organizational structure, occupational careers, and the market.

However, these previous discourses mainly focused on human actors and did not emphasize the advent of digital platforms as major players. As Hutchinson (2023) points out, "cultural production relies on visibility processes by intermediaries to highlight its significance through artefacts that capture, contribute towards, extend conversations about and describe the societies in which we live. While this process has typically been undertaken by human cultural intermediaries" (Bourdieu, 1983; Hutchinson, 2017, cited in Hutchinson, 2023, pp. 3289–3290),

> the contemporary media environment increasingly relies on technological and non-human intermediaries to create and make these digital objects visible. These mechanical, predetermined and automated processes are those that systematically sort, add value and make visible the sorts of content that contain information about the world around us, which is a process many media consumers have lost control over. This environment underpins the processes of digital intermediation, which combines technologies, agencies (e.g. institutions) and automation to amplify the value of cultural production through increased exposure to that information: an automated media production and consumption process (Hutchinson, 2023, p. 3290).

In our contemporary world, cultural production thus implies "the social processes involved in the generation and circulation of cultural forms, practices, values, and shared understandings," as well as "the work of the culture industry" (Oxford Reference, 2019).

While these studies certainly emphasize the recent trend in cultural production, their emphasis does not reflect the growth of digital platforms, which is crucial in cultural production in the 21st century.

Therefore, this book challenges these previous approaches in that digital platforms are working as mediators rather than simply intermediaries. As Gillespie (2010, p. 348) points out, "intermediaries like YouTube and Google, those companies that provide storage, navigation and delivery of the digital content of others, are working to establish a long-term position in a fluctuating economic and cultural terrain." However, as Gillespie

(2018) himself admitted later, the platform is not a neutral entity in the shaping of the creation of content.[5] This book does not consider digital platforms as intermediaries but as mediators (see van Dijck, 2013) that control, manage, and manipulate the entire process of cultural production based on their massive technological and circulation power.

The notion of platformization concerning cultural production certainly proves why we have to study digital platforms in cultural production. Platformization refers to the "rise of the platform as the dominant infrastructural and economic model of the social web," affecting our society through structural changes and new business models (Helmond, 2015, p. 1). Nieborg and Poell (2018, p. 4276) articulate platformization as "the penetration of economic, governmental, and infrastructural extensions of digital platforms into the web and app ecosystems." As an increasingly influential form of digital platforms, OTT corporations have expedited platformization, which reshapes cultural production and consumption processes. OTT platforms mostly began as content distributors as the case of Netflix proves; however, they have now become some of the primary cultural producers as well. As they produce cultural programs, they simply use their platforms as distribution channels, which means that OTT platforms are "central to the production, distribution, and monetization of cultural content," and "the growing dominance of platform corporations over the cultural domain makes [them] vital" in the entire process of cultural production (Poell, 2020, p. 650). This is why we need to use the term mediators instead of intermediaries in conjunction with the role of digital platforms.

What is important is that OTT platforms are technically participating in vertical integration, where they are increasingly controlling the production, distribution, and exhibition of their exclusive content. Vertical integration is "a business strategy where the business itself controls the supply chain and multiple stages of its production process, thus eliminating or reducing third-party vendor dependencies" (Messina, 2022). For example, in the film industry, corporate mergers and acquisitions between distribu-

5. Gillespie (2018, 40) argues that "social media platforms *are* intermediaries, in the sense that they mediate between users who speak and users who might want to hear them, or speak back." However, platforms have grown "larger, more visible, more global, and more commercial," and social media platforms themselves "multiply in form and purpose, become more and more central to how and where users encounter one another online, and involve themselves in the circulation not just of words and images but of goods, money, services, and labor," therefore, it is not adequate to interpret digital platforms as simple intermediaries.

tion and production firms can be categorized as vertical integration, as one company now controls both the distribution and production of content. In the realm of digital platforms, Netflix began mainly as a distributor but now manages production as well, partially via subcontracting local cultural production companies.

OTT service platforms have also invested in artificial intelligence (AI), algorithms, and big data, which are crucial parts of cultural production. Therefore, they have advanced the convergence of popular culture and digital technologies. Traditional cultural industry corporations advance their use of AI technologies; however, OTT platforms have advantages due to their increasing numbers of subscribers. Digital platforms can easily gather user data and appropriate them to advance their business models in cultural production, not only for cultural consumption but also for the production of popular culture (Kim & Jin, 2024). OTT platforms can produce what customers want to watch based on data provided by subscribers. For example, if the majority of subscribers enjoy action or zombie genres, they create more action or zombie dramas or films to appeal to their tastes. They also use subscribers' watching habits based on watching time, ethnicity, gender, age, and location to expose relevant cultural programs to customers. OTT platforms utilize AI algorithms to recommend similar cultural programs to subscribers while producing original programs and licensing already-created programs. OTT platforms play a primary role in the entire chain of cultural production. They certainly appropriate users' consumption habits and utilize user data to advance their business models (Kim & Jin, 2024).

More specifically, as content distributors, producers, and viewing experience providers, global and local OTT service platforms have had significant impacts on cultural production and consumption. On the one hand, digital platforms have reshaped cultural distribution, and more importantly, production. Again, while digital platforms, both domestic and global, began as the distributors of cultural content, including television dramas and reality shows, they have recently increased their roles in the production of cultural content in addition to the distribution of cultural products (Bilton, 2017). Supported by global distribution channels, AI, algorithms, and big data, OTT platforms have tremendously increased their power as cultural producers as well as cultural distributors. Digital platforms are threatening to disrupt the existing order in the global cultural industries. "Their direct-to-consumer services via digital distribution demonstrate an alternative value chain that bypasses the traditional distribution route. By untethering themselves from the traditional structure of trade, such platforms cause the global [audiovisual] business community to be concerned that they may alter the need for the global [audiovisual] markets" (J. S. Choi, 2021, p. 202).

On the other hand, again, OTT platforms have shifted cultural consumption patterns as they expedite the growth of "cord-cutting"—a practice through which media consumers discontinue traditional media subscriptions, while moving on to streaming video content distributed via the Internet (Kim, Chan-Olmsted, Hwang, & Chang, 2021). With the advent of OTT platforms, Netflix and Disney+ have become primary players as cord-cutters. OTT service platforms have consequently played a pivotal role in shifting the cultural content viewing habits of consumers. Consumers can conveniently access content "through features such as watch-lists, locks, replay, resume, and content recommendations tailored to individual tastes and preferences" (Kwak, Oh, & Lee, 2021, p. 1). Cord-cutting has accelerated with the rapid growth of OTT platform subscribers worldwide. In July 2022, for the first time in the United States, streaming platforms took over both cable and broadcast networks as they accounted for 34.8% of viewership, compared to 34.4% in cable and 21.6% in broadcasting (Davis, 2022). The tendency of OTT platform-driven cord-cutting has been observed in many countries.

Meanwhile, OTT platforms act as mediators, controlling and even manipulating entire media systems through monopolistic power; they are not neutral intermediaries that work simply as depositories or conveyors of content in cultural production. In other words, OTT platforms are mediators as they wield their power to manage the entire process of cultural production (van Dijck, 2013). OTT platforms have significantly shifted business and cultural norms. Providing necessary tools and services for the distribution of cultural content, digital platforms become infrastructure at all stages of cultural production, including production, distribution, and consumption (Plantin & Punathambekar, 2019; Zhang, 2021).

The infrastructural control of platforms has reshaped the format of cultural products, such as genre, length, and style. Thus, as Park et al. (2023, p. 2425) noted, cultural producers become "increasingly platform-dependent and [this] shifts governance in the market." As discussed in the remainder of this chapter, the vibrant circulation of Korean Wave content through digital platforms vividly shows how local cultural production is exposed to, and adapted to, the global transformation of media environments driven by powerful digital platforms.

Cultural Production in the Korean Wave Tradition

In Korea, cultural production has been related to the growth of Hallyu. In the Korean Wave context, the platformization of cultural production and consumption has been exemplified by numerous recent cases of Korean content in the global mediascape—the worldwide success of *Squid Game 1* (2021) and *Jung_E* (2023) on Netflix and the global fandom of BTS on social media platforms like YouTube, for example. While the industrialization of cultural production has been noticeable, digital platforms have increasingly been playing crucial roles in the production, distribution, and consumption of Korean cultural content. OTT platforms like Netflix have especially moved from "primarily streaming previously released films and television series to producing original content" (Ferchaud & Proffitt, 2023, p. 2):

> The so-called "streaming era" of television did more than change the television industry; it changed the way people watch TV. No longer was television required to be a ritualized activity where family members gathered around the TV set at a given time to watch a program. Individual viewers could now watch the shows that interest them at the time and on a device (e.g., a television set, a mobile phone, or a computer) best suited for them. While this new technology on its own may not have created culture, it did allow for new cultural expressions. . . . This new era changed not only how people watched television but also what it meant to watch television. (Ferchaud & Proffitt, 2023, p. 3).

In response to the growing distribution and accessibility of Korean cultural content to global audiences on platforms, there is also a proliferation of Korean platforms such as Wavve and Tving, further illustrating global and local interaction. When one emphasizes cultural industries, therefore, the central concern should include digital platforms, cultural producers, cultural policymakers, and consumers who are offering "critical insight into the experiences of cultural creators who play a primary role in the process of cultural production, and therefore Hallyu, within a broader context of sociocultural milieus" (Jin, 2021b, p. 1814).

The recent phase of the Hallyu phenomenon in which digital platforms have played an instrumental role has been referred to as Hallyu 2.0 or the New Korean Wave (Lee & Nornes, 2015; Jin, 2016). This phase of Hallyu has been exponentially facilitated by major digital platforms and their affordances or media logic (van Dijck & Poell, 2013; Jin, Yoon, & Min, 2021). The process of digital platformization has been shifting the ways in which media and popular culture evolve in the global context (Burgess, 2021; Helmond, 2015), and Hallyu has emerged at the center of this transnational process. Digital platforms have changed cultural industries in various ways at different paces. The shift toward digital platforms is most pronounced in the music, film, and broadcasting industries, although their paces and scopes are dissimilar. Across cultural industries, global platforms such as Netflix, Disney+, Spotify, YouTube, and Amazon Prime have gained vital positions, challenging incumbent industry players—content creators, distributors, and national streaming providers—and their business models and practices (Cunningham & Silver, 2013; Lobato, 2019; Sundet & Colbjørnsen, 2021). "National players face the central dilemma of needing to harness the opportunities of streaming—and alleviating the unfortunate consequences—and to do so, they need to make sense of the developments taking place" (Sundet & Colbjørnsen, 2021, p. 13).

Analyzing the cultural production of Hallyu in the context of accelerated and extensive platformization will help effectively explain how the New Korean Wave has emerged, evolved, and will be transformed. The platformization of cultural production entails the extensive penetration of digital platforms into media and cultural environments and eventually reshapes the ways in which cultural content is produced and distributed; furthermore, the process results in the reshaping of the content itself (Poell, Nieborg, & Duffy, 2022). As a result, the production, circulation, and consumption of Korean media and culture can no longer be explained without considering the pervasive influence of major digital platforms, especially the unique affordance or logic of digital platforms.

Despite the frequent use of such terms as "digital Hallyu" (Y. Kim, 2013) and "social media age" (Lee & Nornes, 2015) in the literature on Hallyu, existing scholarship has insufficiently historicized and theorized the digital dimension of the Korean Wave. Therefore, the current literature of Hallyu addresses the instrumental role of digital media primarily by examining the efficient digitization of cultural content that accelerates transnational cultural flows. This partial and instrumental approach to digital media in recent research of Hallyu focuses narrowly on digital technology's contribution to accelerating the existing content. In so doing, the integrative process of digitalization of Korean media and culture remains under-examined.

The majority of studies on Hallyu have primarily addressed three areas—audiences, texts, and industries. As mainly discussed in chapter 2, strikingly, only a limited number of scholars seriously paid attention to the Korean Wave as a cultural or media industry, although the production of popular culture is closely related to the national cultural industries. In other words, scholars have not emphasized the characteristics of the media industries, although they are crucial parts of the Hallyu phenomenon. These studies have been examined separately with no emphasis on platformization; therefore, the proposed book explores the complex and historical ways that the Korean Wave was platformized in the early 21st century.

The current book engages in a structural analysis of the cultural production of Hallyu within the larger context of Korean cultural histories. By examining structural and agentic forces that affect the evolution and trajectory of Hallyu, the current book advances critical insights for understanding and analyzing Korean cultural production as a dynamic process that articulates different meanings and practices rather than as a static entity. This book critically investigates key issues of the digital platformization of Hallyu, such as institutional changes, intellectual property, textual creativity, creative labor, and audience reception. This book analyzes these areas, emphasizing the significant role of digital platforms, in order to determine power relations between platform owners and platform users, as well as global platforms and local cultural creations and audiences who increasingly rely on these platforms. The book's examination of digital platformization in Hallyu is expected to overcome the lacunae of the existing Hallyu studies that narrowly or partially analyze the instrumental roles of digital media in the wave of Korean cultural products. The book examines the digital platform in Hallyu as a process and environment in which structural forces intersect and entail various forms of cultural content and practice. In this way, people are able to understand the increasing role of digital platforms in cultural production within a shifting socio-economic milieu surrounding the changing media ecology itself.

The book's comprehensive and critical analysis of the platformization of Korean cultural production will be the first of its kind in Korean studies, given that existing Hallyu studies have only partially examined the role of digital media in particular areas of Korean culture. The book holistically explores the complex process of digital platformization of Korean media and culture, which informs the cultural production of Hallyu. This book also aims to make an important contribution to Korean Studies at large. That is, it contributes to Korean Studies as an epistemological framework in that it engages in the de-imperialization of Eurocentric perspectives to rethink how the West is no longer a dominant referent for the rest of the world while situating Korea at the nexus of postcolonial studies, globalization studies, and Asian studies.

For this analysis of Hallyu industries in conjunction with their digital platformization, methods of critical communication industries studies are utilized, as fully discussed in chapter 2. In other words, the book has been conducted through highly interdisciplinary research methods, which include historical analysis, political economy analysis, and ethnography. It analyzes local cultural industries through political, economic, and historical analysis. Moreover, for a comprehensive understanding of the Hallyu industries, it includes in-depth interviews with more than 50 policymakers and industry experts, as well as audiences, which were conducted in Korea in the 2022–2023 period. They were mainly introduced through my networks and acquaintances as part of a snowball sampling. Participants were between 23 and 60 in their ages, and cultural creators worked at cultural industries firms or relevant agencies for 7–26 years. We selected cultural creators, including television producers and writers in production firms, who broadly produced cultural content,[6] and we conducted one-hour semi-structured interviews. Respondents were asked about their thoughts on the role of digital platforms, including Netflix, in local cultural industries, their understanding of OTT platforms, and the influence of digital platforms on the continuity and change in major themes and genres of local popular culture. The interviews were transcribed and read through so that relevant themes were identified. With "the political economy's eager embrace of digital technologies" (Yeo, 2023, p. 10) and cultural studies' eager engagement with global audiences, it is vital to combine these two approaches in understanding cultural production and cultural flows. The convergence of critical political economy and cultural studies in both theoretical and methodological frameworks offers new insights in understanding the growth of local cultural industries, and therefore, culture production in the global cultural sphere.

Summary of the Book

The organization of the book is as follows. Chapter 1 provides the fundamentals of the book, including the question of why the Korean cultural

6. Staff, crew members, and actors/actresses/musicians are also cultural creators. Since this book attempts to analyze cultural production, it is necessary to focus on cultural creators who are not only producing cultural products, but also envisioning and actualizing the transnationality of local content (Jin, 2021d).

industries matter in the digital platform era. While emphasizing the increasing role of the cultural industries in the Korean Wave, this chapter engages with the discussion topics, context, major approaches to the subjects, and summaries of the chapters. The chapter shows how the Korean cultural industries can be compared with other transnational cultural industries in overseas markets. It especially attempts to emphasize the ways in which global digital platforms have influenced the continuity and change in the Hallyu ecosystem, which is one of the most significant transnational cultural industries in the Global South.

In chapter 2, we discuss an industry approach to understanding the Korean cultural industries as a theoretical foundation. First, this chapter documents various major theoretical frameworks, such as critical political economy, cultural industries, production studies, and critical media industry studies. Here, we not only discuss their major characteristics but also utilize them to advance a new theoretical framework for understanding the contemporary cultural industries. By historicizing the growth of the Korean Wave, it introduces a new industry approach termed "critical cultural industries studies," which is a meso-approach, focusing on the convergence of political economy and cultural studies. Unlike existing industry approaches, it examines a few new trends as the primary components, including the increasing role of digital platforms and intellectual property as significant economic and cultural elements (Colbjørnsen, 2021). This chapter articulates power relations in the industry, because "the study of media industries has always been part of the examination of the power that media wield on cultures and societies" (Herbert et al., 2020, p. 12), although it interrogates the major differences from existing approaches.

In chapter 3, we emphasize how Korea developed local cultural industries, from broadcasting to film to music, to make them the primary centers for cultural production. Once a very small industry in terms of revenues and jobs in the Korean economy, the local cultural industries, with the help of digital technologies, have advanced a multitude of recognizable cultural products, and the local cultural industries have exported various cultural products. While there are a multitude of significant factors for the recent growth of the Korean Wave, including supportive cultural policies, again, one of the most important yet least discussed elements are cultural industries, which have played a key role in the Korean Wave tradition. This chapter documents the major role of the cultural industries in the Korean Wave in the context of the broader social structure of society. This implies that the cultural industries have to be examined concerning shifting cultural politics. It maps out how the local cultural industries have cultivated local cultural products and foreign exports. Through an analysis of the Korean cultural industries, it discusses the crucial role of the cultural industries globally. In particular, by analyzing the process of the platformization of the local cultural industries, it addresses the ways in which the cultural industries and cultural policies have developed new forms of cultural content.

Chapter 4 focuses on relevant policy measures. As discussed in chapter 3, local cultural industries began to grow starting in the early 1990s, and consecutive government support played an important role. Since the Korean Wave implies the global popularity of Korean cultural content, it is not unusual to focus on enthusiastic global fans and the increasing role of social media as the primary causes for the growth of the Korean Wave; however, we cannot deny the importance of the role of the Korean government, in particular, in the early stage of the Korean Wave, as cultural policies have been considered some of the most pivotal elements. The Korean government has developed a few key measures, including necessary infrastructure while subsidizing local cultural industries, which play important roles in the growth of local cultural content.

This chapter discusses cultural politics by emphasizing the intricate relationships between the Korean government and local cultural industries. It addresses how the Korean government initiated the growth of the local cultural industries, which eventually advanced the Korean Wave. As the cultural industries have played a pivotal role in the Korean Wave phenomenon, it especially analyzes cultural industries policy that the Korean government develops, and therefore, it discusses the differences between cultural policy and cultural industries policy. It then examines whether the Korean government has to redirect its policy directions from cultural industries policy, focusing on the market economy, to cultural policy, emphasizing cultural identity and sovereignty.

Chapter 5 discusses how Netflix, as one of the most powerful global digital platforms, has influenced the local cultural industries in terms of the shift of cultural genres and the industry structure. It explores how Netflix has engaged with the Korean Wave as Netflix has fundamentally influenced cultural production in the Korean cultural system over the past few years. Netflix entered Korea in 2016 when it provided the entire budget for the feature film *Okja*, directed by Bong Joon-ho and released in 2017. Since then, Netflix has funded a series of cultural programs to produce Korean-originated content while licensing numerous existing cultural products. In 2019, Netflix released its first original Korean drama series, *Kingdom*.

The platform went on to produce other original programs, which were global sensations. Along with its direct involvement with production, Netflix has also distributed many Korean dramas, reality shows, and movies. Netflix initially had the role of a global distributor of Korean cultural content; however, it later became one of the largest OTT platforms to manage the country's cultural production. The chapter develops multifaceted methodologies, including institutional analysis to identify major players in the production of popular culture and in-depth interviews with local cultural creators as well as Netflix users to determine people's understanding of Netflix-driven local cultural texts. By examining Korean cultural production in transforming global media environments, this chapter addresses a blind spot within Korean studies. The chapter's research findings will reveal how Korean cultural industries and creators negotiate global media industries and digitalization.

Chapter 6 discusses YouTube, K-pop, and the local entertainment industry. In the early 21st century, K-pop has become one of the most enjoyable local popular cultures emerging from Korea. Korean popular music before the mid-1990s was subjugated under the controlled system as television remained the most important platform for music promotion and talent discovery. The K-pop industry experienced another major shift with the emergence of social media platforms and streaming service platforms. The growth of social media and streaming service platforms has greatly changed the contours of the local music industry in the early 21st century. For example, according to an analysis of YouTube's data, "the country that streamed boy band BTS's music videos and songs the most over the past year was Japan. BTS-related YouTube content—including official music videos and tracks, lyric videos, and fan-made content—accumulated approximately 15.1 billion views between March 2021 and February 2022, 2 billion of which came from Japan" (Chun & Yang, 2022). K-pop's global popularity has relied on social media in the early 21st century.

This chapter examines the emergence of the K-pop industry and the increasing role of entertainment houses by examining the transition of popular music, such as its style, music genre, and structure. It especially analyzes how these entertainment houses utilize social media and streaming service platforms, both nationally and globally, as some of the major elements for establishing global stardom. In other words, it analyzes the role of digital platforms in the Korean music industry and discusses how local entertainment houses have advanced their strategies for digital platforms in the global music market.

In chapter 7, we mainly focus on the platformization of the Korean Wave. Korean cultural industries have been incorporated into overseas media industries—previously, they worked with transnational cultural industry firms, and now they partner with global OTT platforms in cultural production. Global OTT platforms have diversified their business strategies in Korea. While investing in the local cultural industries for the production of exclusive, original content, Netflix has acquired licensing for many other Korean shows and films across different genres, which have been popular among global audiences. Global OTT platforms have joined the Korean Wave bandwagon to create their own original programs (i.e., Disney's *Snowdrop* and *Big Bet*), not only to penetrate the Korean cultural market but also to appeal to global audiences by utilizing Korea-based storytelling. The increasing role of OTT platforms raises concerns for Korean cultural creators and audiences because of the potential subordination of local cultural industries, including the broadcasting sector, to global OTT platforms.

This chapter analyzes the transition of the Korean cultural industries to the platform-driven phase of Hallyu by discussing the highly transnationalized and platformized Korean Wave in the shifting global media environment. It examines how Netflix platformizes and appropriates the Korean broadcasting industry through various strategies, such as investing in original content creation, licensing Korean content, and subcontractualization of Korean production. It also investigates the ways in which Korean cultural industries firms have become subordinated to and rely on global OTT platforms and their implications. In doing so, it explores the implications of the platformization of cultural production for the transnational cultural flows of Hallyu.

Chapter 8 summarizes the major characteristics of the new phase of Korean digital platforms. This concluding chapter proposes how local digital platforms can be theorized and how the growth of local platforms contributes to this theorization. In addition, this chapter delves into the future direction of the local cultural industries and the Korean Wave in the digital platform era based on what cultural creators and cultural consumers alike expect.

2

Critical Cultural Industries Studies: A New Approach

Introduction

The Korean Wave has become one of the most significant cultural phenomena in the global cultural sphere in the early 21st century. The Korean Wave began with a few Korean TV dramas in the mid-1990s, which first gained popularity in a few East Asian countries. The Korean Wave has also been led by the successes of Korean films and a few K-pop musicians, meaning that a few cultural industries have advanced their cultural content to be globally prominent (see R. Kim, 2022; Jin, 2023). The growth of the local cultural industries has facilitated the global popularity of Korean cultural content.

While there are several cultural industries driving the global popularity of Korean cultural content, the increasing role of digital platforms for both local cultural creators and global fans has become a game-changer since the early 2010s, as they play as new mediators for the circulation and consumption of local cultural content. Many local cultural creators, including television producers, filmmakers, and K-pop musicians, work with these digital platforms because they not only substitute for incumbent cultural companies but also function as new cultural agencies in cultural production. Netflix and Disney+ have invested in the Korean cultural markets to attract global audiences who want to enjoy Korean cultural content. Due to the global penetration of Korean popular culture, based on the growth of local cultural industries, followed by global digital platforms, scholars in various disciplines such as media studies, area studies, film studies, sociology, and anthropology have paid attention to the transnationalization of local popular culture but showed different perspectives partially based on their disciplinary programs.

As Mayer et al. (2009) argued, the cultural turn in the social sciences and the ethnographic turn in the humanities over the past three decades have pushed media scholars to look at cultural industries with new eyes, meaning that we may need to advance new approaches to reflect a shifting media environment. It is necessary to utilize the industry perspectives because cultural industries are closely related to a multitude of major actors, such as production studios that create cultural programs, global media conglomerates that possess studios and services, and governmental agencies that allocate necessary funds and set policies. Those studying cultural industries have analyzed the production of a few particular series, the process by which various cultural firms select and schedule programs, the histories of the regulatory agencies and governmental bodies that have shaped the cultural industries, and the textual consequences of international trade practices, among many other aspects of creating and circulating cultural content (Gray & Lotz, 2019). Nevertheless, these emphases still miss a few significant elements, such as the audiences, not only as consumers, but also as producers; the emergence of digital technologies, in particular, digital platforms; and cultural creators, not as individual players, but as connected actors.

This chapter discusses the emergence of the Korean Wave from the media industry perspective in the digital platform era. It first documents a few major theoretical frameworks, including critical political economy, cultural industries, production studies, and critical media industry studies; then, it explains why these existing media industry studies may not fully help to understand the Korean Wave in the digital platform era. By critically historicizing the growth of the Korean Wave, it introduces and utilizes "critical cultural industries studies"—a meso-approach—as a reliable media industry study in tandem with Hallyu studies, and therefore, in the shifting global cultural industries. Unlike existing industry approaches, this perspective examines a few new trends as the primary components, including the increasing role of digital platforms as a significant economic and cultural element. Similar to various existing approaches argued, it articulates power relations in the industry, because "the study of media industries has always been part of the examination of the power that media wield on cultures and societies" (Herbert, Lotz, & Punathambekar, 2020, p. 12); however, it interrogates the major differences from existing approaches as digital platforms play a primary role in the realm of the contemporary media and cultural industries.

The Korean Wave from the Perspective of Industrial Approaches

In Korea, multi-media national cultural industries, such as the broadcasting, film, music, and game industries, have created several well-made cultural products to be exported. Korea exported as much as $11.6 billion worth of cultural products in 2022 (Ministry of Culture, Sports and Tourism, 2022; Korea Creative Content Agency, 2023). Among these, the game industry has been the most significant segment ($8,973 million), given that digital gaming has become popular worldwide. The second largest industry is the music sector at $964 million in 2022, followed by broadcasting ($869.1 million), character ($504.8 million), and animation ($172 million). The film industry has thus far seen the lowest reach in the Korean Wave phenomenon. In 2022, its export value was only $71 million, even lower than that of manhwa ($107 million) (Ministry of Culture, Sports and Tourism, 2022; Korea Creative Content Agency, 2023). Due to the significance of cultural industries, and therefore, the Korean Wave, in the Korean economy and culture, the government, cultural industry firms, and cultural creators have continued to advance new cultural content for both local and global audiences.

As Hallyu has continued to grow, it is essential to understand the increasing role of local cultural industries in the initial stage of the Korean Wave, while digital platforms play a pivotal role in the recent New Korean Wave era. Several scholars and media have paid attention to the industrial aspect of the Korean Wave; however, it is still rare to see academic discourses on industry approaches in Hallyu studies.[1] Some theoreticians emphasized audiences or fans, while other scholars focused on marketing and soft power rather than developing industrial perspectives.

When I analyzed the number of academic papers published in scholarly journals until 2023 via the Communication & Mass Media Complete database, the outcome indeed showed that researchers did not pay atten-

1. According to Yoon and Kang's analysis (2017), the number of Hallyu research papers written in English was 76 until 2016. Based on the study topics those scholars analyzed, audiences of Korean drama and K-pop (34) were until then the most frequently analyzed subjects. The number could rise to 39 when including "people" (or their everyday lives) as the main subject of observation. There were 11 papers on the analysis of media texts, such as videos, lyrics, and blogs. Ten papers were on the media industry; however, as they focused on flows (export/import) and consumer behaviors, they were not directly related to the industry category, such as production and labor issues.

tion to the industrial perspective of the Korean Wave. With the two major keywords, the Korean Wave or Hallyu, the database brought 101 papers written in English from various academic disciplines between 2004 and 2023. Unlike Yoon and Kang's analysis, I did not focus on cultural forms, such as dramas, K-pop, and films, but categorized the papers based on the subject matters, such as fandom studies, audience studies, and cultural production. Among these, papers that examined audience (16 papers) and fandom (15 papers) were the two largest subjects. Globalization/transnationalization (10), public diplomacy/soft power (9), cultural industries/media industries (9), cultural production (9), digital Hallyu (8), and cultural policy (7) were the next-tier subjects. Others included media effects (5), multiculturalism (3), political economy (3), and others (7). As such, only a limited number of scholars have paid attention to the Korean Wave from a cultural or media industry perspective, although the production of popular culture is closely related to the national cultural industries.

Among these, a few scholars utilized political economy to analyze different cultural industries. Ryoo (2008) discussed the Korean film industry, focusing on its discursive strategies, policies, regulations, and other initiatives. Kim (2018) exemplified female idols' proliferation in the K-pop industry. He critically analyzed structural conditions of possibilities in contemporary popular music. Meanwhile, Kim (2014) examined the growth of K-pop and the Korean Wave as the cultural industry by analyzing various legal measures, including the Cultural Industry Promotion Act, which played a pivotal role in the foundation for the development of the Korean Wave.

These existing works, however, did not include the emergence of digital platforms as major forces in the local cultural industries with a few new papers that were published between the late 2010s and the early 2020s. They also did not thoroughly analyze the critical role of global audiences in their industry analyses. Again, various papers were based on audience studies; however, these papers did not make a connection to the cultural industries. Therefore, the current chapter provides new perspectives in understanding the Korean Wave as a potential case of the emergence of local cultural industries in the global cultural industries.

Evolution of Media Industry Studies

Over the past few decades, many theoreticians have developed various approaches in media industry studies. Mainly based on the dichotomy of political economy and cultural studies, they sometimes emphasized critical political economy-based industry studies, while, at other times, they focused on the meaning of cultural text in tandem with media industries. This section delves into the historical development of these approaches based on a few focal points, including the power relationship, between different players in cultural production. It discusses the major advantages and disadvantages of incumbent approaches in media industry studies.

Critical Political Economy Approach

The media industry has been an essential concept in the area of media and communication studies, usually labeled the "political economy of culture" since the 1970s (Schiller, 1989). Among these, the primary approach to the industry can be identified as critical political economy. Based on differing interpretations and adaptations of Marxist theory, political economists have focused on the structural aspect of media corporations and media systems. Policy concerns were often central in this critical, neo-Marxian analysis field (Winseck, 2011).

What the political economy of media has emphasized is the "historical phase of the progressive capitalization of the private-sector media industry, i.e., radical subsumption of the entire media system under the general conditions of the valorization of capital . . . Media production is thus also more intensively subjected to the 'laws of motion' and 'constraints' of production and capital valorization, of profit maximization and competition, as well as of accumulation and concentration" (Knoche, 2021, p. 326). The essential features of this drive for capitalization are a structural change in the media industry, which is evident in "the increasing commercialization of media content production as commodity production" (Knoche, 2021, p. 327).

McChesney (1999) was a critical figure in the political economy of media when it came to the media industry, as he took the media industry as a serious object of analysis. The critical political economy of media has emphasized the increasing role of a handful of media giants, with power concentrated at the top, while not paying enough attention to cultural content and cultural creators—the labor issue (Winseck, 2011). Therefore, Mosco (2009, p. 24) attempted to develop a dynamic view of the political economy of communication, which he defines as the "study of the social relations, particularly the power relations, that mutually constitute the production, distribution, and consumption of resources." Political economy recognizes not merely economic concerns, but political and moral concerns. This means that the political economy is inherently concerned with the ideological (Nichols & Martinez, 2019, pp. 1–2). As Murdock and Golding (2005, p. 60) argued, the cultural industries are important objects of study because "the commercial media play a pivotal role in organizing the images and discourses through which people make sense of the world," while "media corporations are significant economic actors."

More specifically, the political economy of communication is interested in not only understanding the production and distribution of media content but also how we might resist the problems presented by the capitalist control of media and communication (Gandy, 1992; Nichols & Martinez, 2019). It later saw digital technologies as part of a broader range of cultural industries involved in the production, structuring, and dissemination of culture. Dan Schiller (1999, p. xiv) indeed emphasized the significant role of digital media by pointing out "networks as directly generalizing the social and cultural range of the capitalist economy."

Critical political economy is broadly concerned with studying power relations in society during the process. However, critical political economy has not paid attention to content and audiences in general, although some political economists provide their thoughts on consumers as part of the "broad patterns of cultural product, distribution and consumption" (Garnham, 2005a, p. 486). Due to the lack of discussions on cultural creators and consumers, as well as cultural content, other approaches, including the cultural industries school, production studies, and critical media industries studies, have emerged, although their focuses are not mutually exclusive.

The Cultural Industries School

Another primary school to analyze the media industry is the cultural industries school, which can be primarily identified in the tradition of political economy. The rise of the cultural industries was very much bound up with the growth of mass culture. Reacting against what they saw as the misleadingly democratic connotations of the term mass culture, Horkheimer and Adorno, ([1947]1979) developed the idea of the culture industry as part of their critique of the false legacies of the Enlightenment. The term was intended to draw critical attention to "the commodification of art" (Hesmondhalgh & Pratt, 2005, pp. 3–4). The cultural industries approach has been the primary frame that media scholars take to understand the cultural industries and the concept of culture more generally. It also goes beyond the political economy of media to encompass cultural studies components. As Winseck (2011) articulated, the cultural industries school has drawn judiciously from different strands of political economy, differentiating it from the critical political economy of communication.

A significant point of this approach is the shift of the term from the cultural industry to the cultural industries, implying the change in a few important areas. As Garnham (2005b, p. 18) pointed out, "the term now widely adopted—cultural industries—did not now indicate a simple replay of the Frankfurt School's analysis." In its new usage, "the term did not necessarily share either the elitist, cultural pessimism of the Frankfurt School (although some did) or the particular version of the Marxist economics that underpinned it." Garnham (2005b, p. 18) emphasized, "far from rejecting economism, [the Cultural Industries school] took the term 'industries' seriously and attempted to apply both a more detailed and nuanced Marxist economic analysis and more mainstream industrial and information economics to the analysis of the production, distribution, and consumption of symbolic forms."

Accordingly, as Winseck (2011) pointed out, the cultural industries school has advanced the idea that diverse sectors of the cultural industries cannot be treated as the same thing because of the organizational differences that exist between the publishing (e.g., books, music, film), flow (e.g., broadcasting), and editorial (e.g., the press) models (Miège, 1987). However, the cultural industries school still does not pay attention to the roles of audiences, and its emphasis on cultural creators is relatively less focused.

Production Studies

Due to the paucity of discussions on working practices in the media industry discourse, production studies appears to be "an adequate analysis of the organizational forms and working practices associated with the cultural industries" (Hesmondhalgh & Pratt, 2005). This analysis has been characterized in terms of the production of the culture model. The two sets of new entrants to the (sub)field have made their presence in production studies: "one group coming from business and management studies, and in some cases from economics; another group coming from various humanities backgrounds and laying claim to the term cultural studies" (Hesmondhalgh & Saha, 2013, p. 181). For example, with two open-source animation film production cases in Sweden, Velkova and Jakobsson (2017) utilized these two different approaches, as their theoretical approach expands the concept of "moral economies" from the critical political economy with "regimes of value" from anthropological work. Production studies can be situated between critical political economy and cultural studies. Mayer, Banks, and Caldwell (2009) also emphasized the nexus of political economy and cultural studies. Production studies scholars, as contributors to a field of interdisciplinary inquiry, draw their intellectual impetus from cultural studies to look at the ways that culture both constitutes and reflects the relationships of power. This is not an objective unique to cultural studies but is still an objective (Mayer et al., 2009).

Accordingly, the notion of power in production studies has been different from other industry studies. Unlike in political economy, which emphasizes lop-sided power relations between a few mega-media giants, other small media companies, and general audiences, production studies sees that "a centralized and top-down model fails to capture all the aspects of power relations" in cultural production; therefore, "a more productive starting point is that television production necessarily involves negotiation between different participants" (Zeng & Sparks, 2019, p. 56).

Cultural production is indeed tied to questions of power. There are hierarchies of power that enable some actors to move between different spheres and reconcile the different values regimes. The power relationships underlying these work conditions "not only hinge on access to economic capital but are also related to the position of the actor in relation to different regimes of value," which ask researchers to investigate "the multifaceted relationships between the different regimes of value" as well (Velkova & Jakobsson, 2017, p. 27). Therefore, the analysis of relations between creative workers and the other elements, including political participants, data analytics, and global power structures, is central to the production studies approach.

More importantly, production studies takes "they lived realities of people involved in media production as the subjects for theorizing production as culture" (Mayer et al., 2009, p. 4). Because of the evolution of cultural production in different fields, scholars in production studies have offered different approaches. They emphasize that "the production of culture model tends to be focused on organizational relations and the ways in which practices and processes yield specific outcomes" (Havens, Lotz, & Tinic, 2009, p. 240). Peterson and Anand (2004, p. 311) also argue that "the production of culture perspective focuses on how the symbolic elements of culture are shaped by the systems within which they are created, distributed, evaluated, taught, and preserved." Meanwhile, du Gay (1997) points out that cultural production studies adopts a global focus on cultural industries and how cultural products are produced, marketed, and sold.

Production studies also considers not only the "production processes, products and services," but also "the nature of labor markets that enable us to speak of these sectors in a collective sense" (Flew, 2012b, p. 83).

Production studies, however, has not meaningfully considered customers or audiences as part of its analysis, although they are now crucial components of cultural production, in particular with the increasing role of digital platforms, both social media platforms and OTT platforms. As Brooke Duffy (2017) discussed the empowerment of prosumers with the cases of fashion bloggers, YouTubers, and Instagram influencers, several production studies scholars certainly analyzed consumers as creative laborers; however, their analyses mainly focused on individual consumers rather than mass audiences or fans who consume cultural content while providing cultural activities which eventually provide reliable feedbacks and discussions to cultural creators in (mass)-cultural production.

Critical Media Industry Studies

There is another important approach in media industry studies as a mid-level framework that is rooted in cultural studies. The tradition of critical media industry studies can be found in the history of critical cultural media studies, distinguishing it from other forms of industry analysis, particularly macro-level political economy. This relatively recent approach can be part of critical cultural studies, which "emphasizes the complex interplay of economic and cultural forces, as well as the forms of struggle and compliance that take place throughout society at large and within the media industries in particular" (Havens et al., 2009, p. 235). Amid increasing concerns about the lack of its scope in the system and industry in cultural studies, critical media industry studies has emphasized the study of the media as an industry, although the distinction between production studies and critical media industry studies remains somewhat vague (Gray & Lotz, 2019).

To begin with, unlike political economy that predominantly focuses on the significant level operations of media institutions, critical media industry studies is "primarily interested in the production of entertainment programming, thus limiting the usefulness of many political-economic theories and perspectives, which are based on the industrial analysis of news" (Havens et al., 2009, p. 235). Critical media industry studies is concerned with the pivotal role that media institutions play in "organizing the images and discourses through which people make sense of the world," which means that this approach believes that the critical political economy approach to the media industry shows "general inattention to entertainment programming, and incomplete explanation of the role of human agents (other than those at the pinnacle of conglomerate hierarchies) in interpreting, focusing, and redirecting economic forces that provide for complexity and contradiction within media industries" (Havens et al., 2009, p. 235).

Second, critical media industry studies interprets power not as pessimistic but through productive meanings. The notion of power in critical media industry studies proves that this approach "is rooted in cultural studies theories that examine power as it operates within media organizations and allows for the agency of those workers that are negotiated with the macro-level structures of capitalism and the relations of power it creates" (Gray & Lotz, 2019, p. 114). In line with an overall shift in the intellectual discourse away from theories of power as externally imposed, scholars have attempted to give more weight to how cultural workers shape their works in order to construct and deconstruct the existing relations of power (Lee, 2012; Zeng & Sparks, 2019).

"Rather than envisioning power as a form of economic control over media organizations and laborers," it understands power as productive because it mostly "produces particular ways of conceptualizing audiences, texts, and economics" (Havens et al., 2009, p. 237). Critical media industry studies has especially criticized the overall emphasis on economic and institutional power over creative workers. In other words, this school argues that "the emphasis on ownership and market logics elides the complex workings within the media industries where cultural workers negotiate every facet of the production process in ways that cannot be easily predicted by or read off from the interests of those who control the allocative resources of the industries" (Havens et al., 2009, p. 248).

Third, critical media industry studies is a meso-level approach that attempts to account for both media structure and agency, as well as power and resistance in media industries (Cunningham, Craig, & Lv, 2019). A few significant characteristics of the critical media industry studies framework include a mid-level view of industry operations. It focuses on "the ability of individuals to act independently and make their own free choices," while the structure is those "factors of influence such as class, gender, religion, ethnicity, etc., that determine or limit the decisions and choices an agent makes" (Milne, 2013, p. 35)—"within industry operations, a Gramscian theory of power that does not lead to complete domination, and a view of society and culture grounded in structuration and articulation" (Havens et al., 2009, p. 243).

There are some problems in the realm of critical media industry studies. Like production studies, critical media industry studies posits creative workers as one of the major research interests as they are primary players in cultural production. However, it does not much emphasize the audiences as cultural creators, although they actively participate in a meaning-making process. They consume entertainment content, produce content themselves, and provide necessary information to cultural creators in traditional cultural institutions. Unlike the critical political economy, production studies and critical media industry studies put questions of media labor and institutional context in dialogue with debates about identity, meaning, and representation (Johnson, 2014; Mayer, 2011; Mayer, Banks, & Caldwell, 2009); in some cases, these approaches come in the tendency to "treat media industry insularly, artificially cordoning off its work cultures from the realm of consumption" (Johnson, 2014, p. 50). The subsequent two sessions discuss a new theoretical framework in media industry studies, differentiating itself from existing media industry studies, with the case of the Korean Wave and digital platforms.

Critical Cultural Industries Studies Toward the Korean Wave

There are various reasons why media scholars may need to consider the Korean Wave from critical cultural industries studies, which is a form of meso-approach in industry studies, and is neither the political economy nor cultural studies-driven approaches. Scholars in different academic fields still have difficulties in defining the Korean Wave and finding appropriate theories, mainly because the Korean Wave entered public consciousness relatively quickly in the early 21st century. As discussed previously, while the political economy of communication has utilized institutional analysis and historical approaches, most qualitative research on the Korean Wave has been derived from cultural studies, focusing on audience or fan studies, whether they are diaspora Asians or global fans. Much scholarly analysis and discourse about Hallyu argue that they can be understood not only as texts but also as cultural artifacts that are given value, meaning, and position through their production and use by media users (Crawford & Rutter, 2006). Several of those studies using various methodologies have focused on the cultural aspects of Korean cultural content.

To begin with, this new approach is related to the unique position of the Korean Wave in academic disciplines, and it can be applied to transnational cultural flows primarily developed from non-Western regions.

Whereas "critical political economy has been institutionalized within social science" and draws its major practitioners from people trained in economics, political science, and sociology, "departments and programs of cultural studies are still mostly studied in humanities and mainly pursued by scholars drawn from literary and art historical studies, and from anthropology and other disciplines concerned with the micro-politics of everyday meaning-making" (Murdock & Golding, 2005, p. 61). As previously discussed in this chapter, the Korean Wave has been studied in both social sciences, including political science, public policy, marketing, sociology, and communication, mainly focusing on cultural policy on Hallyu and Hallyu marketing, production, systems, and humanities, such as anthropology, geography, Asian studies, and literature, primarily analyzing fandom and cultural text, although they overlap in some cases; therefore, we cannot put Hallyu only within any specific academic discipline. It is essential to advance our approaches by cutting across disciplinary boundaries, and Hallyu studies should be interdisciplinary in both academic fields and methodological approaches.

Second, it is critical to discuss the scope of the Korean Wave, not from the cultural industry as a singular form, but from the cultural industries as a plural form because there are various separate but connected businesses at work. In Horkheimer and Adorno's view (1997), culture and industry were supposed to be opposites, but in a modern capitalist democracy, the two had collapsed together. Again, the French "cultural industries" sociologists rejected Horkheimer and Adorno's use of the singular term "The Culture Industry" because it suggested a "unified field" where all the different forms of cultural production that coexist in modern life are assumed to obey the same logic. The French "cultural industries" sociologists were concerned with showing how complex the cultural industries are and identifying the different logics at work in various types of cultural production (Miège, 1987; Hesmondhalgh, 2012, p. 24).

The Korean Wave cannot be adequately analyzed through a single cultural industry, as a few industries, from broadcasting to music to digital games, work together to establish the contemporary Hallyu phenomenon in the global cultural sphere, although scholars may select a particular cultural sector like film, broadcasting, and music, depending on their unique study plans. More importantly, Hallyu's scope cannot be understood with only a particular media industry or any particular area, as it does not represent the entire Hallyu phenomenon. Korean dramas and K-pop are not symbols of the Korean Wave; they are only parts of the phenomenon. Likewise, the Korean Wave cannot be explained by only cultural policy or audience studies. A few previous works (see Yoon & Kang, 2017) focused on a particular sector like K-pop or Korean dramas, and claimed that they analyzed the Korean Wave phenomenon; however, what they understood was a specific area, not the Korean Wave per se. The Korean Wave phenomenon demands theoreticians to understand the nature of the different industries involved, both audio-visual and digital components, and requires analyzing it as a whole in its relevant historical and sociocultural contexts.

Third, it is crucial to analyze cultural producers as part of industry studies. Unlike production studies and critical media industry studies, scholars in a few different fields have to explore not only cultural creators in mega cultural industries firms but also cultural consumers. What it attempts to argue is that we need to entwine together more complex tales about media in the study of consumers, not only considering them as active audiences but also as viable agencies. In this expansive body of work, scholars see that even the objects of consumption are sites of cultural production as consumers adopt, modify, and re-purpose the cultural meanings of domestic tools and media technologies (Silverstone, 2005; cited in Mayer et al., 2009). The inductive insights of these studies of cultural consumers have "set a new standard for studies of producers" and "the conjuncture of contexts within which they produce meanings" (Mayer et al., 2009, p. 3).

Platform users as customers especially act as cultural producers, which asks theoreticians to analyze their roles in cultural production. In the digital platform era, cultural producers are increasingly platform-dependent; however, platform adoption among cultural producers differs among industry segments (Nieborg, Poell, & Duffy, 2021):

> Historically, some parts of the cultural industries—games and social media entertainment—have been platform-dependent, whereas other segments—news and music—have histories far predating platforms. The latter set of industry segments tend to have more options to operate independently from platforms . . . thus, cultural producers becoming platform-dependent by no means signals an all-encompassing logic; nor does it affect all industries equally (p. 3).

Due to the convergence of popular culture and digital technologies, as well as its relation to digital platforms, it is vital to systematically analyze the Korean Wave as a whole, which can be easily done through existing industry studies.

Last but not least, it is critical to converge two different methodological approaches. The Korean Wave is no longer a discrete and distinct sector. As Hesmondhalgh (2012, p. 5) aptly puts it, "a view of the cultural industries and the texts they produce are much more complex, ambivalent, and contested than expected." Toby Miller (2006, p. 6) also pointed out, "every cultural and communications technology has specificities of production, text, distribution, and reception." Therefore, the converged methodological framework stands to contribute much to moving research and inquiry forward in Hallyu studies, the public sphere of widespread criticism, state and private policy creation, social movement critique, and labor organization. We perceive these parties as those that allow "us to consider who makes the games, who profits from them, how they target audiences, what the games look like, what they are like to play, and how they fit in with social life" (Miller, 2006, p. 8). It is necessary to "employ political economy approaches and combine them with ethnographic research and in-depth interviews gathered in researchers' fieldwork to strengthen their major analytical framework," which necessitates a new theoretical approach (Jin and Chee, 2008, p. 41).

Overall, media theory and methodology must synthesize a wide range of approaches that constitute a multidisciplinary file of research (Wolf & Perron, 2003; Chee, 2008), and these approaches are essential in understanding the complexity of the Korean Wave. It would seem that a complementary structural examination provided by a political and economic approach would satisfy a demand expressed by such cultural researchers of popular culture. It is challenging to cover political, economic, and ethnographic approaches; however, the Korean Wave should be defined "based on specific combinations of technical, social, cultural, and economic characteristics and not on exclusive, essential ones" (Raessens, 2005, p. 373). By examining the Korean Wave as the cultural industries in light of its sociocultural elements and political-economic contingencies, we illuminate some of the underexamined complexities inherent in the conception, development, implementation, and reception of Korean popular culture in the global cultural sphere.

Critical Cultural Industries Studies in the Convergence of Hallyu and Digital Platforms

Digital platforms have been some of the most significant media industries, including in the Korean Wave tradition. As discussed earlier, digital platforms, including OTT platforms, have become primary players in Korea's cultural production, from the production of popular culture to the consumption of cultural content as they work as cultural mediators. Several local broadcasting companies, either individually or collectively, have launched local OTT platforms as their subsidiary cultural agents. They have also produced cultural programs not only for their own channels but also for OTT platforms, as can be seen in MBC's *Physical: 100* (2023) for Netflix, which blurs the boundary between traditional broadcasting companies and digital platforms. For local cultural industries, the rapid growth and use of digital platforms seem to open new possibilities.

In fact, digital platforms play a key role in the entire value chain of cultural production, again, including the production, circulation, and consumption of cultural content. They are not only mere distributors but also powerful producers while working as primary tools for cultural consumption. Therefore, it is vital to follow the development in the light of history, highlighting the intersections with other related concepts, from cultural industries to digital platforms. Understanding the role of digital platforms relates to the broader project that focuses on audio-visual cultural production in general, and especially, those in the Korean Wave (Dwyer & Hutchinson, 2019). Although Korea is not the only country that has developed popular culture, it proves the convergence of popular culture and digital platforms is a new frontline in cultural production, and, therefore, Korea can be worked as an exemplary case at this juncture.

Platform studies have enabled researchers to identify a multitude of seminal aspects surrounding how cultural programs are produced, circulated, and consumed on these platforms. Helmond (2015, p. 1) argues that digital platforms are a prominent infrastructure, noting that platformization refers to "the rise of the platform as the dominant infrastructural and economic model of the social web and its consequences"; therefore, "platformization entails the extension of social media platforms into the rest of the web and their drive to make external web data platform ready."

Here one significant aspect of the novelties-related digital platforms has to do with the articulation of their supply. For a long time, the products of the cultural industries have been available in the market only at certain times. Digital platforms have replaced the logic of traditional cultural industries due to the permanent availability of their products on the web (Colombo, 2018). As for the supply itself, the conventional production of the cultural industries is linked to the specific stability of the genres, which has allowed an efficient, productive articulation. However, "the acceleration of the production-distribution consumption cycle has progressively reduced traditional rigidities in favor of greater fluidity between genres" (Colombo, 2018, p. 143). Due to the increasing impact of Netflix, for example, local cultural creators and cultural industry firms have created new cultural genres, such as zombie (e.g., *Train to Busan, Kingdom,* and *All of Us are Dead*) and Si-Fi adventure (e.g., *Space Sweepers* and *Jung_E*) since the late 2010s, which is unprecedented.

Netflix's effects in the Korean Wave have indeed become significant. The number of Netflix's Korean originals, including dramas, films, and reality shows, has increased from only 6 in 2020 to 25 in 2022. Netflix planned to create 34 original programs in Korea, including 20 series, 12 films, and two reality shows, in 2023, as it wanted to ride the Korean Wave (Toh, 2023). As part of its plan, Netflix decided to invest $2.5 billion in Korea over the next four years, between 2023 and 2027 (Liang & Hoskins, 2023). In addition, there are many licensed programs. For example, as of March 15, 2024, there were as many as 315 Korean movies and television series on Netflix, up from 262 cultural programs as of November 1, 2021 (Netflix, 2021c; 2024b). The primary reason for the growth of Korean cultural content on Netflix is the soaring number of global audiences that increasingly enjoy Korean cultural programs. As of May 2023, among Netflix's subscribers in 190 countries, over 60% have watched Korean content at least once (Ryall, 2023).

Another set of shifting factors linked to digital platforms, therefore, concerns their use and valorization. Integrated users are the most evident novelty of transformations in the media industry. The management of the massive flow of information, which is generated by platform users when they click, share, and upload is elaborated by artificial intelligence (AI) and algorithms advanced by digital platforms, and this can predict and promote personalized consumption options (Jin, 2021b). As H. K. Lee (2024, pp. 1–2) aptly puts it, "by fundamentally disrupting the human monopoly of creativity, generative AI engenders what we can call 'creative precarity' for a broad range of cultural workers—from artists, journalists, and background music composers to film actors—by emulating their creative imagination and communication with audience and by appropriating copyrighted cultural content for its data mining"; therefore, it is essential for cultural and media studies scholars to explore a multitude of "implications of AI in terms of ethics and biases, surveillance, cultural taste formation, datafication of everyday life, the politics of dataset, platform work, deepfake, human interaction with chatbot or voice assistant." Since digital platforms obtain profits "not only through advertising and the sale of products, but also and above all from the increase in network traffic and the sale of users' data" (Colombo, 2018, p. 143), the nexus of digital platforms and AI algorithms has to be critically evaluated.

As Miège (2011, p. 62) pointed out, "the online portals: a conception-production-consumption logic for cultural and informational products increasingly becoming a model. The question of evolution in, and the future of models is part of a larger analysis of the place of cultural industries in contemporary capitalism." For many local cultural creators, therefore, the production of cultural products for digital platforms has become mandatory, which means that they now check whether their products can be released on global OTT platforms. What they want to secure are not only production budgets from global OTT platforms but also guarantees of global consumption.

Meanwhile, with the rapid growth of digital platforms, IP rights versus author's rights and copyright have become some of the most significant issues in industry studies. Global digital platforms influence non-Western countries by penetrating American corporate ideology, which includes entrepreneurship, personalization, and the role of intellectual property. *Squid Game* is undoubtedly a Korean television series; however, Netflix is not only working as a cultural outlet but also is garnering massive profits. While Korea is satisfied with the global success of the locally produced cultural program, Netflix has continued to benefit from Korean cultural products' popularity because the platform maximizes its benefits through the monopolization of IP and as the distribution channel. During my interviews conducted in 2023, one male researcher who is in his thirties in a culture-related government agency stated the importance of IP:

> IPs are becoming popular in all areas of cultural content, including K-pop, dramas, movies, webtoons, and digital games. We do not believe that such IP production capabilities can be created in a short period of time, and therefore, we believe that the success of Korean content will continue for the foreseeable future. It seems that the popularity of Korean content is unlikely to fade away unless companies quickly establish strategies and act. I think the genre that is more promising and can play a key role in the future than the most important one is webtoon/web novel. Many video content IPs are already based on webtoon/web novels. The future content industry will depend on IP competitiveness, and webtoon/web novels will play a big role. Also, given the influence of Naver and Kakao in the global webtoon/web novel market, I think it is a genre that can grow rapidly.

In fact, as is well-documented (Shaw, 2021), Netflix estimated that *Squid Game 1* could create almost $900 million in value for the company. Netflix mainly differs from other cultural industries, such as movie studios and television networks, in that "it does not generate sales based on specific titles, instead using its catalog and a steady drumbeat of new releases to entice customers every week. But the company does have a wealth of data concerning what its customers watch" (*The Economic Times*, 2021). Critics are concerned about whether it is suitable for local productions to allow Netflix to monopolize content rights, based on IP rights, to their shows at a time when the Korean Wave has emerged as a content hub for its globally popular culture (*The Economic Times*, 2021). They argued, "the streaming platforms' huge risk-taking investment may limit the IP rights of Korean creators as the companies demand the entire IP of the shows they invest in" (*The Economic Times*, 2021).

As Hesmondhalgh and Lotz (2020, p. 389) point out, "while a great deal of sociological research has examined the decisions that have shaped media production and circulation, little is known about the corporate arrangements between devices and services, reflecting the opacity of many of the new cultural intermediaries that now participate in media circulation," in addition to the lack of study about cultural industries in the Korean Wave context. It is critical to delve into digital platforms as mediators, which wield their enormous power in cultural production.

In this light, the notion of power in critical cultural industries studies can be differently emphasized. A few existing industry studies have focused on power in analyzing a handful of media industries by highlighting power relations that are primary elements in constructing and deconstructing the relationships between major players, although their significant approaches are different. Unlike other industry studies, the present approach emphasizes multilayered power relations, as distribution power and consumer power (in addition to cultural creators as agencies) play a vital role in the cultural industries.

Hall (1986) already pointed out that within cultural studies, a culturalist perspective, exemplified by Raymond Williams, emphasized human experience and practical activity as the source of culture. In contrast, a structuralist perspective "stressed the structural and ideological features of culture as the ultimate conditions or determinants of human praxis." (Surber, 1998, p. 240). In readings such as Hall's, "Williams is seen as paying too much attention to experience and human praxis as opposed to structural conditions and how they infuse these practices" (Surber, 1998, p. 240, cited in Guillem, 2013). In critical cultural industries studies, one is able to understand the notion of power through the convergence of the structuralist perspective and the culturalist perspective, as the major perspective of this new approach is the pursuit of the accurate meso-level framework.

More specifically, digital platforms' distribution power can be understood through negotiations, cooperation, and conflicts between three major actors, namely media institutions, in this case, digital platforms, but not excluding cultural industry firms, cultural creators, and platform users. Digital platforms act as mediators that control the circuit of cultural production, which means that OTT platforms not only distribute cultural content but also produce their own original programs. Digital platforms allow cultural creators to enhance their position in negotiation with cultural industries firms as cultural creators. They can select broadcasting channels or digital platforms to distribute their cultural content. Platform users can also participate in cultural production as users and consumers. They provide their taste and preferences while clicking and searching for cultural content on these digital platforms. The recognition of customers who "economically support, symbolically reproduce, and thus practically consent to the industry's own construction" of the power has been woefully absent in the otherwise diverse range of research on digital platforms (Mayer, 2011, p. 2). As Johnson (2014, p. 51) points out, therefore, "to most effectively grasp the cultural politics of media work, production studies of the media industries could reinvest in the idea of the audience, asking how the sense- and identity-making practices of professional laborers are tied up in ideologies and social hierarchies extending beyond the bounds of industry and into everyday struggles over consumer identity."

Power relations certainly enhance the roles of cultural creators and audiences. Again, platforms "open up spaces for negotiations, contestation, and even acts of resistance" (Duffy, Poell, & Nieborg, 2019, p. 6). In this light, Nieborg, Poell, and Duffy (2021) argue that the relations and flows of power between digital platforms and cultural creators should be understood as one of mutual dependence. We cannot deny the increasing roles of cultural creators and audiences as meaningful, but not yet fully powered, agencies. In the transnational context, though, it is clear that global digital platforms have reigned supreme in the Global South. A handful of global digital platforms such as Netflix and YouTube are increasing their performance in many parts of the globe; in particular, in Korea. For example, according to the Global Media and Internet Concentration Project (GMICP), which analyzes the transformation of the Internet industry, Netflix has been the biggest online video streaming service in most countries in the Global South. Due to heavy competition among global OTT platforms, Netflix's average share of markets fell from 65% in

2018/2019 to 44% in 2021/2022. However, Netflix has doubled its share of online video streaming service revenue from 29% to 57% over that period (Jin, Han, & Bizberge, 2024).

Of course, this is a complex issue, as digital platforms are becoming central nodes in virtually every cultural industry. Digital platforms equipped with AI and algorithms play a pivotal role, making unbalanced power relations among these three principal actors. The emergence of digital platforms contributes to the institutionalization of a winner-take-all economy practice, and therefore, digital platforms have become front-runners in data and AI capitalism (Verdegem, 2021). As Colbjørnsen (2021, p. 1282) aptly puts it, platform users and cultural creators, in contrast to digital platform owners, "are seen as particularly vulnerable," as digital platform providers "are able to maneuver the network to strengthen their relative position." In other words:

> Users are entirely reliant on streaming providers and must accept the terms specific to the streaming model to gain access, stuck in a network without command over neither database nor device. . . . The data streams to content originators and publishers are provided at the mercy of streaming providers, indicating that the asymmetrical power relations persist (Colbjørnsen, 2021, p. 1282).

Overall, constructing the audience as the primary actor in the Korean cultural industries studies does not automatically mean that they enjoy equal opportunities and, therefore, equal power. The asymmetrical power relations, notwithstanding cultural creators' and platform users' improving negotiation power, have not disappeared and even intensified. However, the analysis in critical cultural industries studies should not necessarily be pessimistic. Instead, by focusing on the shifting power relations, we turn our attention to understanding the increasing role of cultural creators and consumers. While interrogating the necessity of relevant measures to protect local cultural creation from digital platforms, we also advance new cultural industries' norms that emphasize fruitful working relationships between digital platforms, cultural creators, and consumers.

Conclusion

This chapter has discussed the necessity of a reconfigured media industry approach in tandem with the Korean Wave. By developing a new meso-approach termed critical cultural industries studies in the context of the

Korean Wave, it emphasized that we need to analyze the Korean Wave, and in general local cultural industries, more comprehensively and systematically than ever. The Korean Wave is a non-Western-based cultural phenomenon, and quite a few media scholars have utilized existing approaches to examine numerous emerging cultural industries. Scholars in different academic fields can fully comprehend the popularity of local popular culture in the global cultural scene by converging structure, audience, and text in the digital platform era. However, due to the lack of their validity as reliable theoretical frameworks in analyzing the Korean Wave and cultural production, this chapter introduced critical cultural industries studies, which may enhance our understanding of the emergence of the Korean Wave.

It is crucial to acknowledge that an analysis of digital platforms in the Korean cultural industries cannot be the same as traditional cultural industries as digital platforms work as the primary actors in cultural production, from the production of popular culture to the circulation of cultural content. Business and distribution models labeled as digital platforms are no longer a novelty in the cultural industries, which needs to be examined and conceptualized across cultural industries (Colbjørnsen, 2021). Cultural creators should also be considered as the central parts of cultural production as they are primary actors in the meaning-making process. The consumers in the digital platform era are not passive audiences. They are actively participating in cultural production: not only uploading their content on social media but also providing their taste to OTT platforms so that they have fundamentally shifted peer audiences' cultural behavior, although they are not yet gaining equal power.

3

The Evolution of the Korean Cultural Industries

Introduction

Until the mid-1990s, global cultural industries were relatively less developed and small, and they were considered as secondary sectors of national economies. With the growth of digital technologies and globalization trends mainly starting in the 1990s, cultural industries began to expand their scope and magnitude in terms of revenues and the number of employees in the 1990s (Herman & McChesney, 1997). As globalization has been expedited partially due to the advent of digital technologies, cultural industries have experienced unprecedented expansion in the early 21st century. Cultural industries are among "the fastest growing sectors in the world. With an estimated global worth of 4.3 trillion USD per year, the culture sector now accounts for 6.1% of the global economy. Collective art, mass art, the art of modernity, major industrial art of the contemporary 'screenocracy,' the cinema is the most significant cultural industry in terms of economic profitability and symbolic influence" (Vlassis, 2019, p. 4). According to the UNESCO Institute for Statistics (2016), audiovisual services are increasingly becoming the most important cultural service traded. For example, "cinema is the sector in which most of the export and import measures are put in place" (Deloumeaux, 2018, p. 136).

As is fully discussed in chapter 4, studies on cultural policy related to cultural industries in Asia have been given very little attention, mainly because policymakers did not regard cultural industries as a viable object of analysis. Policymakers and media scholars have overlooked the industrial implications of cultural production. However, as the cultural industries became some of the major actors in national economies, as well as in people's daily cultural activities, cultural policymakers, scholars, and cultural creators started to pay attention to the emerging role of the cultural industries. In other words, it was only after the cultural industries became significant areas of the national economy that cultural industries and popular culture became serious objects of study (Keane, 2006; Otmazgin, 2021).

The cultural industries are rapidly increasing their scope and magnitude to become some of the major industry sectors in many parts of the Global North, including the U.S., the U.K., and France. A handful of countries in the Global South have also advanced their cultural industries, and Korea, arguably located in the Global South, has also developed local cultural industries, such as broadcasting, film, music, and animation, making them the primary centers for cultural production. Once very small in terms of revenues and the number of workers in the Korean economy, the local cultural industries have massively produced a multitude of recognizable cultural programs. Based on the growth of local cultural industries, cultural industries firms have also exported various cultural products to many parts of the world. As the Korean government has developed its supporting measures for the cultural industries in terms of the establishment of various cultural industries, including cable and satellite channels, the loosening of strict censorship, and the introduction of various forms of financial subsidies, the local cultural industries have experienced a renaissance era since the early 2010s.

More importantly, the growth of local cultural industries has become one of the primary elements for the recent growth of the Korean Wave. In tandem with the supportive cultural policies discussed in chapter 4 and enthusiastic global fans who enjoy Korean cultural content, the local cultural industries have greatly advanced the quality of cultural products, targeting not only local audiences but also global audiences. A handful of major cultural industries, such as the broadcasting, film, music, gaming, animation, and webtoon industries, as well as local digital platforms like Naver, Kakao, and Wavve, have developed, exported, or circulated popular culture one after another. While the broadcasting and film sectors initiated and led the growth of the Korean Wave until the mid-2000s, the digital game and music industries have grown to become the leading areas in the New Korean Wave era starting in 2008 (Jin, 2016).

Regardless of the importance of local cultural industries, however, only a few works have focused on the shifting role of the local cultural industries. As discussed in chapter 2, many scholars in Hallyu studies focused on either audience studies or global fans as their primary areas, while leaving their analysis of cultural industries behind. When they focused on cultural industries, their scope was closely related to marketing. In other words, one of the most important yet least discussed elements in Hallyu studies is the cultural industries, which have played a key role in the Korean Wave tradition.

This chapter documents the major role of the cultural industries in the Korean Wave in the context of the broader social structure of society. It maps out how the local cultural industries have cultivated local cultural products and foreign exports. It especially examines the process of the platformization of the local cultural industries, and therefore, it addresses the ways in which the cultural industries have developed new forms of cultural content in the New Korean Wave era. Through an analysis of the Korean cultural industries, it critically discusses the crucial role of the cultural industries, in particular, digital platforms, in the Korean Wave phenomenon.

History of the Korean Cultural Industries: Pre-Korean Wave Era

The Korean cultural industries can be historicized based on a few major dimensions, and we divide the history of the Korean cultural industries into a few different eras. While it is not perfect, the historicization of the Korean cultural industries, according to a few major dimensions, can help people understand the advent of the local cultural industries in the Korean Wave tradition. The three major elements, including leading industries in a given period, primary cultural production, and relevant technologies, are used in this categorization of local cultural industries, mainly because popular culture and digital technologies go hand in hand.

The first period is the pre-Korean Wave era between the 1960s and 1990s, which is also categorized as the military regime era. This period showed unique local characteristics that were not seen in other democratic countries, mainly due to the massive control by the government. The second era ran between the early 1990s and late 2000s when the Korean Wave was characterized as the Hallyu 1.0 era. This period is important as the necessary industrial infrastructure was built. The third era started in the late 2000s and goes on until the late 2010s, which can be categorized as the New Korean Wave era or the Hallyu 2.0 era (see Jin, 2016). During this period, the growth of digital technologies, including smartphones and local mobile instant messengers, was peculiar. Finally, the fourth era (Cultural Industries 3.0 era) began in the late 2010s when

TABLE 3.1. Historical Division of the National Cultural Industries (p. 72)

	Period	Major Industries	Primary Cultural Production	Key Technologies
Pre-Hallyu Era	1960s–Early 1990s	Broadcasting	Dramas, News	Broadcasting
Cultural Industries 1.0	Early 1990s–2007	Broadcasting, Film	Dramas, Films, Online Games	Internet, Broadband
Cultural Industries 2.0	2008–2017	Digital Games, Music	K-pop, Mobile Games	Smartphones
Cultural Industries 3.0	2017–present	Digital Platforms	K-pop, Webtoons	OTT Platforms

global OTT platforms gained momentum in the Korean cultural market as the primary actors, while local OTT platforms also vehemently invested in cultural production (Table 3.1).[1]

These eras are not mutually exclusive because diverse elements run over a few different eras. Admitting this duplication exists, it is still legitimate in that we can analyze these four major eras differently based on a few primary standards, such as evolving cultural policies, the emergence of new digital technologies, primary cultural industry areas, and major cultural forms representing each different era. Shifting consumption habits by audiences, both national and global, have also influenced the change in the major characteristics of the cultural industries in different eras.

Unlike many other countries, Korea has advanced two major industries—popular culture and digital technologies—which closely work together to create the necessary synergy effects. Since the production and consumption of popular culture can be practiced with various digital technologies, including smartphones, it is essential to include the advent of digital technologies in the analysis of cultural industries. Cultural industries themselves are benefiting from the growth of digital technologies, while they create necessary digital technologies, such as digital platforms and AI technology. For example:

> the K-pop entertainment industry integrated itself with Korea's digitally hyperconnected society—fast and widespread Internet availability, high 4G LTE penetration, pervasive smartphone own-

1. In order to understand the historical division of the Korean Wave, please see Jin 2016 and 2021a. For the periodization of K-pop, please see Yoon (2022).

ership, and all-around social networking services usage. Korea's entertainment industry took on its current form after 1987—around the same time it laid the foundation for its renowned digital infrastructure. Until the nation's democratization drive of 1987, mass media were restricted by governmental censorship (Yuniya & Marc de Jong, 2021, p. 131).

Most of all, the Korean Wave mainly started in the early and mid-1990s, although the massive scale of cultural exports began in the late 1990s. Until the early 1990s, Korea did not have a tangible force in the audiovisual industries. Briefly discussing the Korean audiovisual industry, it is essential to focus on two major areas: television broadcasting and film, although radio broadcasting and music were important. During this period, music was a big part of radio and television broadcasting as the broadcasters often developed music (competition) shows, such as *MBC Campus Song Festival* (1977–2012) and *Gayo Top 10* on KBS (1981–1988). Until the early 1990s, Korean popular music was primarily limited to two major music genres—ballad and trot (*ppongtchak* in Korean), and the Korean music industry was subjugated under a tightly controlled system as television remained the most important platform for popular music, known as *gayo*. Other than a few concert opportunities, radio and television were the major targets of almost all musicians; therefore, it was not usual to combine the music and broadcasting sectors, although the record industry was one of the key areas in the music sector.[2]

---

2. The Korean music industry then experienced its turning point when the mainstream pop music scene started diversifying through dance-oriented music genres (Lee & Jin, 2019). Debuting in 1992, Seo Taiji & Boys especially shifted the Korean pop music scene. Their music, which included elements of heavy metal, hard rock, and hip-hop in a dramatic departure from mainstream popular music (e.g., ballad and trot), was a sensation. A handful of entertainment agencies, such as SM Entertainment, JYP, and YG, also began producing idol groups. K-pop, differentiating itself from Korean popular music, namely gayo, in terms of diverse music genres, emphasis on dances, and visual effects, has earned fame in the domestic market as Korean youth, followed by global fans since the late 2000s, enjoy this new music trend (Lee & Jin, 2019). Meanwhile, the digitalization of popular music has greatly contributed to transforming the local music industry. For example, Soribada, Korea's most popular file-sharing service, which was developed in 2000, quickly grew into the country's most popular file-sharing service with more than 22 million people registered at its peak. Due to its infringement of copyright, Korea's Seoul District Court ordered it shut down, and therefore, its role diminished (Billboard, 2006). However, the digital transformation initiated by Soribada has fundamentally changed the Korean music industry (see also chapter 6).

Again, this book uses the term cultural industries, plural, rather than the cultural industry, singular, as there are numerous industry areas in the realm of popular culture, including broadcasting, film, music, and webtoon. It is also ideal for scholars to use the term cultural industries related to the Korean Wave because there are various separate but connected businesses at work. Furthermore, it is difficult to segregate one industry from the other, particularly in the digital platform era. Previously, the film and broadcasting sectors were almost separated; however, in the early 21st century, the distinction between film and broadcasting has been blurred, in particular due to the emergence of digital platforms.

As discussed in chapter 2, the French "cultural industries" sociologists rejected Horkheimer and Adorno's (1972) use of the singular term "The Culture Industry" because it suggested a "unified field" where all the different forms of cultural production that coexist in modern life are assumed to obey the same logic. The French "cultural industries" sociologists were concerned with showing "how complex the cultural industries are and to identify the different logics at work in various types of cultural production" (Miège, 1987; Hesmondhalgh, 2012, p. 24). Likewise, one must consider the cultural industries as plural to reflect the shifting nature of popular culture and cultural production. This does not mean that all cultural sectors are equal or should be treated as a whole. Even in the audio-visual sector, broadcasting, film, and music are different in terms of history, government subsidies, labor force, and transnationality. However, as the Korean Wave encompasses all forms of cultural content, it is necessary to understand the general trend, while admitting that the significance of individual sectors' characteristics is different.

More specifically, compared to a handful of countries in the Global North, the broadcasting era was relatively late. In Korea, the first television broadcasting system dates back to May 1956, when HLKZ-TV was established as a commercial television station in Seoul (Gunaratne, 2000). The state-owned broadcasting system KBS, which already operated radio broadcasting, started KBS-TV in December 1961, right after Park Chung-hee took political power as a means of securing the military regime's legitimacy and as an integrative force in nation-building. A commercial television station (MBC) joined the broadcasting industry in 1969. There were a few more television channels, including TBC (Tongyang Broadcasting Company, 1964–1980); however, as the Chun Doo-hwan regime severely controlled the media sector to control the news system that might negatively affect its regime, the Korean broadcasting system was virtually a government monopoly until 1991 when a new commercial broadcasting

(SBS) service began to air (Jin, 2011). SBS became the first commercial television network to be established after the Chun regime reorganized 29 broadcasters into an oligopoly of two public broadcasters, KBS and MBC, in 1980 (Shim, 2008).

The broadcasting and film industries were severely controlled by the government in the name of moral spirit and anti-communism ideology. As is well-documented (Shin & Kim, 2013, p. 262), Korean media were censored in the 1980s. After seizing political power, Chun initiated "the Basic Press Law to control media after his military coup, closed down private stations, and licensed only two state-run TV channels, KBS and MBC." Since the primary concern of cultural policy was arts rather than popular culture during this period (Yim, 2022), the government did not emphasize the importance of broadcasting and film for culture or economy. The major cultural policy of the military regime was censorship to tighten the reigns. The Korean cultural industries between the early 1960s and the late 1980s experienced the longest setback as the military regimes continued to control the cultural industries. There were a few significant breakthroughs, of course. The introduction of color television in December 1980 was one of the most significant developments in the Korean cultural industries. With the economic boom in the 1980s, many Koreans started to purchase color monitors, and broadcasting firms had to produce high-quality programs to meet audiences' expectations (see Jin, 2011).

The Korean film industry also did not achieve any tangible growth during this period. Numerous movies, such as *Deep Blue Night* (*Gipgo puleun bam*, 1985), *Eoh Wu Dong* (1985), *Whale Hunting* (*Goraesanyang*, 1984), and *Prostitution* (*Maechun*, 1988) were domestically successful, but the number of moviegoers was mostly less than 500,000, unlike the Korean Wave era when many movies attracted more than 10 million moviegoers, even almost 20 million viewers (Korean Movie Database, 2023), although COVID-19 fundamentally, perhaps for a while, changed people's cultural consumption habits in tandem with the increasing role of digital platforms.

During this pre-Hallyu era, the Korean government started to implement neoliberal economic and cultural policies that affected the cultural industries, in particular the film industry. The Roh Tae-woo regime (1988–1993) allowed the direct distribution of foreign films—primarily Hollywood films—in 1988, and Korean cinema has been a victim of foreign trade since then. A few major Hollywood studios developed subsidiaries to localize some of their production activity in the Korean film market. Such Hollywood majors as Twentieth Century Fox, Warner Brothers,

Columbia, UIP, and Walt Disney set up branches in Korea, and they imported many Hollywood films. Likewise, the structural transformation of the local film industry was closely connected to neoliberal globalization (Jin, 2019).

The Korean cultural industries experienced a variety of changes that increased their permanence in the ever-shifting Korean society. The introduction of black-and-white television in the 1950s, the emergence of color television in the 1980s, and the implementation of neoliberal globalization played pivotal roles in the growth of local cultural industries, although they did not emerge as a major force in the global cultural markets. Arguably, the Korean cultural industries were in a dark age during this period. Again, as the major concern of cultural policy during this period was arts rather than popular culture, the Korean government did not emphasize the role of cultural production (Yim, 2002). However, the continuous developments of various policy measures and technological advancements in tandem with the growth of the national economy became steppingstones for the emergence of the Korean Wave era starting in the early 1990s. Korea has experienced the sudden growth of the local cultural industries in the midst of several key elements, including new cultural policies, technological breakthroughs, and economic turmoil, as well as globalization strategies.

Cultural Industries 1.0: The Emergence of the Contemporary Cultural Industries

The Korean cultural industries since the early 1990s experienced a dramatic shift as the Korean government decided to allow a new commercial television channel for the first time in decades. Until the early 2000s, the Cultural Industries 1.0 era was characterized by the inception of Hallyu as well, which means the emergence of local cultural industries and the advent of the Korean Wave should be identical. With the introduction of the Internet and cable channels in the 1990s, Korea also experienced the first true digital era, which eventually shifted the cultural industries on a large scale in the following years. In other words, Korea initiated the development of both broadcasting and telecommunications systems—the two pillars for the growth of cultural industries and popular culture, almost simultaneously. Therefore, it is essential to include the growth of local cultural industries as part of the Korean Wave. The Korean Wave has not only considered the global popularity of local cultural content but also the emergence of local cultural industries. One also needs to understand that digital Hallyu has been a major part of the Korean Wave from its inception.

Most of all, the introduction of SBS (Seoul Broadcasting System), which was the first private-owned channel amid democratization between the late 1980s and the early 1990s, became a turning point in the Korean broadcasting industry and, therefore, the Korean Wave. With the introduction of SBS, the broadcasting industry was able to encourage international competition to attract local audiences by creating relatively well-made cultural programs, in particular television dramas. In the early 1990s, a handful of early Hallyu dramas, such as *What is Love?* (1991) and *Jealousy* (*Jiltu*, 1992), were popular in East Asia. These dramas were exported to Taiwan and China to work as the harbinger of the Korean drama boom in China. *What is Love?*—a family drama—was exported to China in 1994, but it was aired in 1997 due to various reasons, including a dubbing issue, and it was eventually made a hit on CCTV (Jin, 2021a).

Korea also introduced cable channels in 1995, and therefore, the country suddenly had more than 100 television channels, followed by more specialty channels in the early 21st century. Some channels have produced dramas, music shows, sports, and reality shows, while airing films. The influx of cable broadcasting channels became another key game changer in the Korean entertainment sector as they produced high-quality dramas and reality shows to become part of broadcasting Hallyu (Yang, 2015). As network channels and cable channels competed to gain more viewers, they had to create quality programs. Korea could consequently expand its foreign export of television programs to Asia and, later, to the global cultural markets. Severe competition also triggered multiple programs that are considered poor-quality content because of the lack of talented producers and actors/actresses. However, the soaring competition between multiple channels eventually helped the production of high-quality programs in most cases.

During this period, there was one peculiar historical and political turmoil, which also greatly influenced the local cultural industries—the 1997 financial crisis. As is well-known (OECD, 2021; Lee & Zhang, 2021), in 1997, Korea experienced its worst economic crisis and had to receive the IMF (International Monetary Fund) bailout program, which asked the country to change its economic policy toward the opening of many industrial areas. In Korea, "it was in the aftermath of the 1997 financial crisis that a new neoliberal subjectivity emerged, in conjunction with the pervasive policy discourse of the 'knowledge economy' and the 'knowledge-based society' ardently advocated by President Kim Dae-jung (1998–2003). As such, the forming of the post-industrial selfhood started as a top-down discursive project" (Lee & Zhang, 2021, p. 524).

Ironically enough, the IMF crisis helped local broadcasters create their programs more than in previous years, as they had to reduce their import of foreign programs. A few broadcasters had to cut down their budget and could not import expensive foreign programs. During the process, cultural creators in the broadcasting sector developed a bunch of quality programs that were popular, both nationally and globally. A few Asian countries, including Taiwan, China, and Japan, started to import Korean cultural content massively for the first time in the history of the Korean cultural industries.

Korea also started to develop the film industry in the mid-1990s. When Korea experienced the lowest market share of domestic films in the Korean film market at 15.9% (Korean Film Council, 2019), the Korean cinema world, including the government and film production firms, had to shift their direction to boost the dying film industry. The Korean government initiated the revival of the film sector by introducing new supporting mechanisms. On the one hand, the government enacted the 1995 Motion Picture Promotion Law to provide various incentives, including a tax reduction incentive, to film production companies. Based on this law, some chaebols, including Samsung, were able to invest in the film sector. Although they did not stay longer than expected in the film sector, these chaebols' involvement in the film industry in the latter part of the 1990s certainly helped the resurrection of the local film sector.

On the other hand, the Korean government loosened its censorship of films. The Korean government controlled the film sector through severe censorship between the early 1960s and the late 1980s under consecutive military regimes. With the establishment of the civilian government starting in 1993, censorship gradually disappeared. In particular, the Kim Dae-jung administration's (1998–2003) slogan for cultural policies was "provide support, but do not interfere"; thus, controls like film censorship disappeared. Kim pledged that he would abolish censorship during his campaign in 1997, and censorship was abolished in January 2001 during his presidency period (H. J. Kim, 2006). The government's support for production and distribution increased markedly.

The Korean film industry has consequently experienced a new boom era. As the number of movie screens also increased from only 762 screens in 1991 to 1,880 in 2006, and to 3,254 in 2021, the market share of domestic films also soared to as much as 63.8% in 2006, although the market share decreased for a while in the middle of the Korea-US FTA (free trade agreement), which was signed in 2006 (Korean Film Council, 2008; 2019; 2022). Back then, the U.S. government asked Korea to reduce screen quotas, and the Korean government arguably scapegoated the screen quota system as part of the FTA negotiation (*The Economist*, 2006). A handful of films, such as *Shiri* (1999), *Joint Security Area* (2000), and *Oldboy* (2003), were very popular in many countries, and the Korean cinema world finally achieved Oscars with Bong Joon-ho's *Parasite* (2019) at the 2020 Academy Awards, including Best Picture and Best Director awards.

The audiovisual industries, including broadcasting, film, and music, have continued to grow since the mid-1990s. Various new media, such as cable channels, the Internet, broadband services, and smartphones, have become part of people's daily activities. People's cultural consumption habits have also deeply changed because they moved from their reliance on television sets and theaters to digital platforms, such as YouTube and Netflix, over the past few decades. Of course, this does not imply that television monitors are obsolete as people use big-size television monitors to watch various cultural programs, including dramas and reality shows produced by networks and cable channels. People are able to diversify their choices of cultural content between traditional broadcasting firms and digital platforms.

Meanwhile, Cultural Industries 1.0 implies that the Korean government took a pivotal role in advancing necessary infrastructure. As discussed in chapter 4, Korean cultural policy has changed toward cultural industries policy. However, unlike the pre-Hallyu era, when the government controlled the cultural industries, the Korean government started to advance diverse policy measures to build infrastructure so that cultural creators were able to create enhanced cultural programs. The government provided necessary foundations, including the launch of a new commercial broadcaster (SBS), cable channels, the establishment of a necessary film act, and the loosening of censorship. Based on the development of these new cultural policies, local cultural creators started to develop their creativity in cultural production, which continues to expand. However, due to the emphasis on commercial imperatives, the Korean government and cultural industries did not emphasize cultural values, which was a big blow to some cultural creators and audiences.

Cultural Industries 2.0: Convergence of Popular Culture and Digital Technologies

The Korean cultural industries have continued to grow in the early 21st century. With the global popularity of local cultural content, a handful of major cultural industries have increased their revenue, exports, and the number of employees. However, the primary dimensions for the growth of the local cultural industries are much different from the Cultural Industries 1.0 era. Starting in the late 2000s, Korea has experienced unprecedented developments in digital technologies, including smartphones, and therefore, the Korean cultural industries advanced their convergence between popular culture and cutting-edge digital technologies. Consequently, Korea has advanced digital Hallyu, in which digital technologies and cultures, such as digital games and webtoons, play a big part in the Korean Wave.

In 2008, the Korean government established the Korea Communications Commission (KCC) as a new media regulation agency, combining the former Korean Broadcasting Commission and the Ministry of Information and Communication. Previously, broadcasting and telecommunications were two separate entities; however, with the convergence of these two areas under the KCC, Korea began to develop a few measures to integrate two different but connected areas, which deeply influenced the Korean cultural industries. For example, the government made The Framework Act on Broadcasting Communications Development in 2008, a basic law encompassing broadcasting and telecommunications, as part of the broadcasting and telecommunications convergence policy (Ministry of Government Legislation, 2008; S.W. Ji, 2008). The local cultural industries were able to increase a few key measures, including the number of employees, their revenues, and the exports of cultural content.

To begin with, the Korean cultural industries, including publication, game, music, and broadcasting, have increased their employees, from 421,087 in 2005 to 453,284 in 2022, a 7.6% increase during this period (Ministry of Culture, Sports and Tourism, 2013; 2017; 2022; Korea Creative Content Agency, 2022). Other than publication and film, all industry areas experienced an increase in the number of employees (Table 3.2). Among these, the field of character showed the largest increase, but game and broadcasting also experienced a noticeable increase. Many global younger generations have enjoyed local digital games, in particular, online games, such as *Lineage I* and *II*, and Korea became one of the largest producers of online games, and later, mobile games. In the broadcasting sector, Korea

TABLE 3.2. Number of Employees in the Korean Cultural Industries (p. 84)

	2005	2012	2016	2022
Publication	214,904	198,262	185,001	184,868
Game	60,669	95,051	73,993	83,698
Music	65,346	78,402	78,393	65,936
Broadcasting	29,634	40,774	43,662	51,016
Character	8,828	26,897	33,323	36,258
Manhwa	9,048	10,161	10,127	14,358
Film	29,078	30,857	28,944	11,556
Animation	3,580	4,503	5,142	5,594
Total	421,087	484,907	458,585	453,284

Ministry of Culture and Tourism, 2006; Ministry of Culture, Sports and Tourism, 2013; 2017; 2022; Korea Creative Content Agency, 2022; 2024.

introduced a handful of new channels in the early 2010s, which triggered the growth of its own employees. However, the film industry experienced a significant decrease in the number of employees mainly because of the coronavirus. The number of employees in the Korean film industry decreased, from 32,566 in 2019 to 10,497 in 2020 (Ministry of Culture, Sports and Tourism, 2022; Korea Creative Content Agency, 2023), although it somewhat increased to 11,556 in 2022.

The Korean cultural industries turned themselves into some of the largest segments of the national economy in the early 21st century, and they have continued to grow in terms of the number of employees, revenues, and the exports of cultural content.

Another major trend that helps our understanding of the Korean cultural industries is the exports of local cultural content. As discussed in previous chapters, Korea continued to expand its exports of cultural products to Asia in the 2000s, and later to the global cultural markets, including North America and Western Europe. The growth of exports clearly demonstrates how Korea advances its cultural industries as driving forces to boost the national economy and digital economy, because it does not only indicate the expansion of the export of cultural content, but also the soaring contribution to the national economy. Although this is not the only element in deciding the magnitude of the Korean Wave, the export of cultural content certainly proves the growth of the Hallyu phenomenon.

Korea started its exports of cultural products beginning in the early 1990s; however, it was in the late 1990s and the early 2000s that Korea could export cultural products on a large scale. Then, due to numerous successful movies and television dramas, as well as K-pop, Korea experi-

TABLE 3.3. Exports of Major Cultural Products, 2000–2022 (Unit: million US dollars) (pp. 85–86)

	2000	2005	2010	2015	2020	2022
Broadcasting	13.1	122	184.7	320	692.7	869.1
Movies	7.1	76	13.6	29.3	54.1	71.4
Animation	85	78.4	96.8	126.5	134.5	172
Music	7.9	22.3	81.3	381	679.6	964.4
Games	101.5	585	1606	3214	8193	8973
Characters	69.2	164	276.3	551	715.8	504.8
Manhwa	3.7	3.3	8.2	29.3	62.7	107
Total	287.5	1,051	2,266.9	4,651.1	10,532.4	11,661.7

Source: Ministry of Culture and Tourism (2006); Ministry of Culture, Sports and Tourism (2011; 2013; 2017); Korea Creative Content Agency (2015; 2018; 2019; 2023; 2024)

enced the sudden growth of local cultural content's global reach, in particular in Asia. Starting in the late 2000s and early 2010s, Korea finally penetrated other countries beyond Asia, and the level of exports soared. As Table 3.3 proves, Korea exported US$287.5 million worth of cultural products in 2000; however, it increased to as much as US$11.6 billion in 2022, which is a 40.5 times increase (Korea Creative Content Agency, 2023). As in the case of the number of employees, a few major industries are broadcasting, music, characters, and game industries. As the film industry experienced a decreasing trend in employment, its exports of local films is relatively lower than other cultural industries, even compared to the manhwa industry.

What is significant is that the Lee Myung-bak and Park Geun-hye administrations, between 2008 and 2017, systematically utilized the Korean Wave as a source of soft power and cultural diplomacy. The notion of soft power was primarily articulated by Joseph Nye (2004a). According to Nye (2004a), power is "the ability to influence the behavior of others to get the outcomes one wants. There are various ways to affect the behavior of others," and soft power co-opts people rather than coerces them, and soft power is the ability to entice and attract. Soft power is related to cultural diplomacy which is a subset of public diplomacy in support of foreign policy goals (Mark, 2009). In relation to soft power, cultural diplomacy is "the exchange of ideas, information, art and other aspects of culture among nations and their peoples to foster mutual understanding"

(Cummings, 2003, p. 1). As Nye (2004b) points out, soft power is a primary element in cultural diplomacy.

The conservative administrations during the Cultural Industries 2.0 era supported Hallyu and utilized it, partially because "popular culture has become a potentially important resource for soft power diplomacy, transcultural collaborations, dialogues and struggles to win hearts and minds of people" (Nye & Kim, 2013, p. 35). The Korean government has continued to advance its soft power and cultural diplomacy strategies as a multitude of cultural performers and productions like BTS, Blackpink, and NewJeans, and quite a few cultural programs, including *Parasite*, *Squid Game*, and *Moving* (2023), continue to reign supreme in the global cultural markets. However, it is critical to understand that the government should not intervene in the process of cultural production. As Otmazgin (2021) points out:

> Highly institutionalized arrangements will not be able to catch up with and accommodate the dynamism of cultural industries and the volatilities of cultural markets. The government should rather keep a free sphere for culture to cultivate, where cultural innovations can freely evolve and interact with the established industry. The emphasis should be on stimulating the growth of small firms engaged in various cultural commodification and production, embedded in the local economy, yet aspiring to export their products and services abroad. More specifically, governmental policy should seek to nurture the development of the cultural industries in a few important areas (p. 224).

Popular culture is deeply connected to people's daily lives. Many people enjoy all kinds of cultural content, from dramas to films to music. It was evident that the local cultural industries expanded their business activities by hiring new employees to produce more and better cultural products, which eventually increased foreign exports. However, since the early 2010s, Korea has faced new challenges mainly because of the soaring role of digital platforms, both social media and OTT platforms, which fundamentally shifted the Korean cultural industries and cultural production. Koreans, as elsewhere, used to watch dramas on television while going to movie theaters to enjoy films; the previous norms are not applicable in the digital platform era. The next section discusses the growth of OTT platforms and their impacts on the local cultural industries.

Cultural Industries 3.0: OTT Platforms in the Korean Cultural Industries

Korea has experienced one of the largest and fastest changes in the cultural industries sector over the past 10 years. The major shift in this particular era is the introduction and expansion of digital platforms, including OTT platforms, both nationally and globally. Although Korea developed its local OTT platforms in the early 2010s, local cultural industries firms have confronted a few unprecedented challenges since Netflix arrived in Korea in 2016. Previously, broadcasters and film companies competed against each other to attract mainly domestic audiences, followed by global audiences. However, as global OTT platforms, such as YouTube, Netflix, Apple TV+, and Disney+, play a pivotal role in cultural production, from the production of cultural content to the circulation of cultural programs and to the consumption of cultural products by global audiences, local cultural industries firms faced severe setbacks in view rates and advertising. In particular, digital platforms, both social media (e.g., YouTube) and OTT (e.g., Netflix), have fundamentally shifted media ecology in our contemporary society, which means that the Cultural Industries 3.0 era can be characterized by the emergence of digital platforms as the primary actor in cultural production.

While Korea already developed local OTT platforms in the early 2010s, due to the increasing role of global OTT platforms in the local cultural market and the Korean Wave trend, the Korean cultural industries have continued to create not only new OTT platforms but also merge existing OTT platforms to make large-scale local platforms that compete against global OTT platforms. A few broadcasting firms and telecommunications companies are major actors as platform owners in the local cultural market, and their activities have greatly shifted the milieu surrounding local cultural production. However, the Korean cultural industries have been influenced by the emergence of global OTT platforms as numerous global OTT platforms take a big part in the local cultural industries. Global OTT platforms have expanded their market shares in Korea mainly because they continue to develop their roles as global distributors, as well as global producers as they create original products while licensing existing cultural programs (H. H. Kim, 2023).

More specifically, the Korean cultural industries have developed local OTT platforms such as POOQ, Tving, and Oksusu, and they gradually influence the business norms of the local cultural industries, although these platforms are not comparable to global OTT platforms due to their small scale in terms of revenue and circulation power. Among these, CJ HelloVision, part of CJ, launched Tving in June 2010. Tving, as the first local OTT platform, has been operated by Tving Corporation, a joint venture of CJ ENM, Naver, and JTBC. In October 2011, two terrestrial channels, MBC and SBS, started their joint platform POOQ, while KBS joined the service platform as the program provider. KBS also later invested in it as a stakeholder (Kil, 2019).

SK Broadband, a wholly owned subsidiary of SK Telecom, also launched its new mobile video streaming service platform Oksusu in 2016. It succeeded SK's old platforms B TV and Hoppin. The move followed Netflix's decision to join the ranks of active players in the Korean streaming market. Oksusu provided real-time TV programs, movies, sports channels, and YouTube-style content (E.J. Park, 2016). A handful of local OTT platforms jumped onto the OTT bandwagon. In 2019, KT, the second-largest mobile carrier in Korea, launched KT Seezn, an online video platform. Seezn attempted to "differentiate the belated service from existing global competitors like Netflix and Disney+ and local rival Wavve launched by an SK Telecom-led coalition of terrestrial broadcasters by merging its mobile Olleh TV service with music platform Genie Music" (Song, 2019). Likewise, in the Korean OTT market, there are three primary industries, including broadcasting, telecommunications, and entertainment corporations, that launch and operate OTT service platforms.

The growth of OTT platforms has consequently influenced the broadcasting industry as many Koreans move to OTTs to watch cultural content. The use rate of OTT platforms for those older than 13 years of age increased from 36.1% in 2017 to 69.5% in 2021(Korea Communications Commission, 2023). Although Korean broadcasters have already begun to wane because of the Internet, digital platforms' surge as the major venues for people to enjoy audiovisual content has also negatively affected television channels and movie theaters on a large scale. Many people don't use television channels to watch dramas and news, and they don't go to theaters to watch movies anymore. Instead, they watch cultural content on their mobile gadgets, including smartphones, via OTT platforms.

What is interesting is that these local OTT platforms could not make tangible power in the global cultural market, let alone the local cultural markets. Although they gradually increased their visibility, they could not compete against Netflix, the largest global OTT platform worldwide. Local OTT platforms attempted to become mega platforms to survive while challenging global OTT platforms. Local OTT platforms, therefore, have developed mergers and acquisitions (M&As), and the government had to support these consecutive M&As. Korea's Fair Trade Commission allowed the merger of POOQ and Oksusu in August 2019, which eventually became Wavve (Shin & Lee, 2019). The consolidation of Tving and Seezn was finished in 2022 as well, as Seezn was merged into Tving. With the completion of the merger, KT Studio Genie, which owned Seezn became the third largest shareholder of Tving, while CJ ENM and Studio LuluLala were major stakeholders. With the addition of Seezn subscribers, Tving became the second-largest video streaming service in Korea. Tving and Seezn together had a combined market share of 18.05% as of December 1, 2022, beating Wavve (N. H. Shin, 2022). As of March 2025, local OTT platforms, including Tving, Wavve, Watcha, and Coupang Play compete against each other, while competing with global OTT platforms, although Netflix and Disney+ continue to expand their market share in Korea.[3]

Interestingly, local OTT platforms, like Coupang Play and Tving have increased their subscribers in very recent years mainly due to pro-baseball and pro-soccer games that they exclusively aired. For example, the market share of Coupang Play increased from 15% in March 2023 to 23% in March 2024, while Tving increased from 17% to 21% as they aired these major sports events. During the same period, Netflix's market share declined from 47% to 35% (Sung, 2024). Although the recent change is not much related to cultural content, but sports events, it certainly shows that local OTT platforms will potentially become major players in the Korean OTT market.

The local OTT market represents an oligopoly due to consecutive mergers among local OTT platforms. Only a handful of OTT platforms control the local market, which hurts diversity. Even after these mergers, they cannot beat global OTT platforms, and the local media industries expect to make even bigger platforms by consolidating Tving and Wavve. As local OTT platforms are eager to develop killer content to attract more

3. In December 2023, operators of Tving and Wavve, two major Korean OTT platforms, signed a memorandum of understanding to push for a merger in an apparent effort to compete with global streaming giants. They plan to sign a formal contract after the Fair Trade Commission, Korea's antitrust watchdog, approves the merger in 2025. Once approved, the integrated platform is expected to have a combined 9.3 million monthly active users (MAUs) (N.Y. Kim, 2023).

users, they emphasize only a few commercial genres, and therefore, people's choices are very limited. Local OTT platforms have not gained profits yet; therefore, the current milieu surrounding local OTT platforms is expected to continue, which means that audiences have no choice but to watch a few commercial genres on local OTT platforms. Local OTT platforms have not gained a sustainable number of subscribers as many Koreans select Netflix and Disney+ as their primary OTT platforms to watch local and global content at the same time.

While there are a few reasons for the slow growth of subscribers on the local OTT platforms, the lack of diversity in cultural forms and genres has been one of the major elements. During my interview with a female webtoonist in the Summer of 2023, she said that she had changed her primary OTT platform from Wavve to Netflix mainly because she wanted to watch more animation programs than other cultural forms:

> Wavve has a lot of content, but especially adult and kids' genres. In the anime genre, Japanese studio Ghibli and American Disney are the two major firms, and Netflix brought Ghibli, and there are many Japanese animes on Netflix. I personally like anime, and Netflix has made it more accessible by bringing a lot of anime works. As a result, there are cases where I found out about anime while looking for interesting and high-quality Japanese anime, so I think Netflix plays a major role in the spread of anime (interview with a female webtoonist, 33).

A female college student (23) also described the content issue between Netflix and domestic OTT platforms;

> Netflix has a lot of quality content that Netflix has produced and monopolized, including *Squid Game*. I think that domestic streaming services are lacking in original content. This is inevitable due to the difference in capital, but in order to survive, it is necessary for domestic streaming services to create their own quality content.

During the interview process, some Koreans, including cultural creators, expressed their concerns about the soaring role of Netflix; however, they also believed the involvement of global OTT platforms provides opportunities for local cultural industries firms under the condition that local platforms and cultural firms diversify their cultural genres.

Meanwhile, the K-pop world has also continued to advance popular music service platforms, also known as online fan service platforms. K-pop has become globally popular since the early 2010s, and a few entertainment powerhouses, including Hybe, SM Entertainment, and YG, have developed or utilized online fan service platforms, including Weverse, V Live, and Dear U Bubble.[4] Among these, Weverse has been the largest music platform. Hybe, as the home for BTS, needed to have its own platform. BTS is peculiar in its social media use, compared to other K-pop idols. BTS members have had the freedom to use social media to convey their daily activities, and therefore, to communicate with ARMY (Adorable Representative M.C. for Youth). BTS members originally used Naver's V Live; however, Hybe had to develop its platform and consequently launched Weverse in June 2019. Weverse became one of the largest music platforms as Weverse and Weverse Shop surpassed 100 million downloads worldwide as of July 2023, while the platform's monthly active users, at 9.8 million, are reaching almost 10 million users using the app per month. Unlike its first stage, the platform is open to both Hybe artists and non-Hybe artists, including NewJeans and Seventeen (Y. J. Cho, 2023a). Non-Hybe artists are also on the platform, including YG's top girl group Blackpink (J. Lee, 2022). Hybe understands the business of fandom. That is why it is a global fandom platform project (de Luna, 2023).

> Weverse, feels so compelling. Envisioned as neither a social network nor a private fan club, Hybe is trying to create a super app that would allow artists to post, livestream, host concerts, sell official

4. During this era, Hybe introduced the multi-label system, departing from the traditional structure where agencies relied solely on major musicians for sustainability in terms of consistency, stability, and external investment. As of May 2024, under Hybe lies BigHit Music, home to BTS; Pledis Entertainment, home to Seventeen; Source Music, home to Le Sserafim; BeLift Lab, home to Enhypen; and Ador, which houses NewJeans (Pyo, 2024). While this new system certainly boosts the K-pop industry, it also causes some competition among labels under the same entertainment house, as can be seen in a battle between Hybe and Ador, led by Min Hee-jin, in the first part of 2024. Ador was established in 2021 as an independent label under Hybe. The conflict between Ador and Hybe started over strategic disagreements concerning NewJeans. "The conflict began to surface publicly when Min expressed concerns over Hybe's overarching control, which she felt stifled her creative autonomy." This conflict eventually made a legal battle between these two units over Min's leadership (K. Kim, 2024). Labels want to get more freedom and independent financial benefits; however, the umbrella entertainment house increases its control over labels, and this new K-pop production system has some tensions and conflicts in the K-pop world.

> merchandise, and more in a single online ecosystem. Thanks to HYBE's ambitious global expansion, including its acquisition of Ithaca Holdings (home to Justin Bieber and Ariana Grande), its merger with former industry livestreaming leader V Live, and partnerships with Universal Music Group and South Korean competitor SM Entertainment, Weverse currently hosts 80 artists and actors from around the globe. (de Luna, 2023)

Weverse allows "fans to connect with other fans around the world, the members of bands themselves, and, much like fancafe, allows them to enjoy exclusive content you cannot see anywhere else handpicked for Weverse members" (Devoe, 2019). Weverse has become popular because it is the exclusive music fan platform where people watch BTS's daily activities. Hybe has been able to utilize its platforms for BTS fans, differentiating itself from other entertainment houses (Kim and Jin, 2024).

Like in the OTT service platform sector, music service platforms also pursued corporate integrations. In 2021–2022, Hybe and Naver worked together to combine their music platforms. Hybe and Naver planned to create a global fan community platform, and the Korea Fair Trade Commission approved a merger deal between Naver's streaming platform V Live and Hybe's Weverse in May 2021. Weverse took over V Live, and Naver acquired a 49% share of the company. Launched in 2015, Naver's V Live became a go-to streaming platform for K-pop fans. K-idols could also upload content, including vlogs, exclusive interviews, and live stream performances; however, it became part of Weverse (H. S. Yim, 2021).

The Cultural Industries 3.0 era can be identified with the growth of digital platforms, which has shifted the scope and magnitude of the local cultural industries. Although digital platforms started to surface in the mid-2000s, their dominance only began a few years ago when Netflix arrived in Korea in 2016. Digital platforms previously worked as distributors; however, they have functioned as cultural producers as well since a few years ago. As OTT platforms emphasize the importance of original programs to attract subscribers, they vehemently invest in the production sector. Therefore, they have fundamentally shifted the local cultural industries that must face these challenges to survive and prosper. This also implies that the global popularity of Korean cultural content is not only related to the growth of digital platforms, but is also increasingly dependent on digital platforms. On the one hand, digital platforms have become new drivers; on the other hand, they have largely controlled the destiny of local popular culture.

Implications of the Advent of Global OTT Platforms in the Local Cultural Industries

Cultural industries in the Korean context have experienced a fundamental shift that cannot be easily seen in other countries. Korea was a small cottage house in the realm of cultural production until the late 1980s; however, the country has dramatically developed its cultural industries, becoming one of the top 10 countries in terms of magnitude based on the export of cultural content, job creation, and overall revenues. With the nascent growth of the Korean Wave in the global sphere, local cultural industries have continued to experience fairytale-like moments as none of the countries in the Global South have achieved this level of progress. Since cultural industries are closely related to people's mentalities and daily cultures, it also means that the growth of local cultural industries and popular culture has greatly influenced people's lives in many countries.

The Korean cultural industries have become some of the major symbols that represent the success of non-Western cultural industries and popular culture, and therefore, for many countries, it is vital to learn from the Korean Wave while developing their own cultural industries and popular culture. As discussed in chapter 4, the success of local cultural industries has been made possible partially when the Korean government and cultural industries firms emphasize commercial values of popular culture rather than enhancing cultural values. Therefore, the growth of local cultural industries does not mean the growth of cultural values and sovereignty. This critical environment asks the government and cultural industries to initiate their attempts to develop cultural values as well as commercial values in the Korean Wave tradition.

A few countries have attempted to develop their local cultural industries. In Asia, for example, Japan and China have continuously developed cultural industries to create cultural content that can be received in other countries. Japan has successfully advanced a few cultural industries, such as manga, anime, and console gaming, while China continues to develop local films to become globally popular. However, these countries cannot penetrate the global cultural markets. Although Japan's socio-economic and cultural milieu surrounding the cultural industries is better than its counterparts in Korea, its global reach is limited to a couple of cultural forms. It certainly proves that the Korean cultural industries in a non-Western realm have reigned supreme in cultural production, at least for now. Over the past 30 years, during the Korean Wave era, local cultural industries have played a pivotal role in producing cultural content that appeals to global audiences. Their know-how, skills, and manpower are unmistakable assets in local cultural production.

The Korean cultural industries have become some of the most significant cultural apparatuses that influence peoples' daily activities and the country's economic and political ideologies. Due to their unique characteristics that control several parts of the country, the cultural industries should be treated not only as cultural agencies but also as socioeconomic and political entities. In other words, seemingly influencing people's cultural behaviors, cultural industries firms take a pivotal role in the national economy and foreign affairs. That's why neighboring countries equipped with massive production money have vehemently invested in their local cultural industries.

The business opportunity of digital platforms has extraordinary implications for popular culture (Lotz, 2022), mainly because it brings about a power struggle between global and local digital platforms, and therefore, the cultural industries. Although audiovisual industries continuously shifted from domestic roots to transnational forces (Steemers, 2004, cited in Lotz and Eklund, 2024), local cultural industries, including local digital platforms, have taken pivotal roles in cultural production. In other words, the nation-state fully understands that streaming is crucial in local popular culture, although technological and business affordances expedite speedy transnationality. Streaming practice does not come uniformly or with consistent effect in different countries. Instead, how it is adopted is shaped by pre-existing individual countries' conditions (Lotz & Eklund, 2024):

> A national lens remains critical because streaming does not erase underlying conditions and histories, or factors such as population scale and wealth. Instead, streaming intervenes in established national sectors with incumbent technological, economic, and regulatory dynamics that structure the array of services—streaming and otherwise—available to a user. Streaming exists alongside established audiovisual sectors that are nationally specific and shape how viewers perceive the need and value of these services, rather than there being some common global appetite for their offerings. National conditions specify a broader audiovisual context of competing and complementary services and supply the basis of pre-existing cultural norms and expectations (Lotz & Eklund, 2024, p. 120).

However, global OTT platforms equipped with their circulation power have become primary actors in Korean cultural production. Although local digital platforms have continued to develop their roles, a few global digital platforms are controlling the Korean market due to their distribution power as well as massive capital. As is fully discussed in chapter 7, the local cultural industries have been severely hit by global digital platforms. Under this circumstance, the local cultural industries have to develop their strategic plans to overcome severe challenges from both global OTT platforms and neighboring countries' growing cultural industries. The Korean cultural industries especially have to create high-quality cultural content that attracts more global audiences than ever. While they work as independent actors, they need to develop collaborative works with global platforms to utilize their distribution networks. As Boccellaa and Salerno (2016) pointed out, developing such collaborations means that the local cultural industries have in mind a clear picture of the deep links between the cultural industries development and the local capital of a country, followed by the collaboration between local and global forces. It is necessary to strengthen close relationships between various actors in order to develop Korea's cultural industries.

Conclusion

This chapter discussed the Korean cultural industries from a historical point of view according to various dimensions. The Korean cultural industries have increased their role in cultural production, and therefore, the Korean Wave in our contemporary society. Cultural industries are closely related to cultural policy, technological developments, and the national economy. Based on these various dimensions, this chapter divided the emergence and growth of the local cultural industries into a few different eras; from Cultural Industries 1.0 to Cultural Industries 3.0, as well as the pre-Hallyu cultural industries era. It analyzed each era according to its major characteristics, reflecting those major elements. There exists some overlap between eras; however, each era certainly shows its unique development.

In Korea, the local cultural industries, mainly audiovisual and entertainment industries, started in the 1950s. The pre-Hallyu cultural industries were relatively static and controlled under consecutive military regimes. The military regimes, from Park Chung-hee to Chun Doo-hwan, tightly controlled and manipulated the cultural industries as they did not earn political legitimacy. As the military regimes did not focus on popular culture, they had no intention of advancing the quality of popular culture as part of the national economy. Of course, the advent of the color television era in the early 1980s and the adoption of neoliberal economic and cultural policies, in addition to severe censorship, also characterized the cultural industries during the dark age, between the early 1960s and the late 1980s.

In the early 1990s, the situation surrounding the local cultural industries dramatically changed. As the country introduced a few broadcasting companies, both network and cable, Korea was able to create a multitude of broadcasting programs, including dramas and reality shows, which were the major parts of broadcasting Hallyu. Simultaneously, Korea developed various forms of film companies, both production and exhibition companies. With the loosening of censorship starting in the late 1990s, Korean cinema created many films that became globally popular. Consequently, Korea has continued to develop its cultural industries in tandem with Hallyu.

Since the mid-2010s, Korea has experienced the new cultural industries era mainly due to the emergence of digital platforms as the primary actors in the local cultural industries. A few local OTT and music platforms were launched, and they competed against global digital platforms. These local platforms have had to compete against local broadcasters and film corporations as well. Local OTT platforms, as of Summer 2025, still faced a difficult media environment due to the increasing role of global OTT platforms, while local music platforms established their own strong forces. In the Korean cultural industries, OTT platforms have recently become new forces in cultural production. The wave of digital platforms is unprecedented, as the local cultural industries have not faced this kind of strong challenge before.

In sum, the Korean cultural industries, which are the foundations of the Korean Wave, have experienced various important changes over the past few decades. This is a unique case in the global cultural markets, as no other country has dramatically advanced its cultural industries more than Korea. From a small cottage house to one of the major cultural hubs that created the Korean Wave phenomenon, Korea has greatly advanced its cultural industries. There have been various setbacks in the process of neoliberal globalization and the power struggles between local and global forces like digital platforms, which means that Korea also experienced various crises; however, the Korean cultural industries are considered as one of the most significant cultural industries from the Global South.

4

Cultural Industries Policy in Korea's Cultural Production

Introduction

While many media scholars and media outlets have analyzed the Korean Wave from various perspectives, they did not focus on cultural industries and relevant policy measures. The popularity of the Korean Wave, as one of the most significant non-Western cultural movements, started in the early or mid-1990s with a handful of supporting dimensions within the country. As discussed in chapter 3, local cultural industries began to grow starting in the early 1990s, and consecutive government administrations played important roles. Since the Korean Wave implies a global surge of Korean cultural content based on the advent of local cultural industries, it is not unusual to focus on enthusiastic global fans and the increasing role of social media as the primary causes for the growth of the Korean Wave. However, one cannot deny the crucial role of the Korean government, in particular, in the early stage of the Korean Wave as cultural policies have been considered some of the most pivotal elements. The Korean government has developed a few key measures, including necessary infrastructure, while subsidizing local cultural industries, which play important roles in the growth of local cultural content.

This does not mean that cultural politics surrounding the growth of the Korean Wave has been the most important factor, nor the sole element. What we have to understand is the ways in which the government has advanced the Korean Wave with its policy arms, such as legal, financial, and political resources, if there are any particular policy measures. We also have to analyze whether a variety of relevant policy measures have always worked positively in the Korean Wave tradition. Many countries, not only Korea but also other countries, have attempted to advance their unique cultural policies. They have developed their supportive cultural policies for their own national cultures with high budgets;[1] however, these countries' cultural contents have not become global sensations, comparable to Korean popular culture, although they allocate more of their national budgets than Korea does in the realm of popular culture. It certainly indicates that there are diverse dimensions other than budget in the growth of the Korean Wave.

Korean cultural policy has experienced a multitude of significant changes over the past few decades. Until the early 1990s, the Korean government focused on cultural identity and cultural heritage in cultural policy; however, it changed its emphasis toward the economic values of popular culture, and their roles in the national economy. Although the Korean governments in the Korean Wave era mostly pursued neoliberal economic policy, they also used their legal and financial powers to develop local cultural industries. The Korean cultural industries have become some of the most interesting areas as the Korean government advances its unique industry policy.

It is vital to analyze cultural politics related to the Korean Wave. This chapter critically engages with various key policy issues to determine their roles in the Korean Wave process. However, instead of utilizing the traditional approach in policy studies, focusing on the notion of cultural policy, it employs a specific policy study approach that terms cultural industries policy in tandem with the Korean Wave to analyze the nexus between the cultural industries and the Korean Wave, systematically and comprehensively. It is not dicey to select the term cultural industries policy over the term cultural policy as the growth of popular culture in Korea is closely related to its new characteristic—the cultural commodity concept. This is particularly the case in Korea, as the government itself does not distin-

1. According to OECD (2020), Korean government spending on recreation, culture, and religion was only 1% of the gross domestic product in 2020, whereas Hungary (4%), Iceland (3.5%), Norway (2%), France (2%), Spain (1.3%), and Germany (1.1%) spent significantly more during the same year. Only a handful of wealthy countries, including the U.S., the U.K., and Japan spent less than Korea. In 2022, the Korean government's spending on culture was 0.6% of the general national budget, while Europe accounted for about 1.3%. More specifically, in 2022, across the EU, approximately 0.9% of total general government expenditure was allocated to cultural services, and around 0.4% of total general government expenditure was devoted to broadcasting and publishing services. This percentage remained relatively stable over time within the EU, although there were considerable differences when analyzing the results for individual countries (Eurostat, 2023; Ministry of Culture, Sports and Tourism, 2023).

guish its policy between cultural policy, emphasizing cultural identity, sovereignty, and society, and cultural industries policy, focusing on the market economy (D. J. Lee, 2022).

This chapter discusses cultural politics by emphasizing the intricate relationships between the Korean government and local cultural industries. It discusses how the Korean government initiated the growth of the local cultural industries, which eventually advanced the Korean Wave. As the cultural industries have played a pivotal role in the Korean Wave phenomenon, and therefore, cultural production in general, this chapter analyzes the cultural industries policy that the Korean government develops, sometimes explicitly, and at other times, implicitly. Then, it discusses the differences between cultural policy and cultural industries policy to address whether the Korean government has redirected its policy directions toward the global success of Hallyu content.

Toward Cultural Industries Policy

State support to cultural industries is provided via a variety of measures that implement cultural policy. Cultural policy as a comprehensive term can be considered as the sum of governmental activities with respect to culture, and cultural policy involves governmental strategies and activities that promote the production, circulation, and consumption of popular culture. Cultural policy encompasses "a much broader array of activities than what was traditionally associated with an arts policy" (Mulcahy, 2006, p. 321).[2] Therefore, popular culture is at the heart of much of the concern about the condition of public life in many countries (Pratt, 2005).

There are a multitude of primary measures of implementation of cultural policy, such as 1) financial (economic): subsidies, tax reductions, and grants; 2) legal measures: laws, decrees, and orders; and 3) socio-psychological supports: recognition, awards, and prizes to boost and develop cultural industries activities (Rimkutė, 2009a, pp. 34–36, cited in Vitkauskaitė, 2015, p. 215). There are also various factors interfering with these activities: various taxes; public condemnation; prohibition legislation; censorship; and various fines (Rimkutė, 2009a, pp.34–36, cited in

2. Arts policy typically "involved public support for museums, the visual arts (painting, sculpture, and pottery), and the performing arts (symphonic, chamber and choral music; jazz, modern dance, opera and musical theater, and serious theater), historical preservation, and humanities programs (such as creative writing and poetry)" (Mulcahy, 2005, p. 321).

Vitkauskaitė, 2015, pp. 215–216). These policy measures are, of course, mainly targeting cultural and/or artistic values. In other words, cultural policy implemented in democratic countries should not have a negative influence on the artistic value of cultural products.

In the early 1990s, a few countries, both in the Global North and the Global South, started to advance progressive measures that highlighted the economic importance of culture. The significance of popular culture in the name of economic values was added to cultural policy in these countries because these governments believed that popular culture might facilitate not only international cultural exchange but also improve the country's image. A few Western countries, including the United States, already defined culture as commodities even in the 1980s. The United States believed in the important role of culture in the national economy as Hollywood films proved, and the American government argued that other countries, both Western and non-Western countries, should accept the market model as the basis for cultural industries policy. The free flow of information has been a primary agenda of the U.S. Department of State, and therefore, the U.S. government used this ideology to demand other countries to open their markets (Schiller, 1975). Here, a significant part of the US strategy for selling its point of view was to merge cultural and information technology issues (Audley, 1994), which means the U.S. emphasized the convergence of popular culture and digital technology:

> by establishing the principle that culture is a commodity, by associating culture exclusively with industry, by formalizing a commitment to the transnational trade in knowledge, by liberalizing trade in information and cultural services, and by initiating the process for a comprehensive undertaking on intellectual property, the United States has furthered its global cultural interests through both direct and indirect means. In the process, it has also set a precedent for follow-up negotiations on culture with Canada and laid a basis for future bilateral and multilateral agreements with other countries (Carr, 1991, p. 29).

In the Korean context, cultural policy used to focus on arts, such as traditional music and local painting, until the early 1990s, meaning Korean cultural policy legitimized governmental intervention from the dimensions of artistic excellence, cultural diversity, and heritage preservation (Yim, 2002; H. K. Lee, 2020). Under the military regimes between the early 1960s and the early 1990s, primary cultural policy strategies were "the rapid establishment of institutions and infrastructures for arts and culture under the tight control of the government, and the insulation of the domestic cultural sector for both protection and manipulation" (Chung, 2019, p. 65). By utilizing various policy measures, the Korean government, until then, supported the arts, but not popular culture.

State intervention in traditional arts was "primarily driven by the desire to preserve the national heritage for future generations and to sustain the consumption of socially desirable goods that are not of interest to private entrepreneurs . . . the government's role was the protection of intellectual property and supporting creative activities and the innovative character of the national economy, which translates into material economic benefits and increasing prosperity" (Kowalczyk & Cichoń, 2021, p. 3). Since the arts and heritage were the government's primary objects in Korea, commercial cultural businesses were mostly left to market forces and subject to general cultural policies instead of specific cultural policies, including competition, tax, and trade (H. K. Lee, 2020). However, the situation fundamentally shifted starting in the early 1990s. Since then, consecutive Korean administrations have emphasized the importance of popular culture, and therefore, increased their support to cultural production. This implies that popular culture has become "the object of state control" (H. K. Lee, 2013, 186).

The situation surrounding popular culture especially changed in the Kim Young-sam government (1993–1998), which turned its policy priorities from artistic excellence to commercial imperatives. The Kim government drove the globalization agenda, known as *Segyehwa*, as one of the primary policy schemas, and suddenly introduced the idea of cultural industries, and therefore, the Bureau of Cultural Industries in the Ministry of Culture and Tourism in 1994 (K. C. Kim, 2013; J. S. Kim, 2018). The establishment of the Bureau marked the turning point from which the Korean government started to formulate serious cultural industries policy. The Korean government did not differentiate between arts policy and cultural industries policy until then. When the Kim government prepared for globalization, the administration finally understood the major differences between the culture and arts sector and the cultural industries sector. This was when the government started to emphasize the significant role of cultural sectors as part of the national economy. This divergence in the Kim administration was considered as the turning point in Korean cultural industries policy that promotes cultural industries from a global perspective (Chung, 2012).

This new concept indeed became a symbol of the shift in the major focuses of cultural policy, from arts to cultural commodities. Korea, for the first time in history, began to massively emphasize popular culture as commodities rather than arts, while initiating the growth of a couple of cultural industries, including broadcasting and film, as well as information technologies. The Kim government certainly viewed the promotion of Korea's cultural industries as one of the primary drivers of economic growth, and the Kim government also "supported the development of Korea's electronics, information storage and telecommunication industries" (Kwon & Kim, 2013, p. 523). Before this, in 1991, the Korean government already established the Korea Foundation, which was a non-governmental organization with the aim of the worldwide promotion of Korean popular culture and language (The Korea Foundation, 2010). The Korean government believed that popular culture could support "the transnational flow of knowledge and artistic creations as well. The growing need for national branding has prompted Korean diplomats to actively seek the exchange of ideas, information and cultural goods on the international stage, and to reinforce the perception of Korea as a democratic, technologically advanced, economically innovative country, open to other ethnic groups and full of tourist attractions" (Kowalczyk & Cichoń, 2021, p. 4). Once seemingly insignificant, popular culture began to be considered as a cure-all element in the Korean context.

More importantly, the Korean government developed the notion of culture as a commodity as the Korean government attempted to develop neoliberal tendencies forced by the U.S. In the early 1990s, the Korean government developed a new economic development framework that aimed to create a knowledge-based economy. New industries were promoted by successive governments through support for advanced technology, such as information communication and biotechnologies:

> Simultaneously to the marketization and accessibility of cultural goods, there was a lively development of the mass media, including radio, television, large-scale press and the newly created Internet network. Advances in information technology have facilitated access to mass audiences, also enabling real-time free communication. The improvement in the coverage of telecommunications channels and the expansion of their offerings contributed to an increase in the number of recipients, and thus the dissemination of broadcast content—including marketed cultural goods (Kowalczyk & Cichoń, 2021, p. 5).

Within this new framework, the cultural industries were selected as some of the key strategic industries for the national economic development of Korea. Consequently, the government provided ongoing and constructive support for the cultural industries. However, in promoting new strategic industries, the government emphasized "a virtuous and mutually beneficial cycle of growth among these industries." For example, the Korean government encouraged "the combined growth of the game and ICT industries and of digital content and electronic industries" to develop new markets (Kwon & Kim, 2014, p. 426).

The Korean cultural industries policy has transformed popular culture into a fictitious commodity via various "intellectual experiments that disembed culture from historical and social contexts and reduced its meaning. In the same vein, the policy's systematic application of industrial strategies to culture results in its assimilation to industry policy and a consequent post-culturalization of the policy itself" to establish pro-business attitudes in the realm of popular culture, while nurturing cultural producers' global ambition (H. K. Lee, 2019, p. 89). The policy goes beyond the normal parameters of cultural policy and shows a fixation on the economic perspective of cultural content:

> The cultural and social significance of commercial cultural products and activities are hardly recognized by the policy as talking about value and meaning is perceived as relevant only for the arts and non-profit culture. Hence it is not really surprising to see the increasing alignment of cultural industries policy to the state's economic development strategy, [a trend that was accelerated by consecutive administrations.] The 'post-cultural' cultural industries policy seeks deepening convergence of culture with ICT, R&D, start-ups and export businesses, inevitably undermining its own foothold as a branch of 'cultural' policy (H. K. Lee, 2019, p. 89).

In other words, the Korean government has promoted the growth of cultural industries to produce popular culture as marketable and exportable commodities. The Korean government has implemented the importance of economic values of popular culture, and therefore, the necessity of the growth of local cultural industries as the new growth engine for the Korean economy and society.

In Korea, cultural industries policy, as a subset of cultural policy, broadly requires the logic of industrial policy, which is difficult to define (H. K. Lee, 2019). While there are a few different positions in understanding cultural industries policy, industrial policy usually involves "the government's use of its authority and resources to address the needs of specific sectors and industries (and, if necessary, those of individual companies) with the aim of raising the productivity of factor inputs" (Okimoto, 1989, p. 8). Chang (1996, p. 60) argued, industrial policy needs to aim at "particular industries (and firms as their components) to achieve the outcomes that are perceived by the state to be efficient for the economy as a whole." Particular industries "implicitly exclude policies designed to affect industry in general" and infer "policies aimed principally at categories other than industry" (Chang, 1996, pp. 60–61). Korea's industrial strategy has a clear target of a few selected industries, focusing on their growth and exports. This explains "why policymakers see it as normative to develop a centrally managed content industries policy that is distinguished from labor market or urban regeneration policies, although there are some overlaps" (H. K. Lee, 2020, p. 545).

Cultural industries policy has become a new policy doctrine in Korean cultural policy since the early 1990s. Although the Korean government has introduced a variety of policy measures and terms, including the contents industries and the creative industries, the major characteristics of cultural industries policy developed in the early 1990s have continued to work as the major policy priority. Different administrations have advanced their unique policy measures; however, there are a multitude of common policy issues concerning the Korean Wave, such as 1) supporting cultural industries for their global entry, 2) fostering cultural experts in local cultural industries, 3) reinforcing intellectual property rights protection, 4) attracting digital content investment, 5) nurturing content start-ups, and 6) promotion of K-content (Ministry of Culture, Sports and Tourism, 2022). Since the notion of cultural industries policy has been discussed in the neoliberal era, the next section mainly addresses the relationship between the adaptation of neoliberalism and cultural industries policy, which are related to K-content promotion and marketing support, as well as K-content monetization model development.

Nexus of Neoliberalism and Cultural Industries Policy

There were various reasons why the Korean government changed its policy direction, from cultural policy to cultural industries policy, in the realm of popular culture, although the overarching umbrella term cultural policy has been continuously used. One of the primary reasons for the utilization of cultural industries policy was the adaptation and expansion of neoliberalism in local cultural politics. In other words, neoliberal tendencies have been some of the primary overarching contexts for the growth of the local cultural industries.

Neoliberalism has greatly influenced several parts of Korean society, and culture is especially dumbfounded. As Milton Friedman (1951, p. 90) already pointed out, "neoliberalism would accept the 19th-century liberal emphasis on the fundamental importance of the individual, but it would substitute for the 19th-century goal of laissez-faire as a means to this end, the goal of the competitive order." Therefore, neoliberalism would attempt to:

> use competition among producers to protect consumers from exploitation, competition among employers to protect workers and owners of property, and competition among consumers to protect the enterprises themselves. The state would police the system, establish conditions favorable to competition and prevent monopoly, provide a stable monetary framework, and relieve acute misery and distress. The citizens would be protected against the state by the existence of a free private market; and against one another by the preservation of competition (p. 90).

McChesney (2001, p. 2) also claims that neoliberalism unleashed national and international politics maximally supportive of business domination of all social affairs. According to him, "the centerpiece of neoliberal policies is invariably a call for commercial communication markets to be deregulated." As these scholars discussed, neoliberalism has been used to bring about the restructuring of national economies, resulting in the transnationalization of local cultural industries and popular culture (Jin, 2006).

More specifically, although consecutive military regimes between 1980 and 1993 gradually implemented neoliberal tendencies, again, it was mainly Kim Young-sam (1993–1998) who actualized neoliberalism reforms in the name of segyehwa (globalization) in the early Korean Wave era. Throughout the 1980s, old Korean economic technocrats developed and supported state-led development schemes (Choi, 2009). However, since the inauguration of the Kim Young-sam administration, neoliberalism supporting economic globalization has been a dominant ideology in the entire Korean society, from economy to culture. Chaebols, referring to the largest conglomerates like Samsung, Hyundai, and SK, were some of the strongest economic interest groups to support the segyehwa strategy, particularly financial liberalization policies. Although these conglomerates were the primary beneficiaries of state developmentalism during the military regimes, they also wanted the maximization of their liberty in planning and developing their own industrial priorities. The Kim government "pursued the internationalization of the Korean economy and severely criticized the state's regulation over business and financial sectors, putting the fundamental feature of the country's developmental state into question" (H. K. Lee, 2019, p. 91).

The Kim Young-sam administration attempted to open the local market, deregulate the industry sectors, and privatize the public sector, which was the primary characteristic of neoliberal economic policy. The Kim government planned to pursue a small government regime to extend the private sector's profits. The Kim government needed to emphasize commercial imperatives by separating popular culture from traditional national arts, allowing it to operate relatively freely in the private cultural market, from cultural services managed by the nation-state (Shan, 2014). As Chung (2019, p. 66) points out, "the Korean CI [cultural and creative industries] policy shift was designed and driven under the dynamics with the two theses being applied to the field of cultural industries policy. The parallel development thesis (i.e., The Third Way) was translated into the 'arm's length principle' and the informational revolution thesis (i.e., The Third Wave) was embodied into the vision of 'CI as a national basic industry.'"

The Kim Dae-jung (1998–2003) government continued to advance cultural industries to boost the national economy in the middle of the 1997 economic crisis. Under the IMF (International Monetary Fund) bailout program, the government had to open the domestic market in return for the IMF program, and "the Korean cultural industries policy shift did not happen because of any natural development in the cultural sector, but as part of an intentional state transformation project that was triggered by and oriented toward the changing international conditions" (Chung, 2019, p. 66). Of course, the shift was initiated by "the state with specific political intentions and objectives, and with the aim of restructuring the cultural sector and policy community in accordance with the rising new economy. Both states promoted CI actively not only as a treasure trove but also as a template for knowledge economy" (Chung, 2019, pp. 66–67). The Korean broadcasting, film, animation, gaming, and music industries have expanded rapidly, giving rise to the Korean Wave, "as successive liberal governments supported them between the early 1990s and 2010s" (Kwon & Kim, 2013, p. 526).

President Kim Dae-jung continued to expand neoliberal tendencies. He had no choice but to expand neoliberal policies in the IMF bailout program period. The Kim government implemented pro-market policies under pressure from the IMF that demanded structural reforms that intended to reduce government control over the business sectors, while fully opening local markets to foreign firms (Crotty & Lee, 2005; Lim & Jang, 2006; H. K. Lee, 2019). In the realm of culture, the Kim Dae-jung government paid attention to cultural products as part of its promotion of growth sectors for the Korean economy (Ministry of Culture and Tourism, 2002; Ministry of Culture, Sports and Tourism, 2010; Kwon & Kim, 2013). When the Kim government enacted the Framework Act on the Promotion of Cultural Industries (1999), it indicated the notion of commodity by saying that "cultural industries refer to the industries related to the production, distribution and consumption of cultural commodities including industries related to film, music recording, video, games, publication, printing, serial, broadcasting program," and others. Here "cultural commodity refers to goods, services, and their combination that create economic added values by embodying cultural elements" (The Framework Act on the Promotion of Cultural Industries, 1999). In order to develop a new, knowledge-driven economy, the Korean government rapidly expanded its cultural industries policy.

While benefiting from public investment and other forms of assistance, the local cultural industries served as a symbol of a knowledge-driven economy. In Korea, the emergence of the entrepreneurial state in cultural policy "was motivated by the unprecedented economic imagination of culture, an essential feature of neoliberal Korea," which means that this new development certainly "sheds light on Korea's embedded nonlinearization, where there is inconsistency across sectors, and the crucial roles played by the state in shaping contexts for the market economy of culture" (H. K. Lee, 2019, p. 92).

Again, the Korean government's policy shift toward cultural industries policy from cultural policy was concurrent with neoliberal economic policies. As many countries, including Korea, wanted to develop their cultural sectors as part of the knowledge economy and digital economy, they had to develop articulated policy measures. Unlike other general industries, the Korean cultural sector has been unique due to its dual roles between cultural creativity/sovereignty and cultural economy. Before the adaptation of neoliberal economic policy, there was certainly a move to analyze culture from an economic lens. This traditional notion emphasized culture as a public good, and therefore, it provided a justification for the government to develop its public intervention (Throsby, 2001; Pratt, 2005). The neoliberal turn asked the government to change the concept of popular culture into commodities rather than public goods, and therefore, the government has developed various industry policies in the realm of popular culture.

However, unlike other industries, such as the textile, apparel, and heavy and chemical industries, cultural industries exist within a complicated context as a few dimensions, including the persistence of the nation-state, multiculturality, and localism, have worked together. Although transnational forces are powerful, domestic actors like national governments and corporations have to play significant roles in protecting cultural sovereignty (Maxwell, 1995). Dan Schiller (1999, p. 2) also claimed that "national governments played a key role in the media sector because unremitting political intervention was, paradoxically, necessary in order to actualize something approaching a free-market regime in the media sector." To examine the rapidly shifting local cultural industries, thus, people need to understand not only the role of transnational corporations (TNCs) but also the role of the government and domestic cultural producers, which means that it is vital to discuss the relationship between neoliberalism and state-developmentalism in Korean cultural industries policy studies. In other words, while it is crucial to understand that the Korean government utilized neoliberalism, the same government also developed unique cultural measures to support local cultural industries although they pursued neoliberal globalization.

Coexistence of Developmentalism and Neoliberalism in Cultural Industries Policy

The uniqueness of Korea's cultural industries policy lies in the coexistence of developmentalism and neoliberalism. Although the Korean government has continued to develop neoliberal policies in the Korean cultural industries, the same government has also utilized state-developmental tendencies. Instead of giving up one particular policy agenda over the other, the consecutive Korean administrations have slightly shifted their priorities between neoliberalism and developmentalism in the realm of popular culture, and therefore, these two major policy agendas have become pillars in local cultural industries policy; some administrations prioritized neoliberalism to developmentalism, and other administrations attempted to shift their positions. Regardless of their priority, they have continued to emphasize economic imperatives more than artistic sovereignty over the past few decades, mainly because the Korean government has pursued entrepreneurial roles in popular culture (H. K. Lee, 2019). For example, Lee Myung-bak (2008–2013) fundamentally developed the cultural industries with the name of "contents industries." Due to his emphasis on the production and the export of cultural contents (plural here, not singular by his administration), "the Lee government was known as a corporate state, and he was called the CEO of a corporation" (Choi, 2013, p. 257).

More specially, the Korean government has to develop protective measures to support and protect local cultural industries because of its unique position in popular culture, although the Korean government has advanced a multitude of neoliberal policy measures to promote the growth of local cultural industries. Fair competition is seemingly implemented; however, government intervention is always necessary in the cultural sector. As can be seen in Europe, the traditional contradiction between "culture" and "economy" in the context of the cultural industries remains topical (Huijgh, 2007). On the one hand, cultural industries are balanced between more economic-oriented and culture-oriented objectives and policies. By considering both, the EU attempts to achieve an internal market for the cultural industries, while simultaneously paying attention to their cultural specifications. In so doing, the Committee on Culture of the European Parliament insists on treating cultural industries under the cultural emphasis to have an active European cultural policy (European Commission, 2006, pp. 2–4; Huijgh, 2007, p. 215).

On the other hand, the interest of the EU was until recently "limited to the case law that verifies respect of the existing competition-regulation framework by the cultural industries and national authorities. Neelie Kroes, European Commissioner for Competition, wants to strengthen the 'European creative industries' in the light of the i2010 Strategy, the European Commission's strategic framework for information communication technologies (ICTs) and media policy. She therefore considers state support as appropriate in some cases, but only when gaps cannot be filled by other means" (European Commission, 2006, pp. 2–4; cited in Huijgh, 2007, pp. 215–216).[3]

---

3. What is significant is that "disagreement on the approach towards the cultural industries has major consequences for the attitude towards state intervention and government support. European cultural industries should have the opportunities to be competitive by virtue of Article 157. But those same cultural industries must also have the chance to call on the exceptions (for example, those on state aid) that are provided

As discussed, Korea cultivated a very strong state-led, top-down developmental model, focusing on an export-led economy. Since military regimes until the early 1990s had to prioritize the growth of the national economy, they did not emphasize the growth of popular culture. Instead, the Korean government regulated local cultural industries through various measures. For example, until the mid-1990s, the government censored popular culture. The government also regulated multiple aspects of the cultural industries, including public ownership of broadcasting and protection of the domestic cultural market from foreign penetration (Ryoo & Jin, 2020).

The increasing role of neoliberalism does not imply the end of state-led developmentalism in the cultural industries. Since the mid-1980s, on the one hand, the Korean government has deregulated and liberalized the cultural industries; on the other hand, it has developed its distinctive cultural policy to support the growth of popular culture. Although the Korean government has executed neoliberal reform, it has simultaneously adopted a state-led development approach in the cultural sector (Jin, 2023). Therefore, it is vital to develop our understanding of Korean cultural industries policy more subtly. We have to "explore the intricate dynamics of the policy by discussing the embedded nature of neoliberal reform in Korea as a background for its arrival and the 'entrepreneurial' roles the state has played during its development" (H. K. Lee., 2019, p. 88). A nuanced analysis of the conflicts between neoliberalism and state-led developmentalism needs to be implemented in examining the Hallyu trend in the global markets (Jin, 2023).

Starting in the early 1990s, each administration had its unique cultural policies; however, there is no single administration that gave up on either state developmentalism or neoliberalism completely. Although these administrations had their priorities, they never fully abandoned one policy direction over the other policy direction. As Dan Schiller (1999) pointed out, again, in order to develop neoliberal policies, the government must deregulate existing policies, which is also a particular form of government intervention. Likewise, the Korean government has utilized these

in the competition policy. This contradiction, between being competitive and simultaneously being excluded, can be situated in a much broader contrast between the Committee on Culture of the European Parliament, the European Commission's DG for Culture and the EU's EYC Council, which are pleading for support to the cultural industries, and the Lisbon European Council and European Commission's DG for Competition, which want to reduce state intervention and move towards further liberalization of the market" (Huijgh, 2007, p. 216).

two major policy directions depending on their strategic choices while still keeping or advancing the other policy route, which makes local cultural policies unique and active.

Contents Industries Policy in Hallyu 2.0 Era

Unlike other countries, the growth of cultural industries policy in Korea between the late 2000s and late 2010s took place in tandem with these industries' rebranding and re-identification as content industries (H. K. Lee, 2019). This does not mean that the Korean government shifted its emphasis on economic imperatives in the cultural industries. Instead, it implies that the Korean government started to fully utilize popular culture to boost the national economy and national image on the global scene. The internationalization of popular culture has continued, and the government not only planned to increase the export of cultural content but also developed various plans to develop related areas. What is significant during this conservative administration era is that the government developed a few supporting measures relevant to these industries, while expanding their utilization of popular culture for soft power and cultural diplomacy.

As briefly explained in this chapter, the Lee Myung-bak administration introduced the notion of "contents industries" in 2008. Lee wanted to develop new policy initiatives during the period of the shift, and he chose the promotion of cultural content as one of the primary cultural policies (K. C. Kim, 2013). As a businessman-turned-into politician, he was aware of the importance of global trade in the realm of culture as well as the growth of the Korean Wave. In order to advance cultural trade while utilizing it to boost national image abroad, Lee pursued the marketization of popular culture through cultural policies. During his meeting with the Ministry of Culture and Tourism in March 2008, for example, Lee stated that we needed "the cultural state" and introduced the term the cultural contents industries as the growth engine of the national economy in the future (Ministry of Culture and Tourism, 2008). Lee supported these areas because he planned to utilize them to advance relevant industries, including tourism, food, and medical *Hallyu* (Y. J. Won, 2012).

More specifically, the Lee government created the Ministry of Culture, Sports and Tourism (MCST) in 2008 as the result of the convergence of the existing Ministry of Culture and Tourism (MCT) and the Ministry of Information and Communication (MIC). When Lee reshaped his executive branch, he planned to advance synergy effects through the convergence of popular culture handled by the MCT and digital technology controlled by the MIC (K. B. Lee, 2009). The Lee administration pursued the growth of information and cultural industries, and "it converged these two areas in order to effectively deal with the industries in the context of contents industries. Through absorbing the software policy function of the (now-defunct) MIC, the government began to directly initiate and support the contents industries" (Jin, 2016, p. 35). This does not mean that the Lee government developed the contents industries due to the issues of national identity or national arts, because it mainly supported cultural contents in relation to Hallyu in the name of economic imperatives (Jin, 2016). The Lee government placed cultural industries policy emphasis on the market, downplaying the significance of collective and citizen-based concerns (Clarkson, 2002). The Lee administration showed:

> a strong discursive leadership in radically reinventing culture as a commodity by dissociating it from social relations and historical contexts and reducing it to 'content', 'digital cultural archetype' and 'story', and developing marketplaces for their trade. The primary code governing the use of culture here is economic value generation rather than aesthetic quality, social representation, cultural identity or creative expression. The idea of content—defined as 'data or information of symbol, text, voice, sound and screen image'—is at the heart of this conceptual exercise. This idea formally entered the cultural policy lexicon in 2003 when the Framework Act on the Promotion of Cultural Industries was revised (H. K. Lee, 2019, pp. 100–101).

Although the Park Geun-hye government (2013–2017) changed the term to the creative industries policy as part of the creative economy, the major policy direction was similar to the Lee administration.[4] For example, in the 2nd Basic Plan for the Promotion of the Content Industry between 2014 and 2016, the Park government set its vision of Korea being

4. The term creative industries started in Australia and the U.K. in the 1990s to emphasize the economic role of these industries. As Flew (2012a, p. 46) stated, "neoliberalism is understood as a global ideological project with its roots in the United States and Great Britain, that has aimed to shift power and resources to corporations and wealthy elites through the privatization of public assets, removal of 'public interest' regulations over large corporations, and tax cuts targeted towards the highest income earners," and the turn to creative industries can be considered as a clear manifestation of neoliberalism (2012b, p.176).

a leading creative force in the global content industry, with an average annual income per person of US$ 30,000 (Jeon & Limb, 2014). When the Park government presented five implementation strategies and 17 key objectives, they all focused on economic characteristics of popular culture, such as building a foundation for investment, loans, and technology; promoting content-related start-ups, job creation, and training creative talent; supporting entry into global markets; promoting the development and use of a healthy ecosystem like fair trade and intellectual property management; and reinforcing content competitiveness and building a cooperation system for industrial growth:

> In the discourse of contents industries, culture is to be deconstructed into digitally flexible data and information ('content') and then modified, mixed and processed to become marketable commodities. Such a conceptual experiment dissociates culture from historical, aesthetic and social contexts and neutralizes it. Content is value-neutral and would be neither politically progressive nor reactionary, and neither conforming nor challenging. This idea also adopts a logic of industrial production: cultural industries produce sellable and exportable commodities by collecting, buying, assembling and processing content as a key input in the production process (H. K. Lee, 2019, p. 101).

Contents industries policy explicitly aims to "develop 'the market economy of culture' and enhance its international competitiveness" (H. K. Lee, 2020, p. 546). Accordingly, the Lee administration developed two distinctive cultural policies: one was the growth of popular culture and digital technology for the national economy, and the other was the enhancement of its soft power strategies. By utilizing the soaring popularity of the Korean Wave, the Lee administration attempted to advance the national image.

Whether "cultural industries policy" or "content industries policy," consecutive governments have focused on the nature of cultural industries as the backbone of policy concerns. Cultural industries policy created "a number of problems and tensions surrounding the role of the cultural industries as a concept and as a real presence in the cultural landscape in cultural policy-making and academic cultural policy studies" (Hesmondhalgh & Pratt, 2005, p. 5). Of course, there are a variety of caveats of cultural industries policy, focusing on the industrial nature of popular culture. Cultural industries policy limits its scope and cannot reflect the global expansion of the Korean Wave. It is essential to understand not only the cultural industries, but also global fans and the media ecology surrounding the evolution of the Korean Wave, such as the roles of the nation-state, transnational corporations, and international agencies such as UNESCO (Jin, 2023).

Cultural industries policy is a difficult process that must combine the elements of the free market and state funding. One particular issue, though, is the inconsistency in state funding between liberal and conservative governments. In this regard, during the interview process, one female webtoonist stated:

> during the Moon Jae-in government, I felt that I received a lot of support; however, during the Yoon Suk Yeol (2022–2027) government, there is too little support. For example, during the Moon government, there were several different financial supports from the government, such as subsidies to freelance workers and Gyeongnam Webtoon Campus subsidies; however, in the new conservative government, such grants have decreased (Interview with a female webtoonist).

A male marketing professional who worked for more than 10 years in a culture-related agency also said:

> Cultural policies supporting the export of popular culture, including the provision of various information on overseas markets and marketing support programs to connect business networks, have had a significant impact on the spread of the Korean Wave. The government efforts to create an industrial ecosystem that enables to produce diverse and competitive content is very important. Creative workforce training programs, content financing support, startup fostering support, content production support, story competitions, creative company incubation support, content technology development support, and policy research support can be considered as government policies to create a healthy ecosystem for the Korean cultural industries. The government needs to develop its cultural industry policy to advance these infrastructural ecosystems to develop the Korean Wave further.

The main task of cultural industries policy is not only to keep the cultural products in the market but to formulate the cultural worldview of the society. As Vitkauskaitė (2015, p. 216) pointed out, cultural industries have to "contribute to the formation of a country's image and its economic welfare," which means that popular culture could attract some foreign tourists to countries, which consequently improves the image of these countries (Vitkauskaitė, 2015). Due to the important role of popular culture, not only as a tool to enhance cultural identity but also as a means to develop the national economy and national image, cultural industries policy in Korea needs to advance effective and well-grounded strategic measures.

Implications of Cultural Industries in Cultural Policy

Cultural industries policy has certainly become a major characteristic of Korean cultural policy. Pratt (2005) pointed out, contemporary cultural policy must take into consideration the existence of the market of cultural industries, and cultural policy must participate in forming them. In other words, he emphasized that the market can be "one of the means to implement CIs [cultural and creative industries] policy" (Vitkauskaitė, 2015, p. 216). As Pratt (2005) argued, art policy developed by nation-states in the 20th century might not be appropriate for dealing with contemporary cultural industries. Therefore, it is not unusual for policymakers to shift their policy priorities, from cultural sovereignty to economic imperatives. One missing point here is the significance of cultural policy in developing cultural identity, even in our contemporary society. Popular culture, even in our contemporary terms, needs to advance cultural heritage and identity.

Cultural industries have shown their distinctive dimensions in Korea due to their close relationship with the Korean Wave. Local cultural industries have continued to grow and contributed to the growth of local popular culture, both nationally and globally. The local cultural industries have advanced their unique stance in the midst of changing media ecology. They have changed the notion of culture, from arts to cultural commodities, as Korea relates popular culture with neoliberal globalization. Again, the Korean government has pursued neoliberal reforms in culture, and consequently, popular culture has become a commodity to be sold. The local cultural industries have followed the path of commercialism and commodification, which prioritizes local popular culture's profits (Jin, 2023).

The local cultural industries have not developed cultural values in conjunction with the Korean Wave, as local cultural industries have not emphasized "the significance of collective and citizen-based concerns for cultural diversity and identity. This means that Korean cultural policies operate primarily in the service of corporate interests" (Jin, 2016, p. 39). As Pratt (2005) argued, popular culture may not need to enhance local identity; however, one must understand that the government has to develop cultural values. The cultural industries need to advance popular culture, not only as cultural commodities but also as enjoyable cultural content related to cultural values. Cultural industries policy has been implemented in Korea to utilize popular culture for several reasons, such as the internationalization of cultural content, the growth of the national economy as an individual industry sector, as sources to help other industries in the global markets, and for the enhancement of the national image. Through the combination of state developmentalism and neoliberalism, the Korean government has successfully fulfilled its mission.

Local popular culture has continuously reflected people's struggles and agonies while portraying rapid socio-economic changes. Contemporary cultural content has been the mirror of the ever-changing Korean society, which means it always reflects Korean people and their cultural preferences. As Druick and Deveau (2015) aptly put it, the industrialization of cultural production has to be duly noted by artists and cultural producers, and therefore, it has provoked a range of responses, not only economic but also aesthetic and political. "Cultural production in Hallyu has been especially unique because each administration pursued different cultural policies, sometimes unpredictably, and negatively influencing cultural creators and cultural industries firms. Of course, one of the most significant elements for the advancement of local cultural content is the creativity of cultural creators" (Jin, 2021b, p. 1827).

Secondly, one particular point related to cultural policy is the increasing role of popular culture as a source of soft power. Mainly starting in the Lee Myung-bak administration, the Korean government has advanced soft power in foreign relations. The Korean government's soft power drive mainly utilized popular culture in relation to the country's economic growth and national image; however, it is essential to develop cultural heritage for cultural diplomacy because other countries' people like Korean cultural content partially based on its cultural values. If cultural products mainly focus on their commodity nature, they cannot secure cultural values that appeal to other countries' audiences. Advancing cultural values must be considered as one of the most significant mechanisms in the country's soft power strategies. Cultural values and economic imperatives in the 21st century may go hand in hand as can be seen in soft power and cultural diplomacy discourses.

The Korean government needs to capitalize on the Korean Wave in two different ways. On the one hand, it develops cultural content as commodities that can be sold. On the other hand, the government has to utilize popular culture as a source of soft power and cultural diplomacy. Since one of the major scopes of soft power is to entice others to follow what we want (Nye, 2004a and b), the government can still help other industries as long as popular culture is attractive; in this case, not only because of its value as a commodity, but also because of its value as cultural content portraying cultural heritage. The Korean Wave as a source of soft power can be addressed and identified as one of the primary elements in cultural industries policy as well.

Thirdly, it is also essential to acknowledge that the Korean cultural industries policy cannot apply similarly to different cultural sectors. Unlike the broadcasting and film industries, the music industry has not been supported by the Korean government, nor have K-pop creators and performers asked for direct government support. In the realm of K-pop, the role of private business is essential, and public support targeting the K-pop sector has not played a notable role. "K-pop idols did not require public support; rather, it was the government officials who needed the fame of K-pop idols for their own political purposes. That said, public support has been at its best when the Korean government invested greatly in the Internet infrastructure—an action that did not specifically target K-pop, but was available to all sectors of the Korean economy" (Messerlin & Shin, 2017, p. 436).

Overall, the Korean government needs to develop various policy measures to enhance cultural values rather than solely focusing on economic values. Korea has continuously developed local cultural industries and the Korean Wave in the early 21st century. The government still needs to support the cultural industries; however, it has to advance well-balanced policy measures so that cultural content can function as both commodities and arts. As discussed, "traditionally, cultural policy legitimized state intervention from the perspective of artistic excellence, cultural equity and diversity, social cohesion and heritage preservation" (H. K. Lee, 2020, p. 546). It does not emphasize that the Korean government must go back to the old days to focus on these issues in cultural policy. The situation has already changed, and it is not possible to focus solely on these issues. Cultural industries are big parts of the national economy, and therefore, it is not time to simply focus on retro-style cultural policy. However, what the government has to develop at this point is to support popular culture in terms of cultural values, as well as economic values. The government has to continue to initiate and support undeveloped areas and areas needing help; however, it is also time for the government to take care of popular culture from a cultural lens.

Conclusion

This chapter has discussed the emergence of cultural industries policy in the Korean Wave tradition. As a subset of cultural policy, cultural industries policy has become one of the major measures in Korea for various reasons, including the adaptation of neoliberal globalization. As Korea started to develop globalization based on neoliberal tendencies, the state's cultural policy also shifted in dealing with culture, from arts to commodities, and therefore, many cultural policymakers developed various cultural industry policies. In other words, the Korean government has developed popular culture as commodities to be exported as in other industries. Instead of focusing on cultural identity and sovereignty, they emphasized economic imperatives when they developed new policy measures. The Korean government has especially advanced the convergence of popular culture and digital technologies to maximize economic gains from popular culture.

Beginning in the early 1990s, Korea adopted neoliberal reforms, emphasizing the minimal role of the government while guaranteeing maximum profits to the private sector. The Korean government also developed its globalization process in order to survive and prosper in the global economy. Korea continued to expand neoliberal economic and cultural policies (Jin, 2023). While their primary policy issues were different, the Lee Myung-bak government utilized the notion of contents industry, while the Park Geun-hye government advanced the concept of the creative economy in dealing with popular culture. The creative economy policy did not last long. With the impeachment of Park Geun-hye, the term creative economy and relevant discourses disappeared. The Moon Jae-in government (2017–2022) began promoting new policy rhetoric such as "the 4th industrial revolution" and "innovative growth" as a fresh direction for the national economy (H. K. Lee, 2020). What is significant is that although these terms were different, the recent Korean administrations have emphasized two major dimensions: one is the export of local cultural content, and the other is the utilization of popular culture as the source of soft power. In the globalized world, the transnationalization of popular culture has been actualized, and therefore, the government planned to develop cultural diplomacy in tandem with soft power.

Of course, the Korean cultural industries policy has not entirely eliminated state intervention. While liberalizing and transnationalizing the local cultural industries, the Korean government has continued to utilize state-developmentalism tendencies. This implies that the government still needs to initiate the growth of local cultural industries, while supporting the expansion of local popular culture in the global markets by using its financial and legal measures. Due to the mix of neoliberalism and state-developmentalism in the Korean Wave tradition, local cultural industries have grown. This does not mean that cultural industries policy as the mixture of two different major directions has become the primary engine for the growth of local popular culture. Instead, it implies that the Korean government along with other elements, including global fans and cultural producers, has become one of the key elements in advancing local cultural power.

The local cultural industries have become some of the major forces in the global cultural markets. With the boom of Korean popular culture, local cultural industries have certainly become some of the major industries in conjunction with digital technologies. One missing area in local cultural industries policy is cultural values. The Korean government may continue to advance its cultural industries policy; however, it also needs to develop and actualize cultural policy more broadly than cultural industries policy. While it is vital for the government to develop policy measures to support the growth of local cultural industries as valuable economic entities, it is also necessary to understand cultural values.

5

Netflix's Effect on the Local Cultural Industries

Introduction

Over the past few years, Netflix has fundamentally influenced cultural production in the South Korean cultural system. Netflix entered Korea in 2016, and Netflix's investment in Korea primarily started when it provided the entire budget for *Okja*—directed by Bong Joon-ho—released in 2017. Since then, Netflix has funded a series of cultural programs to produce Korean-originated content while licensing numerous existing cultural products. In 2019, Netflix released its first original Korean drama series, *Kingdom*—a genre-defining six-episode zombie mystery thriller.[1] Netflix then produced various original programs, including *Squid Game* (2021), *All of Us Are Dead* (2022), and *The Glory* (2022–2023), which were globally sensational. Netflix has also selected and distributed many Korean dramas, reality shows (e.g., *Physical: 100*, 2023), and movies (e.g., *Jung_E*, 2023), which are part of the Netflix system.

Netflix was supposed to play a role as a global distributor of Korean cultural content; however, it became one of the largest OTT platforms to manage cultural production, from the production of cultural content to the consumption of these programs. Cultural producers are more and more platform-dependent (Nieborg, Poell, & Duffy, 2021), and distribution models labeled as digital platforms are no longer a novelty in the cultural industries. In other words, Netflix has developed new business mod-

1. *Love Alarm* (2019)—a webtoon-based drama—was the first Korean series confirmed for pick-up by Netflix; however, *Kingdom* (January 2019) was premiered first, as *Love Alarm* was released later in August 2019. Although it is not a Netflix original, *My Only Love Song* (2017) was recorded as the first Korean drama that aired on Netflix in 2017.

els, including the production and circulation of local cultural content, as well as cultural texts, and implanted them in the local cultural industries, meaning the Netflix effect has been growing. Netflix, as a dominant global OTT platform, wields its hegemonic power, as local cultural creators used to follow Netflix's demand in order to gain global visibility.

Korea is not a mature OTT service market, compared to a couple of Western countries. Before the introduction of Netflix in Korea, there was no tangible OTT service platform (Dwyer, 2018). However, due to Netflix's increasing role, some media scholars (Ju, 2021; Kim, Jang, & Baek, 2021; Jin, 2021c; Park, Kim, & Lee, 2023; Kang, 2024) analyzed a few different perspectives on Netflix, in general, OTTs, in the Korean context, including the structural change in the local OTT market and the influence of Netflix in numerous cultural products.

Among these, H. Y. Ju (2021) pointed out that Netflix expands Korean dramas' speedy distribution and shareability to larger Western audiences, generating new Western viewers' attention. Kim et al. (2021) also analyzed the characteristics of countries that consumed Korean television programs on Netflix by gathering viewing data of Netflix's TOP 10 broadcast programs on Flixpatrol in 80 countries. Meanwhile, Park et al. (2022) mapped out the ways in which Netflix has changed the practices of Korean drama production. They emphasized that Netflix's aggressive international content strategies pose a significant challenge to the Korean cultural industries and concluded that Netflix's strategic use of Korean dramas works to consolidate platform imperialism, referring to the dominant role of digital platforms as primary actors in the global cultural sphere as a handful of American digital platforms, such as Netflix, Disney +, Facebook (now Meta), and YouTube controls the global cultural markets (Jin, 2015). However, few attempts have been made to analyze Netflix's effects on cultural text, particularly in tandem with the Korean Wave.

This chapter discusses how Netflix, as one of the most powerful global OTT platforms, has influenced the local cultural industries in terms of the shift of cultural genres and the industry structure. By employing various approaches, such as critical political economy, focusing on historical and structural elements, and sociocultural approach, emphasizing textual analysis and in-depth interview, it articulates whether Netflix has inroaded Korea due to the Korean Wave. Then, it discusses whether local cultural industries firms change their norms in production to comply with Netflix's orientation. In other words, it argues how the shift in the standard of cultural production has changed the cultural text in genres to determine whether global platforms arguably destroy local specificities and identities, both culturally and structurally. Finally, it interrogates shifting power relationships between a global OTT platform and local players, including cultural creators and platform users, and its implications in the Korean cultural industries.

Shifting Cultural Hegemony in the Digital Platform Era

Global cultural flows have continued changing, and it is not easy to claim that a few Western countries maintain their supremacy amid globalization, unlike several previous decades. Although the U.S. has sustained its hegemonic position in the global cultural sphere, a handful of non-Western countries like Mexico, Brazil, India, Japan, and Korea have rapidly developed their cultural power in the global cultural markets. From Mexican Telenovelas to Japanese anime to K-pop, these countries have significantly advanced their cultural products and exported them to other countries, both regional and Western countries. While American cultural content, including Hollywood movies and popular music, is still globally held, Japanese anime and Korean dramas are meaningfully penetrating Western countries in the early 21st century.

Global cultural flows have changed in the Netflix era, as Netflix fundamentally increases its influence. Netflix started as the distributor of cultural content but added new functions in the 1990s, and now it is one of the most powerful production firms and exhibition outlets. Since it acts as the primary agency in cultural production, including the production, distribution, and consumption of popular culture, its effect in many countries has been tremendous. Although local OTT platforms in a few countries have attempted to expand their presence, Netflix continues to work as a formidable force in the global cultural markets. It implies that cultural hegemony has dramatically changed; on the one hand, the shift of power from the U.S. to a handful of non-Western countries; on the other hand, another shift of cultural hegemony, from the emergence of a few non-Western countries to the U.S. mainly due to OTT service platforms, including Netflix, which asks media scholars to carefully and critically analyze these shifting cultural hegemonies.

Netflix's role is complicated as it works as a double-edged sword. One is that Netflix plays an essential role by making non-Anglophone productions available in many countries and regions, with subtitled or dubbed versions in native languages. With the rapid growth of OTT service platforms, particularly Netflix, the global penetration of popular culture from non-Western countries has been noticeable. As seen in the cases of *D.P.* (2021), *Squid Game* (2021), and *Hellbound* (2021), locally produced cultural products are becoming part of global OTT platforms. The other is that the increasing role of Netflix implies that the platform itself has played a vital role in cultural production, and it is intensifying America's dominant role in the global cultural sphere. Seemingly providing equal opportunities for both Western cultural firms and non-Western cultural creators, Netflix has strengthened its power in the flow of popular culture, as Netflix sets the forms of popular culture and cultural flow on digital platforms.

More specifically, Netflix has started to invest in a few local cultural industries. Netflix funds quite a few local products to make Netflix's original series or purchases many local programs that were already produced to circulate them on the OTT platform itself. Since many cultural creators in non-Western countries desperately want to work with Netflix, these creators have no choice but to develop cultural content that Netflix prefers, while passively accommodating Netflix's business norms. What Netflix attempts to advance is indeed its market control in the global cultural sphere. In this light, Ted Sarandos, Netflix's chief content officer at UBS's 2018 Global Media and Communications Conference in New York, said:

> And our local language original shows now, we're going to be ramping up to 70 original local language shows next year, and those shows have been remarkably relevant in the home country and have been able to get both pan-regional and in many cases global success that has changed the dynamic in a way for international television, which is we're not trying to make more Hollywood content for the world, we're trying to make content from anywhere in the world to the rest of the world (Netflix, 2018, p. 2).

This clearly states that Netflix as "a kind of screen-cultural traffic cop" plans to mediate "a new multilateralism and pluriform interchange of much more heterogeneous content than any previous account of media imperialism, cultural imperialism, [referring to the one-way flow of cultural content from the West to the East, in particular, from the U.S. to the rest of the world, Schiller, 1992], globalization or glocalization has offered" (Cunningham & Scarlata, 2020, pp. 149–150). As Alex Haigh, Brand Finance's valuation director, stated, Netflix also "delivers high-quality and varied programming to anyone with internet access and a credit card." Netflix has "embarked on a disruptive approach to media services and now has incumbents in the market looking over their shoulder" (Spangler,

2019). Netflix has wielded its immense power based on its brand power (Spangler, 2019), strengthening platform imperialism. As Davis (2021, p. 6) aptly puts it, Netflix relates to the four facets presented under the rubric of platform imperialism, reflecting contemporary transnational flow of cultural content: 1) a shift from an explicitly distribution-oriented business model to a vertically integrated business model; 2) the transnationalization of production to scale up its capacities; 3) attempts to leverage both the international financial system and the transnational nature of its production; and 4) dependence on big data to fuel its business model and create its algorithmic process of user engagement.

Therefore, it is crucial to understand the Netflix effect from a media-ecological approach that attempts to "grasp the cultural and industrial dynamics on both the supply (production and business strategy) and demand (consumption) sides" of the impact of transnational OTT services in the global cultural sphere, including in Korea (Cunningham & Scarlata, 2020, p. 159). Netflix's model of internationalization is quite different from previous models that media scholars and policymakers are used to understanding. Without a doubt, "Netflix is now the largest multilingual, multinational commissioner of original scripted screen content the world has ever seen" (Cunningham & Scarlata, 2020, p. 150). It is, therefore, vital to understand the ways in which Netflix has influenced the diversification and transformation of local cultural content in both genres and systems amid the shifting media ecology it pursues.

Netflix is Riding the Korean Wave

A handful of American OTT platforms, such as Netflix, Disney+, and Apple TV+, have continued to expand their footprints in the global cultural markets. K-dramas have long been captivating global audiences. K-dramas make up some of the best-performing content on a variety of OTT platforms, on a regular basis occupying several of the spots on Netflix's weekly Global Top 10 list of the most-watched non-English language TV shows. In 2023, nine out of the top 15 international originals on Disney+ were Korean programs. Global OTT service platforms continue to deliver Korean cultural products; in particular, dramas in response to overwhelming demand by global subscribers (J. Lee, 2024). Among these, Netflix has become a forerunner and, in particular, has obtained hundreds of thousands of global subscribers since COVID-19 broke in December 2019. Netflix has been one of the primary beneficiaries of the pandemic, as many global audiences watch cultural content on OTT platforms due to social-distancing policies. They cannot go to public places like theaters and music concert halls and therefore, they alternatively enjoy cultural content individually with their OTT platforms (La Monica, 2020).

For Netflix, Asia has been a significant market because of a few key reasons. On the one hand, Asia is the fastest-increasing cultural market for Netflix in both the number of subscribers and revenues. Between 2021 and 2022, North America experienced a minus 1% decrease in paid memberships, while the Asia-Pacific Region achieved a 17% increase in paid memberships. During the same period, Europe, Middle East, and Africa (EMEA) and Latin America (LATAM) gained 4%, respectively (Netflix, 2023a). In Asia, subscribers in Japan and Korea have soared since the late 2010s (Netflix, 2021a and d). Korea did not show growth in terms of the number of subscribers in the first few years of its service; however, it suddenly witnessed a surge of subscribers, partially because of the global popularity of a few Netflix original series. When *Kingdom* (2019) was released (and later *Kingdom II* in 2020), many Korean people started to subscribe to Netflix, and subscribers soared with *Squid Game*. As Netflix itself announced:

> There is no better example of this than *Squid Game*, a unique Korean story that first captured the zeitgeist in Korea and then globally. . . . It has become our biggest TV show ever. A mind-boggling 142m member households globally have chosen to watch the title in its first four weeks. The breadth of Squid Game's popularity is truly unique; this show has been ranked as our #1 program in 94 countries (including the US) (Netflix, 2021a, p. 3).

With its high global penetration during the COVID-19 era, Netflix has rapidly increased its revenues. In 2022, Netflix's revenue in streaming services was $31.4 billion, a 7% increase from the previous year, partially due to Asian cultural content, including Korean, Japanese, and Indian cultural programs (Netflix, 2022; 2023a). Due to the increasing role of Asia in the global OTT service markets, Netflix has expanded its strategic investments in Asia. Japanese anime, Indian Bollywood movies, and Korean dramas are globally popular, and Netflix wants to utilize this local cultural content.

Of course, Netflix's riding on the Korean Wave has been the most significant in Asia. As one interviewee (50, male) who works as a voice actor explained:

> due to COVID-19, online content available on digital platforms grows worldwide during a short period. Under the pandemic situation, not many countries have developed digital platform infrastructure and cultural content. I believe that global OTT service platforms, including Netflix, consider Korea as a stable cultural market to produce and consume cultural programs due to the Korean Wave, compared to the scale of their investment.

Netflix is data-driven and "understanding its growth strategy tends to be ruthlessly straightforward: Follow the Money" (Brzeski, 2021a), which is why the company has been interested in the Korean Wave, in particular during the pandemic era.

Netflix is highly interested in Korean television dramas. Vivek Couto, executive director of consultancy Media Partners Asia said, "for sure, these are the two planks—Korean drama and anime—that have been driving a lot of Netflix consumption and subscribership throughout Asia." He continued that the two categories have "been vital for them in South Korea and Japan, obviously, but also powerful in Southeast Asia—and even the U.S. and other global territories to an extent" (Brzeski, 2021a).

Studying the expansion of global digital platforms in the Global South like Korea, India, and Japan "entails exploring the complex web of power relations established among these platforms and domestic actors—not only public but also private actors—and the strategies these various parties implement" (Mattelart, 2024, p. 25). Korea, Japan, and India serve as laboratories in this respect. In fact, Netflix uses Korea's success in exporting its national pop culture to expand its reach in Asia. Since the Korean Wave presents an expandable cultural flow on the global stage, "Netflix seeks to surf this tide positioning itself as a cultural mediator, while simultaneously trying to appropriate the markets conquered by Korea's pop culture" (Meimaridis et al., 2021, p. 18).

Netflix has helped fuel and is fueled by the global popularity of Korean cultural content. Since 2015, Netflix has invested about $700 million in financing partnerships and co-productions. Since late 2019, it has ramped up investments and landed multi-year content partnerships with major local studios and television channels, including CJ ENM/Studio Dragon and JTBC, to access their local shows. More than 70 local-produced shows have been released as Netflix-branded originals which are available in 31 subtitled languages and more than 20 dubbed languages (Li & Yang, 2021). Netflix understands the shifting media ecology. As Korea has continued to expand its global reach with various cultural programs, Korea has become a natural target to work with. Netflix has increased its funds to local cultural creators because it plans to expand its original cultural programs. As K.A. Kim et al. (2023, p. 7018) aptly point out, "Netflix and K-dramas have become inseparable concepts due to the streaming giant's significant influence on the Korean drama industry."

During the interviews, many Netflix users in Korea believed that Netflix has started to invest in Korea due to the popularity of local cultural content. One female (32) participant stated, "I am certain that Netflix developed a variety of original Korean dramas, such as *Squid Game* and *Hellbound*, mainly because of the global popularity of Korean cultural products." Another female respondent (34) also said,

> I think that Netflix understands the increasing popularity of Korean culture. BTS's popularity is enormous, and *Parasite* was globally sensational. Likewise, Korean digital games are played in many parts of the globe. However, Netflix does not have much Korean content, and therefore, it wants to create Netflix originals to get more subscribers.

Cultural producers also agree that the Korean Wave is one of the primary reasons for the entry of Netflix into Korea. A respondent (54, male) who started his career as a drama producer in the network channel in 1993 said that the Korean Wave should be a major issue for Netflix to invest in the Korean cultural market:

> Netflix did not support *The Penthouse: War in Life* (2020)—one of the most successful Korean dramas in terms of its view rate—because the drama had no Hallyu stars appearing. Netflix thought it was problematic as it did not help the show's distribution in the global markets. SBS finally worked with Chorokbaem Media—a local production company—rather than pursuing sponsorship from Netflix and made a tremendous outcome in Korea.

However, a respondent (45, female) who works as a sound director in the broadcasting and film companies said, "the most significant part of the Korean Wave that Netflix is interested in is a Korean style narrative proven through various webtoon-based cultural products. These narratives are not used in the Western cultural markets." Unlike the respondent who emphasized the role of Hallyu stars mentioned above, she highlighted a slightly different aspect of the Korean Wave; "although

Netflix is interested in high-paid superstars, it also pays attention to writers' roles and their capacity as it wants to invest in a good story while finding talented rookies. *All of Us Are Dead* is an excellent example." It implies that Netflix selects new programs based not only on famous stars but also on unique stories. In the contemporary Korean media system, the casting of famous actors is significant in determining the success of the content. The value of a celebrity's name is vital. However, Netflix's original dramas don't seem to have the same strategy. Taking actor Song Kang as an example, he immediately starred in a few Netflix original dramas, including *Sweet Home*, although he has never starred in Korean dramas. Many new actors appeared in *Extracurricular* and *All of Us Are Dead* as well. The production team could elect people who fit the character, instead of their visibility.

Both general users and cultural creators commonly believe the significant role of the Korean Wave in the intrusion of Netflix in the local cultural market; however, cultural creators' interpretations are a bit different. As Minyoung Kim (2021), Netflix's Vice President of Content for Korea, Southeast Asia, and Australia & New Zealand, stated, Netflix pays attention to storytelling:

> Storytelling is deeply rooted in Korean culture. . . . Today, we live in a world where *Parasite* is an Academy Award Best Picture winner, Blackpink plays Coachella, and over 22M households tune into a horror TV series, *Sweet Home*. Audiences around the world are falling in love with Korean stories, artists, and culture. That's why we were investing nearly 500 million USD in Korea in 2021 to add more variety and diversity to our growing slate and to entertain and delight the over 3.8 million Korean households that subscribe to Netflix (Kim, M. Y., 2021).

The Korean Wave demands the OTT platform not only to penetrate this local market but also to work with local creators. As Korean cultural content has been globally popular, partially due to local content's high-quality storytelling, Netflix jumps on the Korean Wave bandwagon.

Netflix also considers Korea a significant player in Asia in its effort to expand in the region. Although Korea has only 51 million inhabitants, the country plays a crucial role in Asia as an influential hub for cultural production and foreign exports. Through Hallyu, Korea accomplished a trend-setting role and a pivotal position in cultural production in Asia. "Korea became not only a potential market but also a bridge to others, facilitating the company's expansion in the continent. As such, licensing and producing Korean content has become one of the streamer's priorities at this stage of Netflix's transnationalization effort in Asia" (Meimaridis et al., 2021, pp. 9–10). Of course, Netflix's expansion in Korea goes beyond the desire to attract regional subscribers. "The popularity of its original Korean productions, in and outside the Asian continent, makes these productions attractive vehicles to win over new subscribers in various parts of the world, an important catalyst for the growth and maintenance of Netflix's transnationalization effort" (Meimaridis et al., 2021, p. 18).

The Korean Wave indeed plays a pivotal role in attracting global OTT platforms. According to Netflix (2023b), the global fandom for K-content continues to grow, with over 60% of all Netflix members watching Korean titles in 2022. One big number that stands out is for the colossally successful Netflix original series *Squid Game*. It was the streaming platform's most-watched non-English language series of all time with a total of 1.65 billion hours watched. In comparison, Netflix's most-watched English language series, *Stranger Things* (season four), was watched a total of 1.35 billion hours. "Netflix is not the only streaming platform that's looking to capitalize on the Korean wave" (Bohdan, 2023a). As K-content is one of the most significant selling points for Netflix, this OTT platform will continue to debut a diverse array of Korean TV series, films, and reality shows in the near future.

While Netflix has reached massive success with Korean popular culture, other OTT platforms, including Disney+, have also jumped into the local market, making Korea a real testbed of global OTTs. Netflix provides a new venue as a mega OTT platform. It means that local cultural production, from the production of cultural content to the consumption of popular culture, has been dramatically influenced by Netflix's corporate business strategies. Temporarily, local cultural producers have increased their opportunity to work with a global OTT platform to circulate their content globally; however, it also implies that they have to follow the guidelines that Netflix implants.

Netflix Effect on Cultural Production in the Korean Wave

Netflix has expanded its influence in the production of local popular culture (Colbjørnsen, 2021; Gómez & Larroa, 2023), and Korea has been one of the most significant places. Netflix has its service in 190 countries, and it is impossible to attract all viewers with only American cultural content.

Netflix wants to have local cultural programs that can be played worldwide. Netflix has many programs from the U.S. that play everywhere; however, it does not play at all in Asia or Europe. Therefore, Netflix is on the search for great local storytellers and great local artists for its own needs (Netflix, 2018).

OTT platforms like Netflix and Disney+ develop a wide range of services, which include both originals and licensing/licensed content. On the one hand, they are generating originals themselves and they fund secure ownership of cultural content through full-funded productions in other countries. In this case, global OTT platforms possess intellectual property. On the other hand, they are licensing catalogs—originally produced in other production companies, sometimes, in different countries—by purchasing exclusive exhibition rights for their own services. When OTTs license content, they pay a flat fee to production companies (Lotz, Lobato, & Thomas, 2018; Lotz, 2022). Netflix partners with content providers in various countries to license streaming rights for multiple television programs and movies while producing in-house or acquiring exclusive rights to stream content, which are called Netflix originals.

Netflix's business model is not what Hollywood has pursued. As Netflix chief content officer Ted Sarandos (2014) stated, "It's been proven that selling Hollywood to the world is a big business." However, "[selling] the world to the world is an even bigger business" (Roxborough & Szalai, 2011). Producing global content and selling it across the globe is "what Netflix has set out to prove possible" (Osur, 2016). In other words, Netflix has been shifting its business model, from simple distribution of licensed programs to the production of new original series as its reaction to customer demand, particularly from global viewers.

Unlike other countries, in Korea, Netflix has diversified its business models, from a simple investment in the local cultural industries, mainly acquiring licensed programs, to the production of Netflix's original series. To begin with, Netflix has increased its local licensing. Netflix has signed an exclusive international licensing agreement with JTBC, a Korean nationwide general cable channel, for the network's new Friday/Saturday TV series *MAN x MAN*, which premiered on 21 April 2017. Apart from being a Netflix original series, *MAN x MAN* is also Netflix's first simulcast of a Korean drama in over 20 languages to millions of subscribers worldwide. Except for Korea and the US, *Man x Man* was streamed globally on Netflix simultaneously (Netflix, 2017). In June 2018, Netflix also licensed the Korean TV series *Mr. Sunshine* from Studio Dragon—a production company in Korea—inspired by historical events concerning a 19th-century US expedition to the Asian country (H. W. Lee, 2018) amid the company's drive to increase its control in Korea.

More importantly, Netflix invested in various local cultural products, including *Okja*. In 2017—its first original film in Korea, Netflix funded $50 million for *Okja*, directed by Bong Joon-ho. Netflix planned to stand out as the company struggled to gain ground in the Korean market during the early stages of 2016 and 2017 (K. S. You, 2021). Netflix did not make a breakthrough in Korea in the first two years due to the lack of original content, other than a very few including *Okja*, and relatively expensive monthly fees (Kang, 2017). Netflix has greatly advanced its business model by expanding its original programs. In 2019, Netflix released its first original Korean drama series, *Kingdom*. Netflix has continued to fund a variety of cultural content. Until February 2021, Netflix has produced over 80 original Korean television programs and films (Brzeski, 2021b). While the majority of originals are dramas, Netflix produces films, stand-up comedies, sitcoms, and reality entertainment (Netflix, 2021b). Netflix's original series *Squid Game*, especially, made it to #1 on Netflix in about 90 countries, the first Korean series to do so.

Regarding dramas, Netflix primarily seems to focus on specific programs, including *Sweet Home* and *Extracurricular*, which teens and young adults are not allowed to watch (K. S. You, 2021). Through its regional offices, Netflix attempts to develop cultural products that "meet the specific demands of audiences in these nations/regions" by commissioning "an interesting solution to create exclusive content that builds audience loyalty in local and regional markets" (Meimaridis et al., 2021, p. 8).

Netflix already had as many as 2,500 original products as of September 2021, which consisted of 40% of the entire content on Netflix. The company wishes to extend the share of original content to increase the gap between Netflix and other OTT platforms like Disney +, which has a lot of original content (*Money Today*, 2021). Consequently, as of July 2023, there are 6,621 movies, series, and specials in the Netflix library. Of those, 3,657 are Netflix originals, accounting for 55.2% (Moore, 2023).

Due to the increasing role of Netflix in the Korean cultural sphere, the Korean broadcasting industry has fundamentally changed its structure. since the late 2010s. In Korea, there were only three terrestrial channels—KBS1, KBS2, and MBC—before SBS (Seoul Broadcasting System) joined in 1990. Cable channels began their services in 1995, while general programming channels began their roles in 2011. Including 658 independent program producers, as many as 1,062 broadcasting-related companies worked to produce and circulate cultural programs as of December 2019 (Korea Creative Content Agency, 2020). Unlike cable channels and general programming channels like JTBC, Channel A, and TV Chosun, three major networks originally made an informal agreement not to sell newly aired television series to Netflix in an effort to restrain Netflix from entering the Korean cultural market.

As is also discussed in chapter 3, in the latter part of the 2010s, a few domestic OTT service corporations, including Oksusu (owned by SK Broadband), POOQ (owned by the network channels, KBS, MBC, and SBS), and Tving (owned by CJ E&M), were primary actors until recent years. Therefore, network channels that owned these local platforms did not want to work with Netflix, although these local OTT platforms combined POOQ and Oksusu to establish the new service platform Wavve due to Netflix's soaring market share in 2019 (S. Y., Kim, 2019). The arrangement also ended in December 2018 when SBS sold the streaming rights for *Hymn of Death* to Netflix. Since then, Netflix has secured shows from network broadcasters, paying a significant portion of the series' production costs through global licensing deals (G.L., Lee, 2020).

Netflix's strategies are apparent. As Osur (2016, p. 105) points out, the programs produced in each country's native language "are tied to cultural peculiarities, and are produced, directed by, and starring local talent." While these programs are local, they are meant to work on a global scale. These programs serve as a source of cultural programs in some countries where Netflix has struggled to make licensing deals, as Netflix produced several programs, including *House of Cards (2013-2018)* to fill a void in its serialized programming library. These local programs, such as films and serial dramas also "help build Netflix's global footprint and develop goodwill and brand recognition in countries that may not otherwise know or approve of Netflix" (Osur, 2016, p. 106). Netflix cannot produce all programs that appeal to niche audiences. By acquiring local programs that mainly target national or regional audiences, Netflix can fill the gap, which is important because Netflix then provides similar programs to broader audiences. Netflix certainly capitalizes on cultural peculiarities and local taste.

Netflix has undoubtedly developed those corporate strategies based on its global distribution power. Many local cultural creators in the Korean TV production industry, including network TV, cable TV, and independent production companies, are partially willing to work with Netflix due to its financial support. They especially want to see the global circulation of their cultural products via Netflix, which cannot be comparable to the export of individual cultural content to a certain number of countries. Netflix utilizes machine learning (ML) to shape its catalog of cultural content by learning characteristics that make local content successful (Netflix, 2019). Netflix's distribution power equipped with AI algorithms has been successful and greatly changed conventional cultural production in the local cultural markets.

Netflix Effects on Korean Screen Culture

As Netflix has continued to develop new business models and implanted them in the Korean cultural industries, local cultural producers have no choice but to comply, which means that Netflix influences the entire circle of cultural production. Korean broadcasters have to select a new system in cultural production. Previously, local terrestrial and cable channels produced dramas that ran two episodes per week for two-three months. However, as Netflix releases all episodes at once so that viewers can watch them back-to-back at any time without waiting for the next episode—known as binge-watching—many local cultural firms now produce drama series and release them at the same time, as can be seen in *Squid Game* and *Hellbound*. The number of episodes in cultural production has also changed. In the Korean broadcasting system, most dramas are 16 episodes or 20 episodes long; however, Netflix's original series used to have fewer episodes than those of Korean programs. These dramas only consist of 6–12 episodes like *Kingdom* and *All of Us Are Dead*.

Netflix also controls the distribution schedule, which means that local networks and cable channels have lost their scheduling power. For example, SBS broadcasted its drama *Vagabond* which aired between September and November 2019. It was initially scheduled to be broadcast in 2018. However, the premiere date of this television series was delayed due to a pending deal with Netflix (Rapir, 2019). *One Spring Night*, which was aired in 2019, also closely worked with Netflix to air the program almost simultaneously on MBC and Netflix, as JS Pictures, the production company of this drama, asked MBC to air it on Netflix as well (*Yonhap News*, 2019). Unlike linear television, OTT platforms are not bound to a programming schedule and provide viewers with a content catalog. "By abandoning the schedule, Netflix can engage more thoroughly in a project of deterritorialization" with a catalog that mixes products from different countries (Jenner, 2018, p. 211). Netflix's recommendation algorithm easily organizes the interface, in which Netflix users access a personalized service based on their consumption habits. As the funding source for content producers, Netflix therefore wields its power to deal with the best schedule for the platform. This new trend is related to audiences' shifting consumption habits. Freedom from the traditional program schedule of classical linear television is the most crucial motive for audiences to use OTT platforms (Jin, 2021c).

Netflix has also influenced the storytelling of local cultural content. Until recent years, producers of Korean dramas used to develop a critical turning point at the end of each episode so that the audiences would wait with anticipation until the next episode. However, program creators don't need to push this traditional norm as they simultaneously produce and release content on Netflix and domestic channels (S. M. You, 2019). In most cases, Korean dramas run for 60–75 minutes, so the final one or two minutes must not only be the climax of each episode but also the focal point for viewers to stick around until the next episode. However, the running time of one episode on Netflix is about 45 minutes, and therefore, it cannot make this form of the ending point. In contrast to the majority of Korean dramas, each episode of Netflix's original dramas ends abruptly. For example, *Squid Game* shows this new trend in a few episodes as they stop the episode with no particular cliffhanger. For many Korean audiences, the final few minutes of cultural programs are cliffhangers. Since Netflix programs are binge-watched, it does not need to develop these cliffhangers.

Last but not least, Netflix has changed the major cultural genres in the Korean cultural industries. Most Korean dramas known overseas were romantic comedies and melodramas (Chua & Iwabuchi, 2008). "Melodrama is an essential facet of East and Southeast Asian TV dramas, especially K-dramas. Similar to Latin American telenovelas, K-dramas employ melodramatic codes to engage viewers" (Meimaridis et al., 2021, p. 15). Netflix has continued to commission melodramatic K-dramas, such as *Love Alarm* (Netflix, 2019–2021), *Crash Landing on You* (tvN, 2019–2020), and *It's Okay to Not Be Okay* (tvN, 2020). In fact, among K-drama audiences, romance dramas are preferred in transnational contexts, and female viewers especially emphasize depictions of love and romance in K-drama narratives as the significant representation of cultural sensibility enables them "to feel comfort from their perception of social marginality" (Ju & Lee, 2015, p. 323). In this way, it is noted that "K-dramas' transnational popularity has established the centrality of both romantic comedies and melodramas, and Netflix's K-drama catalog matches well with this trend" (Ju, 2020, p. 35).

However, as Netflix has invested and is interested in various genres, including thriller, zombie, and stand-up comedy, Korean creators also develop these genres, which are unprecedented. As Netflix is riding the Korean Wave, its most significant investments have been in television dramas, focusing on melodramas, in an attempt to enter the Asian markets. Netflix has also been interested in various genres, which are popular among audiences in North America; therefore, Netflix implicitly pushes local creators to go beyond the boundaries of traditional cultural content offerings (Sohn, 2018). As Stangarone (2019) points out, "Netflix's success is being driven by its catalog of content, but also by the development of original Korean content, something local artists find appealing."

Netflix users and local cultural creators clearly feel the Netflix effect through shifting cultural genres. Although they show some differences, they commonly agree that Netflix has deeply influenced local cultural industries to adopt new cultural genres. One respondent (33, male) who works at a manufacturing company said, "Netflix introduces new genres, which have never existed in the Korean cultural market, and these new genres eventually broaden the scope of diversity in content selection." Another Netflix user (25, female) stated,

> *Space Sweepers* (2021) on Netflix is an excellent example to illustrate Netflix's influence. I don't believe that local cultural production firms greatly create zombie or sci-fin genres. However, local cultural creators, along with Netflix, develop unusual cultural genres.

In this light, an industrial robot engineer (60, male) also said, "in Korea, death game genre content like *Squid Game* has been restricted because it is too violent to show to children and youth. However, after the success of *Squid Game*, similar products are constantly released. It is no doubt that Netflix's influence on the subjects and genres is prominent."

In the 1980s, when there were only three terrestrial channels, they used to create a few genres of dramas, including modern melodramas, historical dramas, period dramas, youth dramas, and rural dramas. Some dramas in these genres, including *The Country Diary*, *A Royal Secret Inspector*, and *The Tree Blooming with Love*, are closely related to the lives and struggles of ordinary people (H. Y., Kim, 2004). Various popular dramas in the early 1990s, including *What is Love* (1992), *Sun and Daughter* (1993), and *Sandglass* (1995), also touched on ordinary people's lives and struggles. In the early 21st century, however, television dramas on terrestrial channels show the rise of unfamiliar dramas to Korean audiences like fantasy, zombie, SF, mystery, thriller, and crime dramas (Jin, 2024).

Television dramas have changed in genres partially because of the advent of new media channels, including OTT platforms like Netflix, in recent years. Due in large part to sharp competition among old and new media outlets, a few media channels, including tvN, JTBC, and OCN, have developed untraditional genres, in particular crime and fantasy/adventure genres, and they greatly influence traditional media channels like network channels. These media outlets believe that they need to create new forms of cultural programs that differentiate themselves from traditional media. They have developed *Guardian: The Lonely and Great God* (2017), *Signal* (2016), and *Stranger* (2017), which are categorized as fantasy, suspense, and crime. Again, Netflix has expedited the introduction and popularity of a few different genres, including zombie, fantasy, and SF. As K.A. Kim et al. (2023, pp. 7030–7031) also analyzed the shift in genres with Korean Netflix originals, "the three most viewed Korean Netflix Originals commonly share dark themes such as class strife, revenge, death, and judgment; therefore, it can be argued that Netflix helps shape a new K-drama identity, because these dark K-dramas are a significant departure from the history of successful romantic genres," which means that "Korea's positioning is a significant departure from countries with an average (Spain, Mexico, France, Brazil) and high concentration (Japan, United Kingdom)."

Cultural creators expressed similar observations and said that they had to adjust to this new trend. A researcher who works at the content-related agency (43, female) said, "Netflix has expanded the subjects in numerous ways. Unlike previous years when family-oriented themes and romantic comedies were popular, Netflix likes horror and high-school genres." A female respondent (38) who works as a scenario writer in the broadcasting industry stated:

> Netflix-supported cultural content has developed adventurous stories with the rapid development in narratives. Also, the way of representation became less strict. *Seonam Girls' High School Investigators* is an excellent example.[2] Some audiences backlashed it once the episode was aired. In contrast, OTT platforms have a broader representation of LGBTQIA2S+, which is what Netflix influences.

The shifting trend of genres in Korean popular culture can be witnessed in many countries as the outcome of the change. In Japan, for

2. A television series aired on JTBC from December 2014 to March 2015, notably featuring the first on-screen lesbian kiss on Korean television.

example, people enjoy Korean dramas and films emphasizing melodrama and action. *Winter Sonata* (2002), *Joint Security Area* (2000), and *Shiri* (1999) were some of the first Korean popular cultures that attracted many Japanese audiences. However, in November 2021, the situation was quite different. According to FlixPatrol, eight programs were Korean cultural content among the top 10 cultural programs on Netflix in Japan, while there was one Japanese program and one American program on the list. Genres in these Korean programs are diverse, from thriller to romantic comedy. Japanese audiences still like drama, romantic comedy, and romance genre programs, such as *The King's Affection*, *Touch Your Heart*, *Crash Landing on You*, and *Hometown Cha-Cha-Cha*. However, they also like thrillers and horrors like *Hellbound* and *Squid Game*, although they are not traditional genres that Korea used to produce. Netflix has played a vital role as a mediator (van Dijck, 2013) in the Korean cultural industries by influencing cultural creators to develop various drama genres, and consequently, Korean cultural content attracts much broader audiences than ever.

Power Relations between Local Cultural Industries and Global OTT Platforms

Due to Netflix's heavy influences, local cultural creators recast their production norms to comply with Netflix's preferences instead of relying on local cultural standards. Local cultural creators have to adopt Netflix's corporate model that would lead local cultural industries. It is not surprising to acknowledge that many parts of the world have lost their local specificities due to the dominance of American cultural products. As Kraidy (2010, p. 138) argued, a few Arab countries had to "abandon their traditions wholesale in order to adopt Western modernity wholesale." Although the same logic could not apply to the Korean cultural industries partially because of the increasing role of cultural creators, it is not dicey to claim that Korea has been losing its ground to hold national production norms in terms of genre specifications as can be seen in previous sections. Netflix has indeed challenged the existing broadcasting models and delivered television content via digital platforms. Content producers must establish cooperation with OTT service platforms to offer their products to a much broader spectrum of audiences or customers interested in multi-screen consumption of cultural content (Radošinská, 2017). Korean creators have to greet the new world, driven by Netflix. The early 21st century witnessed the increasing dominance of Western digital platforms like Netflix, equipped with capital, AI algorithms, and cultural content. As Benjamin Han (2023, 6938) points out, "the growing number of independent production companies also had its drawbacks. Given the saturated and competitive television market, independent producers struggled financially to sustain their operations as they had to pitch their ideas for new dramas to get selected for broadcast on a network," and global OTT platforms have expedited the deterioration of these local independent production companies.

Therefore, many Netflix users and cultural creators are concerned about a few caveats, although their perceptions of the Netflix effect vary. One respondent (45, female) who works in the entertainment industry said,

> the recent popularity of Netflix originals looks brilliant; however, I am concerned about the situation as many cultural producers seem to take only the successful formula. It is also shameful to see some cultural content that Netflix produces illustrate and spotlight the dystopiatic aspect of Korean society. This would become a stereotype in the representation of Korea that has been made by the West.

One male participant (32) also said, "Netflix originals are more provocative than content created by domestic networks, and therefore, they influence the subjects and genres at the same time." Cultural creators seem to have similar perspectives. Like general Netflix users, one respondent (35, female) who is a writer stated, "both the subjects and genres are deeply influenced by Netflix. Once sexual and violent content is suddenly famous, and many other shows portray violence, which is not right."

More importantly, as Netflix takes Korea by storm, its growing presence raises some concerns about Netflix's control over the local content. This asymmetrical power relation seems to occur, as many local producers, with all kinds of scripts, knock on the door of Netflix. "Netflix receives so many content proposals, so they get to review and select which to work on and turn down," one production company official in Netflix Korea said during his interview with a local media outlet: "The deep-pocketed company is likely to become the dominant source that monitors and selects the content available to audiences, shaping the market" (G. L., Lee, 2020).

What is interesting is that respondents who have been working in the cultural industries commonly expressed their concerns about the lopsided power inequality rooted in the monopolization of intellectual property. A drama producer on the major network channel (53, male) said, "the most significant structural influence is monopolizing intellectual properties (IPs). By utilizing IPs, Netflix will continue to produce the second season and the third season of episodes. However, once IPs are taken by Netflix, there would be no expansion in content production, which is not what the Korean cultural industries expect to see." In this regard, Park, Kim, and Lee (2023) also emphasize:

> It is premature to claim that Netflix's involvement in the Korean drama industry leads to the further advancement of the Korean Wave. On the contrary, Netflix's aggressive international content strategies pose a significant challenge to the Korean media industry. Because Netflix acquires all IP rights to Netflix Korean originals and the global streaming rights to numerous Korean dramas, neither production companies nor Korean television stations gain profits commensurate with the global popularity of Korean dramas . . . Insofar as Korean production companies continue to be swayed by Netflix's financial clout and Netflix financially benefits from the global success of Korean dramas, the Korean drama industry may ultimately be relegated to a subcontractor role and alienated from its own shows' overseas profits (p. 85).

Surely, Netflix's power can be understood through negotiations, cooperation, and conflicts between three major actors, including Netflix, cultural creators, and platform users. Netflix allows local cultural creators to enhance their position in negotiation with cultural industries firms as cultural creators select either broadcasting channels or digital platforms to distribute their cultural content. This is a complex issue, though. Empowering cultural creators and the audience as the primary actors does not mean that they have equal opportunities and, therefore, equal power. Netflix acts as a mediator who controls the circuit of cultural production. As Flew (2021, p. 229) aptly puts it, the status of digital platforms, including Netflix, does not work as "pure intermediaries, which have no relationship with the content deposited on their sites beyond hosting it," as they are increasingly controlling the entire process of cultural production.

There are certainly various resistances against Netflix. For many local cultural creators, it is unavoidable to work with Netflix primarily due to its global distribution power in many countries. However, the production company of *Extraordinary Attorney Woo* (2022) did not sell its IP rights to Netflix and decided to broadcast the program on a small domestic channel ENA. Due to its huge hit in the Korean market, Netflix later had to license the program. While it is not effective, local OTT platforms have continued to expand their magnitude to compete with global OTT platforms. As the latest merger case, the Fair-Trade Commission in Korea approved the merger between Tving owned by CJ ENM and Seezn owned by local telecom giant KT Corp, in July 2022 to make a bigger local OTT platform to potentially compete with Netflix, which is the dominant player in the Korean market as well (S. H. Park, 2022).

Netflix will continue to play its dominant role in cultural production in the Korean Wave tradition. Regardless of enhanced opportunities for local cultural producers and audiences, the disproportionate power relations between Netflix and these local actors still exist, potentially resulting in the sub-contractorization of the local cultural industries. In other words, the close connection between a global platform, Netflix, and local cultural creators remains as they develop mutual interests—the capitalization of popular culture. During the process, local cultural producers get some benefits; however, it is not avoidable to witness the subordination of local forces to global platforms.

Conclusion

This chapter discussed the increasing role of Netflix in the Korean cultural industries, as Netflix has rapidly become one of the largest and most important OTTs in the Korean Wave. Regardless of the continuous attempts by local-based OTT platforms to expand their market share, Netflix as a global OTT platform has built its brand in Korea over the past few years, and its impact continues to grow due to its unique business models in utilizing an ample amount of capital, data, and algorithms. Only six years after its launch in Korea, Netflix has become a formidable force to transform the Korean cultural sphere. It has controlled the vicious circle of the cultural sector and actualized its status as a global platform, reshaping local cultural production.

Netflix and local cultural industries seemingly work together in the midst of a shifting media ecology in which OTT platforms reign supreme. Netflix needs cultural content that the American cultural industries do not have, while local cultural producers need to secure production costs and distribution channels. However, it is still Netflix to set standards, as they have money and distribution power. As Meimaridis et al. (2021, p. 19) argue, we need to analyze Netflix's position as "mediator of narratives to and from the rest of the world through frameworks as decolonial studies and Platform Imperialism," which means that Netflix "occupies the very center in the streaming war, in a movement already known by the old imperialist rhetoric of its country of origin. Different times, new strategies, same goals."

Overall, Netflix creates itself as a new media ecology that local cultural industries reside in. Regardless of the growth of local OTT platforms, they cannot compete against global platforms like Netflix as they do not secure worldwide distribution channels. It is not only about money but also about the distribution power, which asks local cultural producers to work with global OTT platforms.

6

Local Fan Music Platforms, Global YouTube, and K-pop

Introduction

Since the early 21st century, Korean popular music has become one of the most enjoyable local popular cultures around the globe. The country has had a long history in the popular music scene; however, it was not long ago when Korea started to reign supreme in the popular music area—not at the same level as the U.S., but from the Global South. The Korean music industry has witnessed dramatic changes over the past few decades due to various elements, including the advent of idol groups and digital technologies. Although it is necessary to analyze the entire music history, this book focuses on the relatively recent history of the K-pop world, before and after the 1990s, but mostly in the early 21st century, as the book itself emphasizes the nexus of the local cultural industries and the Korean Wave.

Korean popular music (K-pop) before the mid-1990s was subjugated under a controlled system as television remained the most significant medium platform for music promotion. The record production process was also closely controlled by the studio system (Shin & Kim, 2013). The Korean music industry has experienced a series of shifts in the digital technology era. The digitization of music is almost everywhere; however, Korea has advanced unique growth due to the recent popularity of K-pop in the global music sphere, as well as the emergence of diverse digital technologies, including broadband, the Internet, wi-fi technology, and smartphones, which are all in globally leading positions.

The Korean music market was relatively small and static as only a few music genres, including ballad and trot, dominated the entire local music market. The turning point of Korean popular music toward the contemporary K-pop era was the mid-1990s. Numerous entertainment houses, including SM Entertainment (SME), JYP Entertainment (JYP), YG Entertainment (YG), and Hybe, started to nurture young musicians and the music industry. These entertainment agencies began producing idol groups targeting teenage fans (Lie, 2012). K-pop, differentiating itself from previous Korean popular music in terms of diverse music genres, emphasis on dances, and distinctive visual effects, has gained fame in Korea as youth enjoy this new music trend. K-pop has gradually penetrated other music markets, firstly in East Asia in the early 2000s, followed by other parts of the planet in the 2010s (G. T. Lee, 2016; Lee & Jin, 2019).[1]

The K-pop industry experienced another major shift with the development of social media platforms and streaming service platforms, although digitization already started prior to this aspect of its popularization. While Korea began to use the Internet in the late 1990s, the K-pop music era had already started in the early 1990s, even before the massive use of the Internet. Until 2000, the sales of physical CDs, LPs, and cassette tapes still grew, but this started to decline beginning in 2001 (Korea Creative Content Agency, 2011).

The growth of social media and streaming service platforms has greatly changed the contours of the local music industry in the early 21st century. Whenever Korean idol groups and artists release their new songs, they utilize various social media platforms like YouTube, and a few entertainment houses use social media platforms, such as Hybe-developed Weverse as the major platform for BTS. According to an analysis of YouTube's data, "the country that streamed boy band BTS's music videos and songs the most over the past year was Japan. BTS-related YouTube content—including official music videos and tracks, lyric videos, and fan-made content—accumulated approximately 15.1 billion views between March 2021 and February 2022, 2 billion of which came from Japan" (Chun & Yang, 2022). K-pop's global popularity has relied on social media in the early 21st century.[2] However, as the transnational

1. K-pop can be categorized as "a fusion of synthesized music, sharp dance routines, and fashionable and colorful outfits," and as part of K-pop, the catchy music in itself could be described as "a fusion of electro, disco, hip-hop, R&B, and rock sound" (Rousse-Marquet, 2012). K-pop has learned from Japanese pop culture and American pop music since the 1990s. In many cases, "Korean singers are cute and innocent, but project stronger personalities than their Japanese counterparts and sexually teasing, though not as provocative as the American pop stars in order to appeal to conservative Asian markets" (Rousse-Marquet, 2012).

2. Until early 2022, eight K-pop acts that garnered as many as 1 billion views on

popularity of K-pop is a relatively recent trend (J. O. Kim, 2016), and the reliance of K-pop on YouTube is a new phenomenon, little research has dealt with the specificity of the K-pop boom on music streaming service platforms, either global or local.

This chapter examines the emergence of the K-pop industry and the increasing role of entertainment houses by examining the transition of popular music, such as its style, music genre, and structure. It analyzes how these entertainment houses utilize social media platforms like YouTube and streaming service platforms, including Spotify, both nationally and globally, as some of the major elements for establishing global stardom. It especially discusses the major characteristics of music fan platforms, which are unique features of the K-pop world, differentiating it from Western music scenes. In other words, it analyzes the role of digital platforms in the Korean music industry and discusses how local entertainment houses have advanced their strategies for digital platforms in the global music market.

The Growth of the Korean Music Industry

The Korean music industry has experienced dramatic shifts over the past few decades. Korean popular music before the mid-1990s was very limited in production and reception. Korean popular music was not received in other countries, and many young people in the country used to enjoy American pop music until the 1980s. There were only a couple of music genres in Korea. Traditional Korean *Gayo*—also called pop music, including ballads—was mainly influenced by Western countries, but mostly Japan. In other words, *Gayo* was "a popular music genre created under Japanese and American influence" (Oh & Lee, 2014, p. 78). There were only 24 recording companies in 1981, and the studios controlled the songs and the hits (Shin & Kim, 2013). However, various music genres were developed in the 1980s, such as trot, ballad, dance, and rock, while the emergence of the color television era opened the visual music era, instead of simply listening to music on radio (see also chapter 3).

As in the case of broadcasting and film, the Korean music industry also

YouTube drew the most viewers from outside of Korea. For Blackpink, the second-most-viewed K-pop artist at 8.59 billion views, following BTS, the country with the largest viewership was India, with 820 million views. Twice, ITZY and Seventeen were famous the most in Japan, while Stray Kids was popular in Mexico. Only IU and aespa, among the top eight groups or artists, got the most views in Korea (Chun & Yang, 2022).

started to become one of the major cultural sectors in the mid-1990s. The Korean music scene especially experienced a significant change with the emergence of Seo Taiji & Boys who debuted in 1992 in the midst of loosening censorship on cultural content. Seo Taiji & Boys' music included some elements of hard-rock and hip-hop, which made them a national sensation. Structurally, with this group achieving enormous success, a few entertainment houses began to train and nurture new musicians, including H.O.T., Fin.K.L, S.E.S., and Shinhwa, which means that Korea began to develop idol groups. In 1996, SM Entertainment debuted its first idol group—a five-member boy band called H.O.T., followed by SME's first girl group, S.E.S. Both groups were popular and inspired other up-and-coming groups (Seabrook, 2012).

Ever since then, idol groups have dominated the Korean popular music industry, although there are many famous solo artists. K-pop has developed a few major characteristics, again, such as diverse music genres, emphasis on dances, and diverse visual effects, and increased artists' fame in the domestic market, triggering the global popularity of K-pop music (G. T. Lee, 2016; Lee & Jin, 2019). Eventually, the Korean music industry started to export K-pop to neighboring countries in the late 1990s, and later, K-pop gained global popularity in different regions, including North America and Western Europe in the 2010s.

What is significant in the process is that music entertainment houses become driving forces in the local music industry. While music record firms were the major players in the Korean music industry in the late 1980s, a handful of entertainment houses, such as SME, JYP, and YG, suddenly became major actors. These entertainment companies have never operated as conventional "record labels." They have driven "the direction of the Korean popular music by adopting a way of working that seeks to deal 'in-house' with all aspects of a performer's education and music and performing skills. In certain respects, this might be seen as an extension or elaboration of both the classic Hollywood studio system and the production methods developed by Motown Records in the early 1960s" (Negus, 2015, p. 8).

Among these, SM Entertainment—Lee Soo-man created SM Studio in 1989 and changed its name to SME in 1995—has especially become the leading force in the K-pop world. SME has grown into a major conglomerate in the local cultural industries. SME was the first company in the music industry "to introduce systematic casting, training, producing, and management systems, and it has been discovering unique content by pinpointing demands for music and cultural trends" (SM Entertainment, 2023). SME has continued to expand its global reach (Lee & Jin, 2019). As *Forbes* (2013) aptly put it, SME "kicked off the K-pop phenomenon in the 1990s. With its boot-camp-style training for the performers and production-line approach to the music, it perfected the model for churning out acts that storm the Top 40 charts and pack concert halls across Asia and beyond. An S.M. report lays out the industrial scale of the enterprise."

A few other major entertainment agencies, such as JYP and YG, also created contemporary K-pop. JYP is owned by Jin-Young Park who is a musician himself. He has trained many popular idol groups and solo artists, including Wonder Girls, 2AM, miss A, Suzy, TWICE, and ITZY. YG Entertainment has also created various idol groups and solo musicians, including BigBang, 2NE1, G-Dragon, PSY, and Blackpink. These local entertainment houses managed several important roles, such as songwriting, production, and recording, before Hybe, formerly Big Hit Entertainment, started to play a key role due to the global popularity of BTS in the mid-2010s. By implementing the Japanese idol system, these local entertainment houses nurtured television-friendly young talents—talents not just with singing ability, but dancing and general all-round entertainers' capabilities (J. Y. Lee, 2009).

While there are a few industrial activities, the most significant role of these entertainment houses has been recruiting and training young artists who might turn into leading idol members. The training process has been rigorous and influential in the music industry. The training period varies among K-pop idols from less than one year up to 15 years (Lee & Jin, 2019). In the K-pop world, "to become a trainee is to have one foot in the door, making it [as] an idol is a far tougher proposition. With contracts spanning an average of seven years, an agency will assess a trainee's talent, his or her ability to blend into a group, withstand the hardships of 'idol life', and avoid trouble" (Sunio, 2020). As *Forbes* (2013) points out:

> For spots in its groups, it receives 300,000 applicants in nine countries every year. Its training facility in Gangnam is 2,550 square meters. It collaborates with 400 songwriters worldwide and samples some 12,000 songs a year. From 2010 through 2012 its artists played to a total audience of 2.5 million. Its YouTube page gets 1,000 views a second.

There have been many solo artists as well; however, it is safe to claim that contemporary K-pop has become popular with idol groups who are mostly trained by entertainment houses more than solo artists (Lee & Jin, 2019). As explained, in 1981, there were only 24 recording companies. In 2020, there were as many as 33,138 music firms and 65,464 employees working for these music companies (Ministry of Culture, Sports and Tourism, 2022). The growth of the music industry has been remarkable.

Regardless of its sudden growth, the Korean music industry has shown a handful of socio-cultural issues, including the training system. Due to the rigorous and sometimes dehumanizing characteristics of in-house training systems, including the images of standardization and assembly lines, several parts of society were concerned about the star system in these entertainment houses. Jong-im Lee (2023), a music scholar and critic, for example, raised a big concern as major entertainment houses mainly focused on the growth of K-pop rather than developing fair and constructive training systems. A variety of issues, including unfair contracts and settlement matters, continue:

> Incidents resulting from physical assault under the guise of discipline, invasion of privacy, and conflict between members have also occurred recently. As the industry grows, so do the burdens and sacrifices of idols, such as the difficulties of living in a dormitory, the absence of friends of the same age, communication problems where only communication is possible with agency officials, and the burden of dieting and public attention (J. I. Lee, 2023).

As Keith Howard (2014, p. 408) also claimed, "the open, global market of K-pop today comes at a price. Entertainment companies segment and fill markets with songs produced on an assembly line and based on pre-masticated formulae."

Several foreign media outlets occasionally emphasize these concerns. *BBC News* (Oi, 2016), for example, claimed, local entertainment agencies have a hands-on approach to their trainees' daily lives. They are concerned about how their musicians are perceived by fans. *BBC News* (Oi, 2016) reported, "if you go to the agency, every young trainee will give you a very polite bow and there are notices with the company rules on the wall to remind them how to behave." The K-pop world is globally shining; however, behind this glory, several caveats should be resolved. K-pop idols and trainees mainly start their music careers in their mid-teens, and therefore, it is essential to protect them, both mentally and physically, with legal and ethical standards, while nurturing the music sphere.

The Korean Music Industry and Digital Music Platforms

Korea has greatly advanced its popular music since the mid-1990s, mainly due to the growth of digital technologies, meaning that the Korean music industry has turned into a digital music-driven market. In recent years, the music industry has shifted its direction one more time due to the increasing role of digital streaming service platforms. As is well-documented (Anderson, 2014; Morris, 2020, p. 2), "the cultural industries continue to experience ongoing aftershocks in the light of digitization. While the early stages of this transition were marked by concerns about the digitization of individual products or cultural commodities, digitization has now extended to all facets of the industries themselves. Not only is music that was once available in physical retail packages like CDs or cassette tapes, digital, but so too are the means of accessing, discovering, acquiring, and using those goods." YouTube, Spotify, and Apple Music are new mediators in the music sphere.

Digital music streaming is the big driver of growth in the recorded music business. Global recorded music revenue increased to US$36.1 billion in 2022, up from US$23.2 billion in 2018. Digital music streaming rose 11.6% in 2022 to US$25.8 billion, up from US$12.7 billion in 2018. Indeed, Spotify added 10 million net paying subscribers in the fourth quarter alone to push its global premium subscription base to 205 million at the end of the year. Spotify increased its paying subscriber audience by 14% from the prior year. Apple Music, Tencent Music, and Amazon Music each had estimated premium subscriber bases of close to 90 million at the end of 2022 (PricewaterhouseCoopers, 2023). Interestingly, the live music segment is also rebounding from COVID-19 lockdowns.[3] The live music

3. As PricewaterhouseCoopers (2023) indicates, this segment comprises consumer spending on music, including both physical and digital recorded music and live music played at concerts, as well as revenue from sponsorship of live music, but does not include revenue from merchandise or concessions at live music events. It also includes revenue from consumer spending on radio license fees and all advertising spent on radio stations and radio networks. Finally, it includes revenue from podcast advertising, podcasts being defined as a piece of principally spoken-word recorded audio content delivered over the internet, excluding audiobooks, that can be either downloaded or streamed. The recorded music component comprises physical and digital. Here physical recorded music covers any retail or online purchase of official physical albums (i.e., CDs), single sound recordings or music videos. Digital recorded music considers the sale of any licensed music distributed digitally to connected devices (including PCs, tablets, smartphones and dedicated music players), and is split between streaming and

sector was hit by COVID-19 lockdowns, which slashed global revenue by 74.8% in 2020 ($6.83 billion). The music market in 2022 delivered a significant rebound, although performance restrictions remained in place across many markets. Live music revenue was expected to be US$25.3 billion in 2022 and $28.5 billion in 2023, respectively, compared with US$27.2 billion in pre-pandemic 2019 (PricewaterhouseCoopers, 2023).

Cultural distribution in the digital era is "undergoing changes so profound that they can be difficult to trace, both empirically and theoretically," and cultural distribution has "long known that distribution is much more than a purely functional practice—the middle ground between the far more interesting practices of media production and consumption" (McDonald, Donoghue, & Havens, 2021, p. 1):

> Rather, distribution acts as a shaping force in the industrialized practices of cultural dissemination. Distribution does more than just "move," "relay," or "transmit" content. For critical studies of media industries, distribution holds dual significance, inviting interrogation of the systemized processes by which the media industries supply cultural content between parties (i.e., how are media distributed?), but also the time and space over which that content is spread and made available (i.e., when, where, and to whom are media distributed?) (McDonald, Donoghue, & Havens, 2021, p. 1).

In the global music industry, digital music streaming service platforms, including YouTube, are expected to become an even bigger contributor to total worldwide recorded music revenue, as more consumers switch to streaming services and as physical revenue contracts. In 2022, "streaming accounted for 71.7% of all recorded music revenue and is forecast to be responsible for 80.3% of segment value in 2027. The live music sector has done remarkably to bounce back from lockdowns and shuttered venues and festivals. While streaming will drive long-term growth in the music sector, the live category is providing a large, short-term spike to revenue as it rebounds from the pandemic" (PricewaterhouseCoopers, 2023).

In the Korean market in the early 21st century, K-pop experienced a

---

downloads. Streaming comprises revenue from subscription and advertiser-supported streaming services (such as Spotify). Performance rights revenue is generated for record companies and performers by the use of recorded music by broadcasters and in public venues. For live music, consumer spending on tickets is included along with sponsorship revenues (PricewaterhouseCoopers, 2023).

dramatic change, as the digital download process of music consumption decreased as the use of digital streaming platforms, such as YouTube, Spotify, and Google Play Music, soared. "Music streaming services allow access to a virtually unlimited library and make owning the music unnecessary" (Oh & Choeh, 2022, p. 805). This implies that music streaming affects local music consumption habits on a large scale. As Prey (2020, p. 8) aptly puts it, these music streaming platforms "analyze user behavior and provide dynamic curation and personalized recommendations."

Music streaming platforms control the vicious circle of cultural production, from the production of popular culture to the consumption of cultural content. Digital streaming service platforms have controlled the production and distribution of popular music, and music fans enjoy their favorite music on these streaming service platforms. These music platforms "become essential in promoting songs," and therefore, "many artists create an official channel on YouTube and encourage their fans' engagements" (Oh & Choeh, 2022, p. 804). Numerous global streaming platforms, such as Spotify, YouTube, and Amazon, have gained vital positions, thus challenging incumbent industry players and their business models and practices (Cunningham & Craig, 2019; Poell et al., 2022, cited in Sundet & Lüders, 2023, p. 223). As Cunningham and Craig (2019) pointed out, social media entertainment creators harness those platforms to create new content separate from the old model of IP control in the traditional music industry. Digital platforms have changed the contemporary media environment in that digital platforms reign supreme. What is significant is that "these developments challenge national media players, who need to make sense of a shifting world and take action to stay relevant" (Sundet & Lüders, 2023, p. 223).

The growth of digital streaming service platforms has been peculiar in our contemporary society, and "the Korean music market is or has been 'leading the world' in the move towards a completely digital 'model', and sometimes suggest that this may provide 'lessons' (Mulligan, 2013, cited in Negus, 2015) for the rest of the world" (Negus, 2015, pp. 4–5). As Bolin (2017, p. 44) points out, "each potential generation is born into a different media landscape. There will be media that are already established at the point of birth, and that all individuals take for granted and act naturally in relation to. And new media forms, genres and styles will develop, as well as new technological platforms that each individual will encounter during their life course." Here "a metaphor for the media landscape is often used to describe the mediatized space in which people live and act. It is a spatial metaphor that indicates a phenomenological 'world' perspective, just like the metaphor of the media environment" (Bolin, 2017, p. 45). This means that "the media and platforms taken for granted by those born since the turn of the millennium are often interpreted as causing unprecedented competition for national and legacy media players" (Sundet & Lüders, 2023, p. 223). Millennials and Generation Z easily adopt global streaming services as an integral part of cultural activities.

Music streaming for the Millennial and Z generations has indeed become a popular way of listening, sharing, and downloading their favorite music and new songs. During the COVID-19 era, music streaming platforms especially became a primary resource. Although many people around the world started enjoying music on various streaming services, including YouTube and Spotify, streaming music has deeply changed the global music industry since the pandemic struck in late 2019, allowing any genre or style to become more affordable. Music streaming has made it easier for people, particularly younger generations, to discover new musicians who would not have the opportunity for such exposure. Distribution of music on streaming service platforms makes it much easier for musicians to spread their music as well. Music streaming has benefited consumers with the ability to listen and discover various songs and musicians (Tamera, 2021).

When the global music market grew by 9.0% in 2022, subscription streaming was the leading driver of growth (+10.3% to US$12.7 billion). Overall streaming (including subscription and advertising supported) accounted for the highest proportion of the market, increasing to a 67.0% share of the overall market in 2022, up from a 65.5% share the prior year. During the same year, the Korean music market ranked 7th, only behind the U.S., Japan, the U.K., Germany, China, and France (International Federation of the Phonographic Industry, 2023).

More importantly, K-pop is different in its own market structure:

> First, it has enjoyed a continued run of success for the past 15 years—a longer span of time than the golden years of the Hong Kong movie industry (from the late 1980s to late 1990s) or the Japanese J-pop wave (during the 1990s). Second, it has drawn in huge audiences in Japan and across Southeast Asia since the early 2000s, paving the way into the rest of Asia and other parts of the world since the late 2000s. Last, but not least, a significant number of K-pop groups have achieved regular chart hits around the world, prompting Billboard to launch a global chart entitled "K-pop Hot 100." Furthermore, YouTube created a specific K-pop entry to its

existing musical entries. All combined, these trends give the impression that the popularity and success of K-pop are developing into a true global force (Messerlin & Shin, 2017, p. 410).

In K-pop, music streaming service platforms have also played a pivotal role in disseminating locally produced popular music in the global music sphere. However, the situation is different. It is not unusual to claim that streaming platforms are major drivers for the global popularity of K-pop; however, CD sales and music concerts are still relevant and important, which means that the K-pop industry is showing a different trend. As in many countries, digital music has become a dominant force in the local music market. In 2015, of all music sales, 84.3% were digital, while the sales of physical formats, including CDs, consisted of 15.7%. However, the proportion of the sales of physical formats went up to 29.4% in 2017 (Korea Creative Content Agency, 2018), and the trend has continued.

The recent surge in the sales of physical formats has been based on the popularity of numerous idol groups, including EXO, Twice, Blackpink, BTS, and Seventeen (Jin, 2020). According to the Circle Chart (2023), previously known as Gaon Album Chart, which records the sales of physical music formats among the top 400 albums starting in 2011, the sales of physical albums have soared, from only 7.3 million copies in 2014 to as many as 115.1 million copies in 2023 (until the second week of December)—a more than 15 times increase during this period (Figure 6.1). As the chart explains, during the COVID-19 era, the sales of physical albums soared partially because people who practiced social distancing bought albums instead of going to music concerts, which were all canceled.

As Figure 6.1. proves, Korea's CD sales have been consistently on the rise since 2015. The majority of Koreans mainly listen to music digitally, like people in most other countries; however, the K-pop industry is unique because its physical CD market is also alive. There are a few primary reasons for buying CDs in the K-pop world, including CD collection and fandom activities. Among these, K-pop fandoms have a strong notion that people are true fans only if they buy the physical CD. When their favorite musicians release new albums, many fans think "it's their duty to help its success by purchasing physical copies to make it reach No.1 on music charts," which is part of the fan activity. In particular, "first-week sales indicate the size and loyalty of fandom because it means that fans bought the CD unconditionally and immediately upon its release" (Yang, 2021). Since first-week sales are a standard of an idol group's popularity, some fans, including global fans, buy multiple CDs fans. Many entertainment

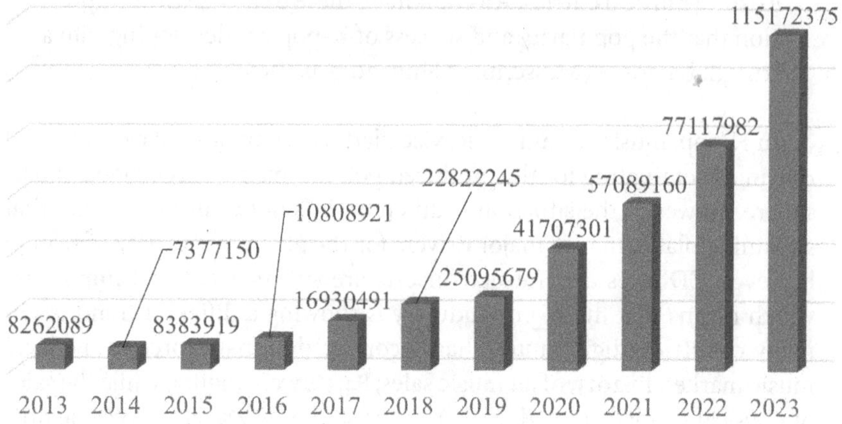

Figure 6.1. Sales of Physical Albums, 2013–2023

agencies actively employ various business strategies, including meet-and-greets, to appeal to dedicated fans in an attempt to boost sales. "The more CDs fans buy, the higher the chance of winning an invitation to the meet-and-greet. Loyalty is what makes CD sales a steady industry" in the K-pop world (Yang, 2021).[4]

Globally, K-pop achieved exponential growth during the COVID-19 pandemic, as K-pop has boosted its global presence over the past couple of years. Many people around the world "are known to have fallen under K-pop's spell during the global health crisis, as they came across a tsunami of Korean entertainment content on social media platforms like Twitter and YouTube while staying at home due to social distancing" (Dong, 2023). In the early 21st century, Korea has become a testbed where digital platforms, both local and global, examine their business models and new functions as the majority of Koreans rapidly adopt new technologies in their daily activities. Understanding the Korean music market is essential for many countries and cultural creators as they can

4. Music entertainment houses' marketing strategies have sometimes gone too far. As can be seen in a court hearing between Hybe and Min Hee Jin in April 2024 (see chapter 3), Min Hee Jin said, "Hybe suggested the tactic of 'advanced purchasing' 100,000 albums," upon the release of *Get Up*, NewJeans' new song, in July 2023, in particular, to beat aespa, a girl group by SM Entertainment, in first-week sales with this tactic (allkpop, 2024). When Seventeen, a male idol group, released its new album *17 IS RIGHT HERE*, in April 2024, many CDs were thrown away on the street in Tokyo, Japan. It was speculated that fans purchased multiple CDs to get photo cards that are inserted in CDs; however, they did not possess CDs other than photo cards (S.H. Ji, 2024).

more easily determine what may work and be successfully developed for different countries.

How Digital Platforms Shape the Korean Music Sphere

When the Korean music industry experienced a variety of significant changes, the emergence of YouTube fundamentally influenced the Korean music sphere. For example, *Gangnam Style* was "one of the most notable phenomena in the world of popular culture" mainly thanks to YouTube. PSY's new song was released on YouTube on July 15, 2012, and it reached number two on the Billboard Hot 100 chart in less than two months (Jung & Li, 2014, p. 1932). More importantly, PSY's *Gangnam Style* made online video history as his viral video smashed all of Billboard's records and became the first video ever to reach one billion views on YouTube, while breaking the 800-million-views record of Justin Bieber's *Baby* on December 21, 2012 (Gruger, 2012; YouTube Trends Team, 2012) and remained at the number one spot of the world's most watched video on YouTube as of August 2014. The impact of the *Gangnam Style* phenomenon extended beyond PSY's singular music video. According to a YouTube Trends report (YouTube Trends Team, 2013), the view counts of Korean music videos increased threefold from 2012 to 2013 (Jung & Li, 2014).

As can be seen with PSY's *Gangnam Style*, social media, especially YouTube, has become a new outlet for popular music, and many K-pop musicians, such as Twice, BTS, Blackpink, and NewJeans, have penetrated both regional and Western markets due to social media platforms. *Gangnam Style* is catchy and ridiculous enough; however, it might not be globally popular without YouTube. PSY's *Gangnam Style* became globally popular due to the convergence of its unique musical characteristics, including comical horse dance, and social media platforms. As Mattelart (2024, 28) aptly puts it, social media platforms, including YouTube, are not only working as the facilitators of cultural production in the countries where they operate, but they are also playing as contributors to the restructuring of content creation. Streaming service platforms are eager to increase their "user base at a transnational scale and the advertising revenues associated with" them, while they try to formalize, through a comprehensive set of training tools, the practices of their "amateur content creators wanting to professionalize themselves."

As such, it is not a secret that social media has become one of the most important drivers for the emergence of K-pop in the global cultural markets. Social media is for everyone, including American and Japanese musicians, and therefore, any musicians can utilize social media. However,

> K-pop entertainment agencies and musicians deliberately utilize social media platforms to penetrate the global music markets. Several social media, in particular YouTube make it easier for K-pop musicians to reach a wider audience in the global music markets. In fact, social media has expedited the growth of K-pop's presence in many parts of the world. It is not dicey to argue that the global K-pop phenomenon in the 2010s can be maintained mainly because social media makes K-pop easily accessible (Lee & Jin, 2019, p. 28).

It is certain that the K-pop phenomenon around the globe has been made possible because of big entertainment agencies' social media strategies while engaging with audiences through on-and offline promotions (Ahn et al., 2013). As Ahn et al. (2013,) aptly put it,

> focusing on the business potential of social media, the K-pop entertainment industry utilizes various channels to promote music videos and to communicate with global audience. Along with releasing new music videos and related teasers on YouTube, entertainment agencies open and manage Facebook and Twitter accounts to meet their overall social media strategy. Though each social media (YouTube, Facebook, and Twitter) serves a specific purpose, agencies try to integrate the channels under their business strategy and maximize the potential (pp. 775–776).

A variety of idol groups and individual artists were globally popular on YouTube, as Table 6.1. shows. PSY still holds the position as the most-viewed music video by Korean artists as of January 6, 2024. PSY's *Gangnam Style* music video surpassed 5 billion views on YouTube as of December 30, 2023, the first time a K-pop music video reached this milestone (All K-pop, 2023). Other famous idol groups and individual artists, including Blackpink, BTS, Lisa, and Jennie, also attained top-ranked positions. Interestingly, BTS and Blackpink are the two most popular idol groups representing Korean boy groups and girl groups on YouTube. Other musicians, including Twice, Big Bang, EXO, and ITZY, also made the top 50 list with their famous songs.

The K-pop world has developed its unique strategy of utilizing You-

TABLE 6.1. Most Viewed Music Videos by Korean Artists, January 6, 2024 (p. 194)

Ranking	Video	Views
1	PSY—GANGNAM STYLE(강남스타일) M/V	5,007,106,686
2	BLACKPINK—'뚜두뚜두 (DDU-DU DDU-DU)' M/V	2,156,780,110
3	BLACKPINK—'Kill This Love' M/V	1,911,872,814
4	BTS (방탄소년단) 'Dynamite' Official MV	1,779,882,321
5	BTS, '작은 것들을 위한 시 (Boy With Luv) (feat. Halsey)' Official MV	1,736,576,635
6	BLACKPINK—'붐바야 (BOOMBAYAH)' M/V	1,663,084,000
7	PSY—GENTLEMAN M/V	1,592,848,771
8	BTS, 'DNA' Official MV	1,562,149,846
9	BLACKPINK—'How You Like That' DANCE PERFORMANCE VIDEO	1,556,422,630
10	BTS, 'MIC Drop (Steve Aoki Remix)' Official MV	1,395,000,886
11	BLACKPINK—'마지막처럼 (AS IF IT'S YOUR LAST)' M/V	1,345,914,011
12	BTS, 'IDOL' Official MV	1,262,793,391
13	BLACKPINK—'How You Like That' M/V	1,261,859,020
14	BTS, 'FAKE LOVE' Official MV	1,253,477,378
15	JENNIE—'SOLO' M/V	987,905,171
16	BTS, '피 땀 눈물 (Blood Sweat & Tears)' Official MV	960,458,530
17	LISA—'MONEY' EXCLUSIVE PERFORMANCE VIDEO	949,426,550
18	BTS, 'Butter' Official MV	933,454,455
19	BLACKPINK—'Ice Cream (with Selena Gomez)' M/V	886,734,928
20	BLACKPINK—'휘파람 (WHISTLE)' M/V	875,576,543

Source: https://kworb.net/youtube/topvideos_korean.html

Tube as one of its most significant distribution channels. In June 2009, SM Entertainment opened its official YouTube channel to upload music content on social media. This was the first move among the Korean entertainment agencies, and other agencies followed to have their own social media accounts on YouTube and Facebook. They focused on a few leading social media platforms, including YouTube, Facebook, and Twitter (now X) (Lee & Jin, 2019). As for their primary promotion platform, "they opened official YouTube channels to promote new music videos and leveraged other social media such as Facebook and Twitter to communicate with their youth audience. At the same time, to facilitate communication with the audience, major K-pop labels manage individual dedicated YouTube channel[s] for their artists" (Ahn et al., 2013, p. 776).

Since K-pop has reached the global cultural scene, YouTube has become a barometer for the success of K-pop. Many global K-pop fans and media outlets check YouTube to determine the success or failure of K-pop groups and new songs. For example, when BTS broke records with their new single *Dynamite*—the first BTS song to be released completely in English—which amassed 101.1 million views in its first 24 hours of release in 2022, it became one of the major entertainment news stories around the globe. As ABC News (2022) reported, the clip had "the most views for a music video in its first 24 hours on YouTube, while the video also set a new all-time record for the biggest music video premiere with over 3 million peak concurrent viewers immediately upon release." Digital platforms have certainly transformed the Korean music industry as music labels, musicians, and music fans have had to change their production and consumption strategies in order to adjust to the platform-driven media environment.

Growth of Local Music Platforms

While YouTube as a global platform plays a major role in Korea and elsewhere, a handful of local music platforms have also taken significant roles in the growth of K-pop, both nationally and globally. Unlike many other major countries, Korea has advanced unique music platforms, including music streaming platforms and fan service platforms. Music streaming platforms, like Melon, Genie Music, FLO, VIBE, KakaoMusic, and Bugs! are some of the major music platforms that offer rich libraries of Korean music. In the fan service platform category, a handful of platforms, such as Weverse, V Live, Dear U Bubble, and Universe, have developed local-special platforms, which are not found in a few Western countries. This section discusses these two different music platforms in order to fully understand the Korean music industry, where digital platforms have become a new value chain in music production, distribution, and consumption.

Local Music Streaming Platforms

As the Korean music industry has rapidly turned its direction toward digital music as in many other countries, local music platforms continue to grow. Local K-pop fans do not buy CDs and cassette tapes with some exceptional years while enjoying their favorite music on music streaming platforms, such as Melon and Genie Music, as well as YouTube. Among these, Melon has been the largest local music streaming service platform since 2004, when SK Telecom developed it. In 2016, Kakao acquired a 76.4% stake in the company for $1.55 billion. Kakao has been pushing to "expand its platform business to a wider range of industry commerce, mobile games and mobile banking," to gain "a major boost in securing entertainment content and a global market presence" (S. W. Yoon, 2016). Melon, with 28 million subscribers, in 2016 was "the largest music content service here with more than 50% market share over KT Music's Genie, CJ ENM's Mnet.com and NHN Entertainment's Bugs Music" (S. W. Yoon, 2016).

Due to the increasing popularity of YouTube in Korea, local music streaming platforms have experienced a decline in the number of users and their market share in the local music industry. Until a few years ago, Melon did not seem to have rivals in terms of market share, with its share nearing 50% in 2018 (S. H. Dong, 2022). Local music platforms, such as Melon, Genie, FLO, Vibe, Bugs!, and Kakao Music, were the go-to-streaming platforms in Korea until Korean music listeners shifted to YouTube and Spotify (S. Ha, 2022). The situation has changed, as YouTube Music threatens Melon's dominance in Korea:

> According to the big data platform Mobile Index, as of December 2021, YouTube Music held the third-largest market share in Korea (19.22%), only after Melon (37.28%) and Genie (19.24%). The relatively new service, which began with a 1.7% share in 2019, edged out other homegrown platforms such as FLO (13.31%) and VIBE (4.08%). It also saw a dramatic rise in the number of monthly active users (MAU). Its MAU was about 630,000 on Jan. 1, 2021, but the number spiked to 1.26 million on Dec. 1—a 97% increase in just a year (S.H. Dong, 2022).

The competition among streaming services has been tough in very recent years. "Melon is preparing to enhance its music recommendation system based on users' personal data and Genie is set to showcase content that blends music and its audio services. The latter is also planning to kick off new businesses that involve artificial intelligence (AI), the metaverse and non-fungible tokens (NFT)" (S. H. Dong, 2022).

According to a survey conducted in Korea in 2022, around 59% of respondents stated that they used YouTube to stream or download music

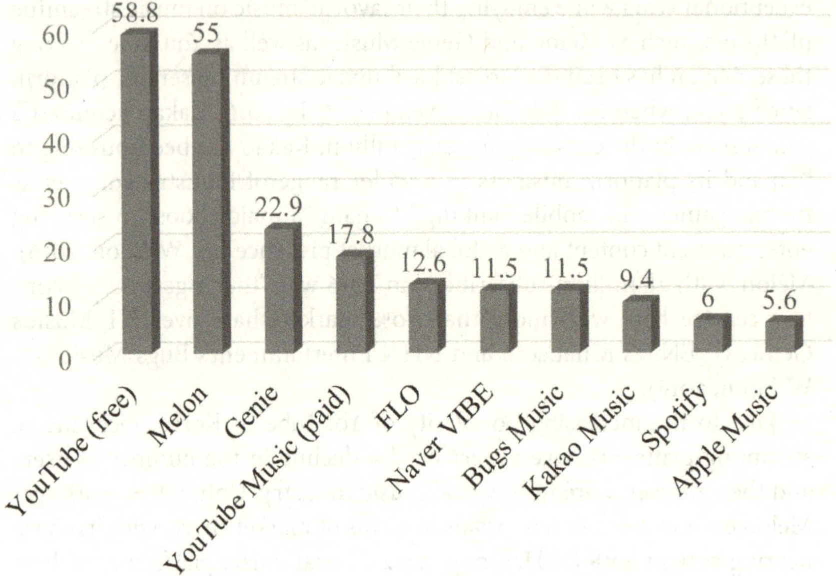

Figure 6.2. Most Frequently Used Music Streaming or Download Services in South Korea, August 2022 (Unit: %)

content. A similarly popular service, at around 55%, was the Korean music streaming platform Melon. YouTube's paid music streaming service, YouTube Music, was used by around 18% of respondents (Statista, 2023) (Figure 6.2).

Until recent years, Melon stood atop the summit of Korean streaming platforms; however, 2023's user statistics revealed a new twist: Melon is no longer the reigning champion in the Korean music streaming market. YouTube Music has become the leading player. "This overtaking by YouTube's service underscores the global platform's increasing dominance not just on international soil but in Korea's own backyard. While Melon saw an increase of 90,000 users from last year, YouTube Music enjoyed 1.12 million others joining the platform" (Koreaboo, 2023).

There are various elements that account for these shifts. Most of all, user interface and subscription prices become significant factors. Melon users pay ₩10,900 (comparable to US$ 8.34) per month to use the streaming and offline playback features. YouTube Music's service fee is ₩8,690 per month, but if users pay ₩10,500, they gain access to YouTube Premium as well. Young people who love music don't just want to listen to music. Instead, they want to listen, watch, interact, and share. YouTube's interactive interface and extensive catalog cater to young music fans' desires (Koreaboo, 2023). Local platforms, however, didn't fare as well. Several local music platforms, such as GenieMusic, FLO, VIBE, Kakao Music, and Bugs, have experienced a decline in user numbers in recent years. While they offer rich libraries of K-pop music, platform users might find "their interfaces less intuitive or their subscription prices less competitive compared to international juggernauts like YouTube Music and Spotify" (Koreaboo, 2023). Compared with other music streaming service platforms, "YouTube has dominated the online multimedia market and distributed a substantial amount of music through music videos and lyrics videos released in connection with albums" (Oh & Choeh, 2022, p. 805).

The K-pop industry shows two different power struggles in the digital platform era. On the one hand, the K-pop industry has increased its reliance on local music platforms that have been established and operated by a handful of local mega-platforms and telecommunications companies, including Naver and Kakao. K-pop labels and local music platforms seem to build "a symbiotic relationship"; however, this also indicates that "the technological and financial advantages" that local platforms like Kakao and Naver enjoy in the platformization of K-pop production, which results in power asymmetry between K-pop producers and mega-platforms (Park, Jo, & Kim, 2023, p. 2433). On the other hand, the K-pop industry has witnessed the power dynamics of platformization in local cultural production because global music platforms, in particular, YouTube, have become the major player regardless of the growth of local music platforms. The asymmetrical power relations between global and local music platforms in the K-pop world show the continuing dominance of global cultural industries, in this case, global music platforms, in the Korean music sphere. This lopsidedness eventually threatens the local music industry as a viable popular music center, which emerges from the Global South.

Fan Music Platforms

The K-pop fandom has been one of the strongest in the global music sphere. As ARMY exemplifies, many fans, locally and globally, form and practice very strong fandom activities. They watch new songs together, while sharing their feelings and emotions on social media. They also systematically organize various fandom activities to show their loyalty to their favorite musicians. In Korea, numerous fans follow BTS, Blackpink, and Twice in various ways: they send birthday cards and presents; they purchase concert tickets and goods; they request radio plays. Some groups even host a variety of competitions where their fans win items if they purchase their music in support (BBC, 2021).

The fandom platform, which is created through the convergence of fandom culture and the media industry, shifts the arena of fan activity, from offline to online, as the fandom platform offers a multitude of products and services related to idols and artists. A fandom platform refers to an online space where people can consume and exercise in fan activities. Previously, music fans conducted their activities on multiple channels. However, with fandom platforms, fan activities, such as fan recruitment, management, announcements, and self-management, that used to be scattered are now gathered on the fandom platform. From content distribution to merchandise sales to event booking, all fan activities are carried out through the fandom platform (S. G. Kang, 2022).

The technology of fandom has changed as well. As Stitch (2021) points out, "parasocial relationships—a largely one-sided relationship between a fan and a public figure they feel close to due to social media—are everywhere online." Quite a few music companies have advanced online platforms to help K-pop fans feel connected. That access helps shape the way K-pop fans interact with their favorite idols and how they engage with other fans. The firms behind some of the biggest acts in K-pop pioneer "a new way to monetize them" (Stitch, 2021).

As is well-known, before the rise of social media accounts and fan platforms, most fans for K-pop idols and artists basically were

> locked into direct engagement through fancafes—a kind of digital fan club that often required fans to prove their knowledge of a particular artist before gaining access to artists. Initially hosted on platforms like social networking site Daum, these fancafes allowed fans to connect with idols directly, and they could become even more intimate when connected with the official paid fan club memberships. While the DAUM fancafes for many idols are still up and running, there has been a shift away from them over the past two years, especially for English-language fandoms. In their place, several companies have created new social apps for their artists, entirely bypassing third-party platforms like Twitter or Facebook (Stitch, 2021).

Of course, "parasocial interaction demonstrates a shift in interaction as internet communication technologies enable fans to readily interact with artists. The nature of parasocial interaction has extended from a one-sided, passive interaction to a two-way interaction between the fan and the artist" (Kassing & Sanderson, 2009, cited in Kim, Hwang, & Kim, 2021, p. 4). Fans' parasocial interaction in the social media era "is demonstrated by not only role-modeling sports figures but also actively expressing gratitude, providing advice, and suggesting play behavior. Internet technologies are thus extending offline fan club events to the online platform and encouraging fans to form efficient interpersonal relationships with celebrities" (Kim et al., 2021, p. 5).

Numerous entertainment houses and local media firms establish fan service platforms in order to initiate these activities while providing venues for fans to actively organize and conduct fandom activities. Local platforms have advanced various online fan services, which drive the growth of K-pop in the global cultural markets. In particular, Weverse, which Hybe has operated, has been the primary fan music platform (see chapter 3). Hybe planned to use Weverse for BTS and Seventeen, which is a boy band formed by Pledis Entertainment. BTS originally used V Live—Naver's fan music platform:

> Along with the strong influence of global platforms in spreading K-pop, Korea's local platform V Live has also increased its presence in approaching overseas fans. Launched in 2015 by Korea's search portal company Naver, V Live is a live video-streaming platform for K-pop idols to conduct personal broadcasts and interact intimately with fans. V Live is different from other platforms as celebrities can operate their own channel and upload original content that is not seen elsewhere. The platform encourages artists to conduct live broadcasts that are usually streamed in waiting rooms, in cars, and at home. By revealing their off-stage persona in comfortable settings, celebrities on V Live have better opportunities to minimize their performative images and talk casually with fans. In addition to live-streaming content, V Live offers premium content and offline opportunities for fans to actively interact with their favorite artists (Kim, Hwang, & Kim, 2021, p. 3).

Hybe launched its own platform Weverse in June 2019 as BTS became a global star. Weverse "has changed the way people connect with others online by making it easier for fans to message each other regardless of which country they're from," since its inception. Previously, "most K-pop artists used a Korean forum called fancafe to communicate and share exclusive content with fans" (Devoe, 2019). However, fancafe, which has been operated by Daum, was not easy for global fans to access or use due to a language barrier (Devoe, 2019). Hybe's Weverse has been systematic in developing fan engagements. On Weverse, "all of the interactions between artists and fans (and among fans) can be translated into nearly a dozen languages. At the same time, Hybe debuted a sister app Weverse Shop, which sells exclusive gear from artists, from branded pajamas to K-pop's signature light sticks, as well as concert tickets"; therefore, in 2021 alone, "licensing and merchandise accounted for a quarter of Hybe revenue. Fan clubs brought in an additional $37 million" (Farley, 2022). Likewise, Weverse allows global fans to connect with other fans while offering exclusive content that fans cannot easily see anywhere else. The platform is available in a few different languages, such as English, Korean, Japanese, Chinese, Spanish, Portuguese, Indonesian, Malay, and Thai (Devoe, 2019).

Weverse has become popular because it is the exclusive platform on which global fans watch BTS's daily activities. Hybe has differentiated itself as it is "investing in digital technology that makes it possible to stream concerts virtually and own the artist-fan relationship, from ticketing to merchandise shops to live artist broadcasts, shows, and message boards. Weverse, where fans can go for all things related to Hybe artists," is a new platform for musicians (Bruner, 2022). Hybe emphasizes its own platform that it can fully manage without broadcasters, Naver, Kakao, and other Internet platforms.

Other entertainment houses have created their own fan music service platforms. In 2020, SM Entertainment launched Dear U Bubble under Lysn—a fan community service—as a subscription-based fan communication platform (Y. J. Jun, 2021). NCSoft, one of the largest digital game companies in Korea, also created Universe in January 2021 and recorded 21 million downloads globally in a year. It competed with two other platforms, which were Weverse under Hybe and Dear U Bubble under the affiliation of SM Entertainment. However, Universe decided to shut down its service in January 2023 and planned to transfer its registered artists to Dear U Bubble (J. L. Lee, 2023). One of the major reasons that music fans like these local fan platforms is proximity, meaning that "fans can feel as though they're seeing a different, more personal side to the idol they're following on less direct platforms like Twitter or Instagram." In other words, "these company-run apps don't just offer fans the ability to receive comfort from the artist. For some fans, the appeal is in getting to offer support when an artist is going through a health issue, a scandal, or simply when they're bored on their rare downtime" (Stitch, 2021).

Ironically, the COVID-19 pandemic era facilitated the growth of local fan music platforms. As is well-documented, the pandemic caused the suspension of all in-person events, including live performances and world tours, all of which are essential for building stronger fandoms for musicians. As COVID-19 spread, it was impossible for the idols and artists to interact with fans in-person, so Weverse helped people to connect with their favorite musicians (C. Y. Oh, 2021). As the latest development, Kakao acquired SM Entertainment in February 2023, so, therefore, SME's K-pop fandom platform Dear U Bubble is expected to collaborate with Kakao's entertainment agencies to compete with Hybe's fan platform Weverse (Kim & Cha, 2022). Since Kakao has already acquired a few entertainment houses and cultural production companies, this recent decision implies the platformization of cultural industries in the Korean context.

As such, the growth of K-pop fandom is closely related to digital platforms, and digital platforms have greatly increased K-pop's visibility in the global music sphere. Since music production and consumption can occur on digital platforms on a large scale, music platforms are expected to grow further in the future. Unlike the case of OTT platforms, local music platforms, in particular, music fan service platforms, play a pivotal role in the Korean music industry. They actualize the platformization process in order to maximize their market shares, and therefore, profits. As Kim, Hwang, and Kim (2021, p. 3) point out, "advancements in technology and strategic uses of social media has transformed K-pop into a more fluid and opportunistic ecosystem," and the K-pop world itself benefits from the platformization of the music industry, although platforms have destroyed the traditional forms of the music ecosystem.

What is significant is that it is easy for entertainment houses to expand their businesses to support global fandom. Fan platforms are a virtual space, and therefore, there are no borders or nationalities. The features of the platform mean that one can expand one's business area and expand one's activity area without space limitations. The fandom platform attracts fans from all over the world. The fandom platform provides information and content to fans constantly, and multifaceted communication occurs from time to time (S. G. Kang, 2022). Given the significance of social media platforms in the K-pop industry, participatory fandom has taken on an important position, and fan service platforms play a key role in this particular juncture (Yuniya & Marc de Jong, 2021). K-pop fandom is unique as fans play a key role in both online and offline spaces, and the growth of fandom platforms has become a new participatory culture that global musicians and music corporations pay attention to. Unlike the music streaming platform sector, in which global platforms like YouTube and Spotify have increased their market shares in Korea, the music fan platform area indicates that local platforms like Weverse still play major roles, which characterizes the platformization of Korean music fan activities.

There are various caveats. While K-pop has deeply influenced the global music sphere in the early 21st century, there are various concerns as well, such as the commercialization of popular music, the platformization of popular culture, and the necessity of transparent and careful training systems. The most significant issue is the utilization of user data. On the fandom platform, participants engage in various activities, and during the process, all data is collected in time series, not only user-related information such as conversation history, but also information about various purchases made within the platform. In other words, the fandom platform is based on personal information and participant experience, and the data collected in such a way is customized for marketing purposes (S. G. Kang, 2022). Although the appropriation of user data is not new, it is critical in fandom platforms as the users are mainly teens and people in their early twenties. Providing enjoyable fandom platform culture is one thing, and protecting users from potential harm is another.

Conclusion

This chapter has analyzed the increasing role of digital platforms related to the K-pop industry. It documented the significance of local entertainment houses that have become primary players in advancing K-pop, both nationally and globally. By analyzing two major forms of music platforms, including global music streaming service platforms, mainly YouTube, and local music fan platforms, mainly Weverse, in tandem with K-pop, it also discussed the ways in which digital platforms take pivotal roles in the value chain of the K-pop industry, from music production to consumption.

K-pop in the early 21st century has witnessed its growth based on the increasing roles of local entertainment houses and music platforms, which are unique factors. Local entertainment agencies have driven the K-pop phenomenon in the global music markets. Numerous entertainment houses have advanced their production systems, including the idol training prototype, which has contributed to the K-pop phenomenon. They have also created various business models that have not been seen in other countries' music industries. These entertainment houses have not only utilized local specificities but also global standards because they target global music fans. Due to the timely growth of various digital technologies, from the Internet to music streaming platforms, K-pop has expanded its global reach.

While the local entertainment houses work as the major players in music production, music platforms are certainly playing as the new mediators that circulate K-pop systematically. As can be seen in the case of PSY's *Gangnam Style* and Blackpink's Rosé's and Bruno Mars' APT, 2024, which have been globally popular on YouTube and other social media platforms, digital platforms have played pivotal roles in the K-pop world since the early 2010s. Without music service platforms, contemporary K-pop does not exist. The Korean music industry has closely worked with music platforms, both local and global, while uniquely creating music fan service platforms. Digital fandom is everywhere these days; however, local fandom culture driven by music fan platforms has been peculiar.

The convergence of entertainment houses and streaming platforms has been crucial, as the role of entertainment houses is vital in helping musicians succeed online:

> Besides the comprehensive support in producing hybrid music and opportunities to perform on global stages, entertainment companies' promotional and management support is needed in online media platforms. Given how artists' online exposure is a mix of authenticity and professionalism, entertainment companies need to ensure that artists maintain the equilibrium by following appropriate guidelines. To consistently engage fans, entertainment companies need to make sure that the artists have opportunities to expose distinct personas in various contexts (Kim et al., 2021, p. 11).

Global music fans have witnessed the shift partially due to K-pop over the past decade. They enjoy popular music created in the non-Western region on various streaming platforms simultaneously. These fans are able to watch music performances online, while communicating with musicians and other fans in different countries. In particular, due to the growth of fan platforms, which are very unique local inventions, global fans develop their solidarity, although they are not physically connected. K-pop, entertainment houses, and fan platforms certainly represent local specificities that global fans and music creators/performers are keen on. The new nexus of AI, music platforms, and music production in the K-pop world will be offering a new testbed that global music creators and fans alike pay attention to.

7

Platformization of the Korean Wave

Introduction

In the early 21st century, a multitude of Korean cultural programs, both television dramas and films, have been globally acclaimed since a handful of cultural products, such as *Parasite* and *Squid Game* earned prestigious awards. Many Korean cultural programs have also become top-ranked foreign-language programs on Netflix and Disney+. The surge in popularity implies that global audiences enjoy well-made Korean cultural content partially because they sympathize with the themes reflected in local cultural products. For example, *Squid Game* and *The Glory* portrayed the bleak nature of contemporary Korean society—the dog-eat-dog world of capitalist competition and traumatic childhood violence. Whether historical or contemporary, these cultural products dexterously express Korean identities and themes, appealing not only to local but also to global audiences. These shows' global popularity illustrates the crucial convergence of Korean popular culture and global OTT platforms.

In particular, since its launch in Korea in 2016, Netflix has invested in Korean cultural industries to produce original series, films, and reality shows, exclusive to the platform—e.g., the success of one of the first Korea-made Netflix Original programs, *Kingdom*, a zombie genre drama, which has been followed by numerous examples of Korea-made original content like *D.P.* (2021), *Hellbound* (2021), *All of Us Are Dead* (2022), and *The Glory* (2022–2023).[1] During the start of the COVID-19 era in late 2019, global

1. A couple of dramas were made as Netflix originals. *Love Alarm*, which was adopted from a famous webtoon was planned to be the first Netflix original, but *Kingdom* was aired on Netflix in January 2009, while *Love Alarm* was aired in August 2019. *My Only*

OTT platforms have substantially increased their interest in the Korean cultural industries, seemingly riding the Korean Wave. The Korean Wave, again, referring to the rapid growth of national cultural industries and cultural production followed by the soaring global popularity of Korean cultural content, including television dramas, films, and K-pop, started in the mid-1990s (Jin, Yoon, & Min, 2021). While the Korean Wave was originally represented by made-in-Korea cultural products and celebrities, its latest phase involves far more complex processes in production and consumption due to global OTT platforms. Korean cultural industries have been incorporated into overseas cultural industries. Previously, they worked with transnational cultural industries firms in the U.S., China, and Japan, and they now partner with global OTT platforms in cultural production. Against this backdrop, various forms of Korean cultural content, such as television dramas and K-pop, have penetrated both Western and non-Western markets via OTT platforms in the early 21st century.

Among several cultural production sectors, the broadcasting industry has become especially important in the digital platform era because OTT platforms have greatly transformed television dramas and reality shows in terms of production systems and content, including genres and themes. In other words, broadcasting Hallyu has grown via digital platforms in the global cultural markets in recent years. For instance, approximately 4.8% of content library titles on Netflix are from Korea despite its relatively small market size, underscoring how OTT platforms are capitalizing on Korean content (Lotz, 2022).

Global OTT platforms have diversified their business strategies in Korea. While investing in the local cultural industries for the production of exclusive, original content, Netflix has acquired the licensing for many other Korean shows and films across different genres, such as *Mr. Sunshine* (2018, historical epic), *Vagabond* (2019, spy action), *Crash Landing on You* (2019, romantic comedy), *Itaewon Class* (2019, drama), *Hometown Cha-Cha-Cha* (2021, romantic comedy), and *Extraordinary Attorney Woo* (2022, legal drama), which have been popular among global audiences. Other global OTT platforms, such as Apple TV + and Disney+, have joined the Korean Wave bandwagon to create their original programs like Disney's *Moving* (2023, action and fantasy drama), not only to penetrate the Korean cultural market but also to appeal to global audiences by utilizing Korea-based storytelling. The increasing role of OTT platforms raises

---

Love Song was aired on Netflix in 2017; however, it was created by FNC, a Korean production company, and was titled as a Netflix original other than Korea.

concerns for Korean cultural creators and audiences because of the potential subordination of local cultural industries, including the broadcasting sector, to global OTT platforms. Despite Netflix's increasing influence on Korean cultural industries (Park, Jo, & Kim, 2023), there is a lack of studies that critically examine the platformization of Korean cultural production in tandem with the Korean Wave. As fully discussed in chapter 1, platformization refers to the "rise of the platform as the dominant infrastructural and economic model of the social web," affecting our society through structural changes and new business models (Helmond, 2015, p. 1). Nieborg and Poell (2018, p. 4276) further articulate platformization as "the penetration of economic, governmental, and infrastructural extensions of digital platforms into the web and app ecosystems."

By employing the platformization of cultural production in relation to a critical cultural industries studies approach, this chapter analyzes the transition of the Korean cultural industries to the platform-driven phase of Hallyu by discussing the highly transnationalized and platformized Korean Wave in the shifting global media environment. It examines how Netflix has platformized and appropriated the Korean broadcasting industry through various strategies, such as investing in original content creation, licensing Korean content, and subcontractualization of Korean production. It also investigates how Korean cultural industries firms have become subordinated to, and rely on, global OTT platforms and their implications. In doing so, this chapter explores the implications of the platformization of cultural production for the transnational cultural flows of Hallyu.

Local OTT Platforms in the Korean Wave

The Korean Wave has fundamentally shifted with the advent of digital platforms, including OTT and social media platforms since the 2010s. On the one hand, domestic and global OTT services have contributed to expediting the shift characterized by cord-cutting consumption of cultural content. On the other hand, local stakeholders, including Korean OTT platforms and their collaborations with network TV sectors, have played a significant role in this new phase of Hallyu, while Netflix has played a leading role in the recent global rise of Korean content.

Diverse local actors, such as Korean broadcasters—network, cable, and general programming channels (JTBC, TV Chosun, Channel A, and MBN)—telecommunication companies, and big entertainment houses, began to establish their own OTT platforms in the early 2010s, while a multitude of global OTT platforms have penetrated the Korean market since 2016 when Netflix began its business in Korea. The history of local OTT platforms indeed goes back to 2010 when Tving allowed consumers to view cultural content on smartphones, smart pads, and PCs. Tving, which was acquired by CJ ENM in 2016 as the first local OTT platform, allows real-time viewing of many channels—some network channels and some cable channels. In 2016, Tving provided a total of 147 live channels, including tvN, Mnet, and OnStyle, and more than 16,000 opinions for video-on-demand content, including movies (S. W. Yoon, 2016).

Meanwhile, a few local network broadcasters and telecommunications corporations began developing their OTT platforms one after another in order to compete with global OTT platforms while sustaining their market control in the Korean cultural sphere. As discussed in chapter 3, in 2011, MBC and SBS launched the local platform service POOQ, allowing real-time viewing of all programs on the two broadcasters' six channels on smartphones and iPad. The service also includes subsidiary cable channels, such as MBC Drama, MBC Everyone, MBC Game, and SBS Plus (S. J. Choi, 2011). KBS—the most extensive network broadcaster—joined as program provider, although it later invested as a stakeholder. SK Telecom developed its mobile video streaming app Oksusu as well.

Since the late 2010s, local OTT platforms have sought corporate integration to compete with global OTT platforms. The Korean government acknowledged the increasing role of digital platforms in the cultural industries and the necessity of local-based OTT platforms in order to effectively compete with global digital platforms, such as YouTube and Netflix, and approved numerous mergers (E. J. Kim, 2019). Early local OTT platforms were combined under the new OTT service brand Wavve, which became one of the country's largest OTT platform providers with 14 million subscribers. Its name was created by combining the Korean Wave and wave of the sea, and it hoped to grow into "Netflix of Asia by supplying Korean contents to overseas markets amid growing popularity of Korean pop culture across the world" (Shin & Lee, 2019).

As these local OTT platforms attest, in Korea, three major industry sectors in Korea—broadcasting, telecommunications, and entertainment corporations—have continuously invested in the OTT service platform business. Local OTT platforms compete against each other in the domestic cultural market while competing with global OTT platforms, including Netflix, to expand their market share and influence not only in the domestic market but also in the global cultural markets. Of course, global OTT platforms, including Netflix, Apple TV+, and Disney+, have significantly increased their market share despite several existing local OTT platforms since 2016. These global OTT platforms have become tremendous forces in the local cultural industries as they are not only distributors of global content in the local market but also producers of local cultural content, significantly contributing to the platformization of the local cultural industries.

The increasing role of OTT platforms in the Korean cultural market as elsewhere is uniquely related to the recent surge of the Korean Wave. Both local and global OTT platforms are riding the Korean Wave as the country's popular culture and digital technologies are gaining popularity in the global cultural markets. As was briefly discussed, OTT platforms have become alternatives to traditional media outlets, including broadcasting channels and theaters, as they function as the primary distributors. During the COVID-19 era, people were forced to stay at home or socially distance, and OTT platforms—especially those including Korean content—gained increasing subscribers. For example, Kocowa, a U.S.-based streaming platform launched in 2016 as a collaborative venture between major networks like KBS, MBC, and SBS, and SK Telecom experienced 40% audience growth during the pandemic (Littleton & Layne, 2022). The number of OTT platform (including YouTube) users in Korea also doubled between 2019 and 2022. In particular, the number of paying users rapidly increased during the pandemic period, from 5.6% in 2017 to 50.1% in 2021 (Y. H. Kim, 2022), even though local-based OTT platforms, such as Wavve and Tving, are not gaining enough users to make profits in the domestic market.

Despite their relatively short histories, OTT platforms have developed new business models with which global platforms expand their subscription bases and efficiently enhance culturally diverse catalogs (Lobato, 2018). Instead of emphasizing their role as distributors, which are digital intermediaries in storage and distribution, they have increasingly focused on their role as producers (Bilton, 2017). In doing so, the platform corporations have enhanced their control over the entire value chain in the cultural industries to maximize their profits and influence. Global OTT platforms have especially developed three different business models in their collaboration with the Korean cultural industries: 1) original programs, 2) licensing, and 3) subcontracting. As further discussed in the next three sections, these three models categorically show how global OTT platforms utilize their hegemonic positions to expand their influence in the Korean cultural industries.

Development of Platform Originals in the Korean Cultural Industries

Global OTT platforms have expanded to produce original programs as exclusive content to appeal to global audiences. They have significantly advanced their local originals in a few countries, including Japan, Mexico, India, Spain, and Korea. Due to the soaring popularity of Korean cultural content, such as television dramas, reality shows, films, K-pop, and webtoons, global OTTs especially target Korea as an outpost to produce original programs.

Most of all, Netflix, as the primary actor in the Korean cultural market, has continued to develop its originals since 2017. Netflix invested US$ 50 million in *Okja*, although it was not released in theaters, unlike other films (Buchanan, 2017). Since then, Netflix has developed a multitude of successful originals in Korea, and due to the soaring popularity of these original programs, Netflix has continued to increase its investments in Korea. In 2021 alone, Netflix made about 80 Korean originals, including historical zombie thrillers and horror series (*The Korea Times*, 2021). Consequently, Netflix has sustained its leading position in Korea. As of December 2023, the monthly active users (MAU) of Netflix in the Korean OTT market were 11.64 million, followed by Coupang Play (6.64 million), Tving (5.21 million), Wavve (4.04 million), Disney+ (3.04 million), and Watcha (0.55 million). Netflix continued to be the largest shareholder in Korea, while Disney+ increased its MAUs from 1.95 million in 2002 (55.8% increase) due to the popularity of *Moving* (2003), its original series (*The Economist*, 2024).

This drastic move emphasized how Netflix was increasingly doubling down on Korean cultural content as global audiences continued to buzz over it. According to Netflix, the majority of Netflix subscribers watched Korean content, and therefore, the platform rolled out more than 30 new and returning titles in 2023, from 15 Korean originals in 2021 (Toh, 2023). In this regard, Don Kang, the company's vice president of Korean content, stated:

> The global popularity of K-content has continued apace over 2022, with Netflix bringing a wider variety of stories and genres to fans around the world. Over the last year, Korean series and films have regularly featured in our Global Top 10 list in more than 90 countries, and three of Netflix's most-watched shows ever are from Korea (Toh, 2023).

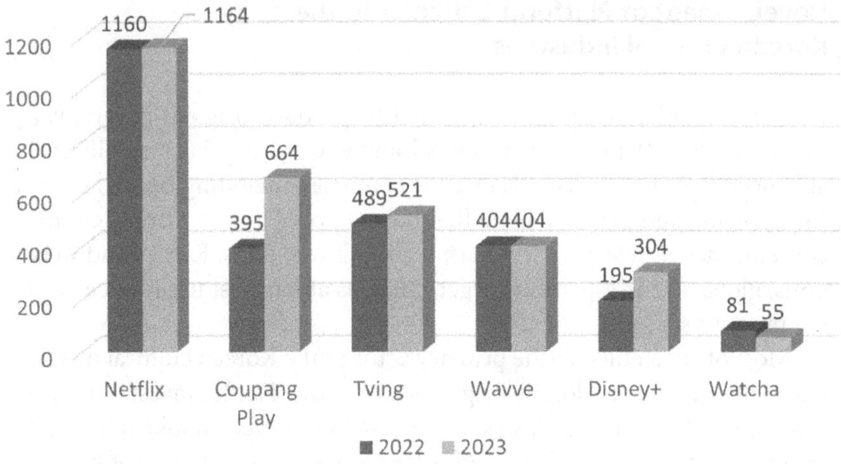

Figure 7.1. Monthly Active Users (Unit: 10 thousand)

Netflix has benefited from these originals, as well as licensed Korean content (to be discussed in the next section) as the platform has dramatically increased its subscribers. Again, Netflix provided US$21.4 million to produce *Squid Game*; however, it generated about $900 million in impact value for Netflix based on the high number of subscribers (Shaw, 2021). According to Netflix (2021), its subscriber base grew by 4.4 million in the third quarter of 2021, propelled in part by *Squid Game*, which the company called its "biggest series launch ever." The growth helped Netflix earn $7.5 billion in revenue during the same time, up 16% from the previous year. Netflix understands that the global OTT platform markets continue to experience severe competition among OTT platforms, and therefore, it is essential to secure originals in order to win. Needless to say, as long as the Korean Wave continues to grow, Netflix will develop Korean originals.

The number of Netflix's paid subscribers has indeed continued to grow, from 221.8 million in 2021 to 260.2 million in 2023. Among these, the Asia-Pacific region showed the largest growth rate at 38.9% during the same period, followed by Europe, the Middle East, and Africa (19.9%), Latin America (15.1%), and the U.S. and Canada (6.5%), as the reflection of the significant role of Asia, including the Korean Wave (Netflix, 2024a) (Figure 7.2). While it is not easy to identify people who started to subscribe to Netflix because they wanted to watch Korean cultural content, the recent surge of Korean dramas and films on Netflix, including the *Squid Game* series, certainly proves the increasing popularity of Korean content for both Netflix and global audiences.

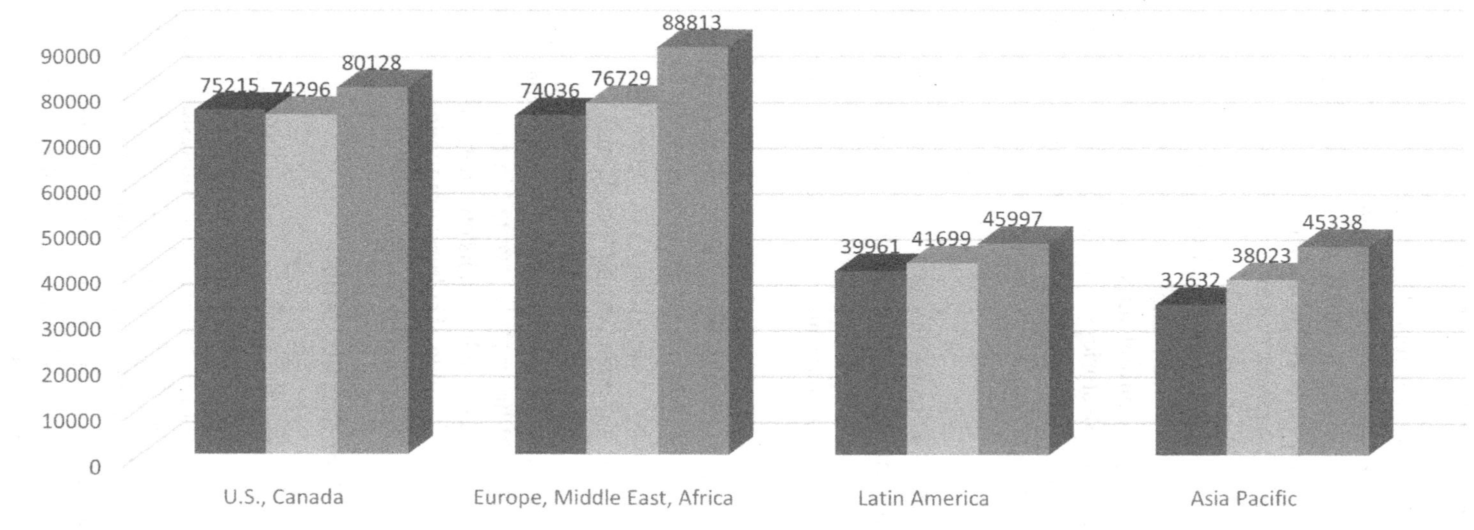

Figure 7.2. Number of Paid Subscribers, 2021–2023 (Unit: thousands)

Global OTT services aim to appeal to a wide range of global audiences, including local audiences, by developing certain formats and catalogs; therefore, it is vital to have new originals that mainly target regional audiences, but eventually appeal to global audiences. As TV critic MacDonald (2019) commented on the recent rise of K-dramas:

> With audiences developing an appetite for programming set in other cultures, the expanded catalog makes it easier to sample more Korean TV and films. Cultural authenticity also matters. The company's streaming success stories show that the more local a program is, whether it is French, Brazilian, or Korean, the better it seems to travel. Ideally a production is culturally authentic but also explores universal themes.

In fact, Kim Minyoung, Director of Content at Netflix Korea, attempts to find, develop, and commission a multitude of original programs. While the storytellers she attempts to find maybe are Korean, the stories she selects must have an appeal that transcends national borders:

> Overall, it comes down to basics. What is the story? Is the story unique? Is the story strong? What is the creative vision? That's where we lean toward. When it comes to Korean content, for now, we're trying to find Korean storytellers and stories that are going to resonate well in Asia and even beyond (MacDonald, 2019).

As the statement suggests, Netflix has grown based on its global circulation network; however, it has rapidly invested in the production of cultural content to create and capitalize on its own network, and therefore, it has platformized the entire circle of cultural production.

Digital Platform Licensing Strategies

Global OTT platforms have continued to expand their global reach by providing existing cultural programs from many countries, and Korea is one of the most significant production hubs. Alongside originals, licensing has also been vital as licensed cultural products mainly focus on already proven cultural content that found success during the New Korean Wave era, starting in the late 2000s (Jin, 2016). While original programs need a lot of time to be produced, licensed programs can easily be distributed to many countries because OTT platforms can secure these programs immediately for global audiences.

Netflix has inked a multi-title licensing deal with JTBC, a Korean national television network, to have broadcasting rights to 600 hours of programming, which included shows like *Something in the Rain* (2018), *The Beauty Inside* (2018), *SKY Castle* (2018–2019), and *My Country: The New Age* (2019). These JTBC dramas were introduced as Netflix originals in the country as Netflix had exclusive distribution rights (S. H. Lee, 2019). The agreement between Netflix and JTBC included the network's signature titles, such as *Chef & My Fridge*—a cooking show—and *Abnormal Summit. Beating Again* and *Can We Get Married*, both of which were popular in Korea, were globally available on Netflix in 2017. While Netflix has expanded its slate of Korean originals as discussed in the previous section, it continues to increase its library of licensed titles from Korea as well (H. Y. Lee, 2017).

Netflix, again, was not initially welcomed by the local entertainment industry. Several major players, such as network broadcasters and large media and telecommunications firms that controlled domestic streaming services in the Korean market, declined partnership requests, aiming to prevent Netflix from becoming a dominant player in the local market; however, a few Korean entertainment firms agreed to license content to Netflix (Stangarone, 2019). Terrestrial networks' refusal to collaborate with Netflix ended in 2018 when SBS Contents Hub sold Netflix overseas streaming rights for *Hymn of Death*, an epic K-drama so that the show could be released on Netflix on the same day it aired on SBS (G. L. Lee, 2020).

Furthermore, in 2020, Netflix and CJ ENM and its subsidiary Studio Dragon also entered into a strategic partnership, highlighted by a multi-year content production and distribution agreement. This arrangement included licensing contracts to air programs that were streaming in Korea, such as *Stranger* (2017), *Mr. Sunshine* (2018), *Memories of Alhambra* (2018), *Romance Is A Bonus Book* (2019), and *Arthdal Chronicles* (2019). Netflix said, "our members love great made-in-Korea stories. We are thrilled to present the depth and variety of best-in-class Korean stories from JTBC" and other studios (Brzeski, 2019).

As is well documented (Meimaridis, Mazur, & Rios, 2021, p. 7), unlike linear television, Netflix "is not bound to a programming schedule and provides viewers with a catalog of content." The platform's recommendation algorithm organizes the interface, in which each user accesses a personalized version of the app based on their consumption habits on the service. Although different in certain countries, the streamer's catalog is a significant lure to win new subscribers, keep them satisfied, and avoid turnover (Robinson, 2017, cited in Meimaridis et al., 2021). As global digital platforms seek to build diverse catalogs, they have obtained exclusive global distribution rights through license deals with local productions that promise high-quality content, such as major Korean productions.

OTT Platform Subcontracting Model

While Netflix has developed originals and its licensing models, it has also recently benefited from the subcontracting business model, which speaks to the subcontractualization of the Korean cultural industries. This does not mean that subcontracting is totally different from Netflix originals and the licensing models, as they are also parts of the bigger concept of subcontractualization. However, there is a new trend, which cannot be explained by either original programs or licensing models, which is the subcontracting model. This business model does not receive production funding from OTT platforms, nor secure IP rights, as many local networks and cultural creators voluntarily produce cultural content for Netflix.

As one of the latest examples, *Physical:100*, a Korean reality show, which was aired on Netflix beginning in January 2023, brought a shock to cultural producers and consumers at the same time. *Physical:100* gathered 100 highly athletic people in Korea to compete with each other in a series of physical challenges to eventually find the most athletic person. Similar to the severe competition for survival in *Squid Game* (2021), participants in this reality show competed to win 300 million Korean won (Reality Tidbit, 2023). Notably, the reality show was produced by MBC, one of the largest network channels in Korea, along with Luyworks Media—an independent media company—not for its own network but for Netflix. The intellectual property of *Physical:100* also allegedly belonged to Netflix (Yu, 2023). As discussed, MBC, alongside other network channels, was initially concerned about the penetration of Netflix in the local market. However, its business attitude toward Netflix dramatically changed. In this regard, Seong-je Park, CEO of MBC, stated on Facebook on January 23, 2023:

> many people say Terrestrial TV is over, but I always say this to our employees, 'MBC is no longer terrestrial TV. It is a global media group that owns terrestrial channels.' *Physical 100* is a full-fledged

challenge for MBC to meet with viewers around the world through global OTTs, and the same challenge will continue throughout this year.

Prior to this, MBC produced another program, *The Hungry and the Hairy*, for Netflix in 2021. Television director Kim Tae-ho who had produced a couple of the longest-running and most successful variety shows, including *Infinite Challenge*, produced this reality show as a Netflix original entertainment series, starring the artist Rain and comedian Noh Hong-chul. As a popular producer with MBC then, Kim Tae-ho's involvement with Netflix was quite a surprising move because it was his first non-MBC program (S. J. Lee, 2021). As such, MBC has changed its business model and decided to work with OTT platforms. That is, to survive in the rapidly shifting media environment, MBC plans to work as a content provider to not only national audiences and OTT service platforms but also global OTT platforms. MBC plans to continue producing cultural content for OTT platforms to overcome the disruption caused by the Netflix effect (S.Y. Park, 2023).

Domestically, MBC had already supplied its content to local OTT platforms. MBC produced *manjjijnam*—a man that is unrealistically good-looking as if he popped out from a book called pretty boy in English—and supplied it to Tving, operated by a domestic OTT owned by JTBC and CJ ENM. A terrestrial broadcaster supplied content to an OTT platform operated by a competing broadcasting channel, not to its own. In the case of comprehensive programs, JTBC supplied original content, such as *Solo Hell*, to Netflix (S. Y. Park, 2023).

When MBC provided *Physical:100* to Netflix, many people expressed their concerns because domestic production firms would become subcontractors for OTT platforms. The Korean Broadcasters Association (2018) already claimed, "in the end, the domestic content production industry would become a production subcontracting base for Netflix, and Netflix would use its global network to distribute Netflix original content produced in Korea" (G. L. Lee, 2020). Global OTT services can be helpful as they expand distribution channels while providing necessary production costs; however, as they secure IP rights in the content production process, their involvement in the Korean cultural industries eventually makes Korean cultural firms, including major networks, into subcontractors.

This kind of business strategy can be considered as coproduction between Netflix and local cultural industries firms, known as "cross-platform coproduction, a collaboration that pairs national broadcasters with transnational or multi-national premium networks" (Dunleavy, 2020, p. 337). However, while collaborations between local cultural industries firms and global OTT platforms bring cultural and economic benefits to both parties, subcontractualization is not based on mutual benefits, because global OTT platforms wield enormous power in the process of production and distribution, which makes local cultural industries firms as mere contractors as can be seen in outsourcing. This business model can be categorized as subcontractualization similar to outsourcing rather than cross-platform coproduction. However, as outsourcing is a business practice in which a company hires a third party to perform tasks or provide necessary services for that company, it is not the right business model to explain the local broadcasting sector as local cultural creators perform part of "all of the obligations," meaning the entire production process, from pre-production to post-production.

Of course, subcontracting is not a new trend in the Korean cultural industries. Numerous other cultural industries companies have worked as subcontractors for other countries' cultural industries corporations for several decades. Animation has been peculiar as many Korean animation firms worked as subcontractors to American and Japanese animation companies in the 1970s and the 1980s.

> Japanese outsourcing work tended to be split by the Japanese prime contractor and assigned to a group of both Japanese and Korean subcontracting studios. A division of labor between these subcontractors was more flexible. Who does what varied by project, and was adjusted depending on the workload and capacity of each studio. Many Korean suppliers assumed a limited part of main production functions, such as in-betweens and coloring, and relatively advanced tasks, such as layouts and key animation, were initially done only by Japanese studios (Masuda, 2007, pp. 205–207, cited in J. K. Lee, 2011).

Mega global cultural firms started contracting some of their work out to Korean studios "as they confronted rising wages and the depleted pool of Japanese animators as well as cost-cut pressure trickled down along the chains. The size of these studios is relatively small, maintaining a small group of staff (around 30) to keep their internal production lines in operation as well as managing subcontractors both at home and abroad" (J. K. Lee, 2011, p. 181). Likewise, subcontracting has become more prevalent in the Korean cultural industries. The complex production process of video games, such as programming and visualization, also "requires professional regional studios to be subcontractors. At the same time, game publishers in the United States have to maintain not only their standard of programming, but also the quality of the artwork across their subcontractors, which requires standardization" (Fung, 2016, p. 47).

However, the current subcontractualization in the Korean Wave tradition is dissimilar from these existing business models as the most significant cultural industries firms, including network channels (MBC), CJ ENM, Studio Dragon, and JTBC, voluntarily produce in-house cultural content for Netflix. They are trend makers in popular culture, and other small and mid-sized cultural firms must follow this new trend, which is worrisome for the Korean cultural industries. Since Netflix became popular, numerous local cultural industries firms have increased the cultural programs they supply to global platforms. Koh Chan-soo, a KBS producer highlighted the importance of Netflix in the Korean media industries:

> until now, the three terrestrial broadcasters have regarded Netflix as an object to be overthrown as it dominates the Korean broadcasting market. However, Netflix occupies the No. 1 spot in OTT in almost every country. PDs at domestic broadcasting companies want to have their content evaluated in the global market. It would be nice if Wave or TVing could play that role, but it's not easy at the moment. Overseas viewers will be able to see my content, and a completely different opportunity will arise (S. Y. Park, 2023).

Cultural creators are desperate to circulate local cultural programs globally, as the Korean market is relatively small. Quite a few original cultural programs have become some of the most popular cultural programs around the globe.

When the Korea Communications Commission (2023) surveyed to identify the use of OTT platforms to enjoy Korean audio-visual content in four countries, such as the U.K., Japan, Mexico, and Brazil, in 2023, Korean dramas and films were the third most popular cultural content in all these countries, reflecting the growth of Korean cultural programs around the globe. Although these countries mainly enjoyed their countries' cultural programs, followed by American cultural content, Korean content was selected as one of the most popular cultural programs more than cultural programs from other countries, including Japan, France, and Spain (Figure 7.3). This data shows not only the global popularity of Korean cultural

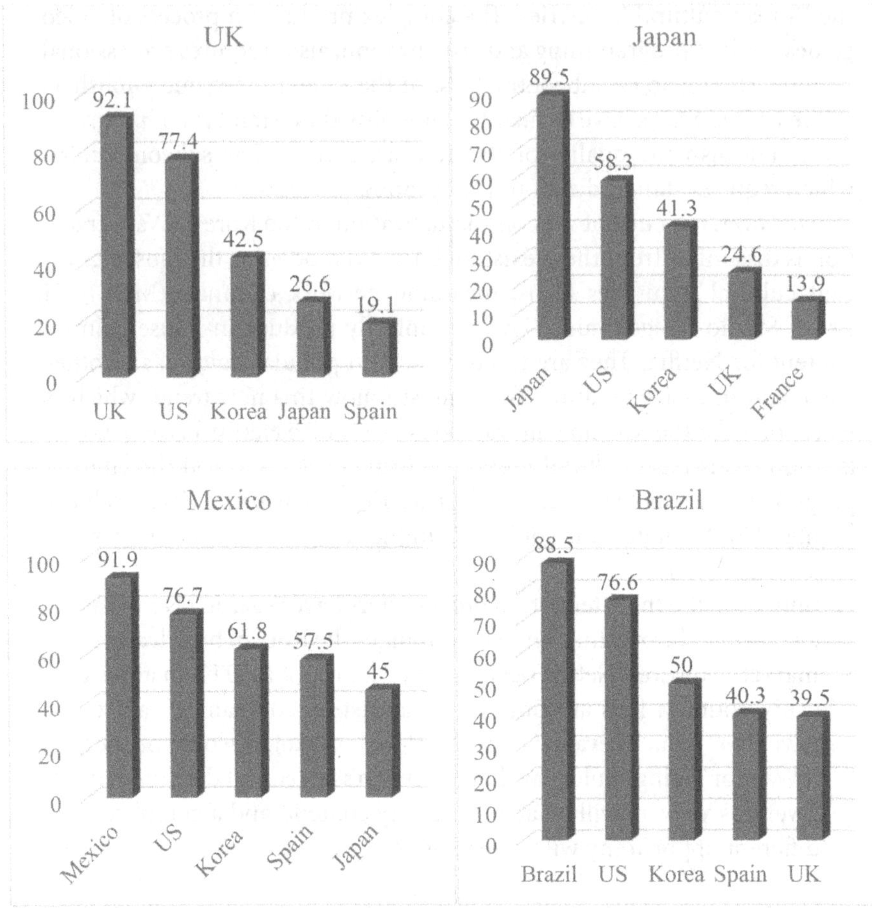

Figure 7.3. The Popularity of Korean Content on OTT Platforms (Unit: %)

content but also the significant role of OTT platforms in enjoying popular culture, which asks Korean cultural industries firms to focus on OTT platforms to distribute their cultural programs.

As the latest example, Netflix's revenge drama series *The Glory* became the most popular globally just three days after the release of the first season's remaining episodes in March 2023. According to FlixPatrol, a Netflix ranking tracker website, *The Glory* ranked No. 1 in 38 countries on March 13, including Korea, Indonesia, Japan, Malaysia, and Mexico, and No. 3 in the U.S. and the U.K., making it the overall No. 1 show globally. "Netflix app usage in Korea also hit an all-time high following the release, according to the data analysis company WiseApp and Wise Retail, with the app's active users reaching 4.88 million users on March 10, the day of the release, and 5.32 million users on March 11, a 61% increase from the 3.31 million users recorded on March 9" (Y. J. Cho, 2023b).

As in the case of *Squid Game* whose IP rights were held by Netflix, *The Glory*'s IP rights were also not owned by the Korean production but by Netflix in return for its investment in production cost. During the conference titled How to View Netflix's Korean Investment held in Seoul in May 2023, Seong-min Lee, a media scholar, outlined how Netflix became the biggest beneficiary of K-content with its strategy of securing IP through global investment. Netflix has continued to invest in content in Korea, but on the other hand, it has been a problem with the contract method of taking content IPs. In this way, Korean content industry firms produce quality content for Netflix as subcontractors (Kwon, 2023). Without securing IP rights, original programs are nothing but outsourced cultural products, which expedites the subcontractualization process.

Even worse, as can be seen in *Physical:100*, local cultural industries firms now have to provide their plan to Netflix, not for their own channels, while voluntarily losing their IP rights to Netflix in return for global distribution. Although the Korean production owned the production title, the ownership has technically moved to Netflix. Global cultural industries corporations such as Disney and Nintendo have increasingly subcontracted to small-to-medium studios that cost-effective cultural labor (Fung, 2016). In the Korean cultural industries, the subcontracting system has been different, again, as local cultural producers volunteer to produce the entire program, not only parts of it, for global OTT platforms. Therefore, they have put into practice the subordination of local cultural industries to global OTT platforms, fundamentally shifting the Korean cultural industries.

Ostensibly, Netflix may not force local cultural creators to accept Netflix's business models; however, local cultural industries firms voluntarily followed the path that Netflix carefully designed. During an online meeting with the press held in January 2022, Kang Dong-han, Vice President of Netflix's Korean content, promised that Netflix would make efforts to maintain good relationships with local cultural industries firms as partners when he was asked about concerns that domestic creators and producers are becoming Netflix's subcontractors. He said that Korean content is good enough that Korean cultural creators cannot be mere suppliers as subcontractors (Noh, 2022); however, the subcontractualization of Korean cultural production has continued and even intensified. Seemingly, local cultural creators choose their destiny—they might work with Netflix or not based on their business decision—however, the current media ecology surrounding the Korean cultural industries has changed according to Netflix's global business strategies. Netflix is not only riding the Korean Wave, but also providing the route local cultural creators step onto. Netflix has become a formidable force in wobbling the local cultural industries in the early 21st century.

Critical Understanding of the Platformization of the Korean Wave

OTT platforms have substantially increased their dominant power in the vicious circle of cultural production. In particular, a few global OTT platforms, including Netflix have shifted the major characteristics of the Korean Wave, from production to consumption. While local cultural producers have to rely on digital platforms to secure production costs and circulation networks, global Hallyu audiences increasingly access these platforms to consume Korean-made cultural content. In the Korean broadcasting industry, OTT platforms have advanced three primary business models, namely originals, licensing, and subcontracting, which expedite the platformization process of local cultural production.

Netflix has consequently reshaped K-content—helping to promote Hallyu abroad in a way that no Korean cultural industries firms could advance, as Netflix attempts "to become a channel to introduce Korean content to people around the world" (Stangarone, 2019). OTT platforms like Netflix and Disney+ have helped to boost the circulation and consumption of Korean movies and dramas by making them more accessible to foreign audiences. Besides an internet connection, there is no barrier to global audiences in different countries sampling Korean cultural content, since all that is required is a subscription. The algorithms used by Netflix have also helped to bring in new fans. Any viewers who watch *Mad Men* (an American TV series, 2007–2015), for example, might be recommended to *Okja*, Netflix's original Korean movie, because they are in the same taste cluster (Stangarone, 2019).

The platform-driven Korean Wave in the early 21st century has fundamentally transformed the local cultural industries. As Chalaby (2023, p. 72) aptly puts it, "national media systems have progressively integrated with one another and embedded in transnational networks of consumption, distribution, and production. Cross-border media flows have intensified and become more complex." A few years ago, digital platforms were not essential components; however, cultural creators, cultural production firms, and global audiences all rely on digital platforms, which control cultural production processes. In the broadcasting sector, cultural creators have recently developed new forms of drama, such as seasonal series, different time ranges, and various subjects and themes, which mainly target global audiences.

Consequently, Netflix has greatly influenced media texts, including the genres and formats of Korean cultural content. The majority of Korean dramas which are popular internationally are romantic comedies (Bohdan, 2023b). However, as Netflix has invested and is interested in diverse cultural genres, such as thriller (e.g., *Stranger*), zombie (e.g., *Kingdom*), and stand-up comedy (e.g., *Yoo Byung Jae: Discomfort Zone*), Korean cultural creators have to develop these new genres. For cultural creators, again, the global reach of their content is the new norm, and they hope that Netflix will help them to take off in the global cultural markets (Jin, 2021c).

Another platformization trend is the blockbusterization of Korean cultural content in terms of production cost. Local cultural creators plan to develop big-scale cultural products comparable to Netflix-produced blockbuster-level content in order to target global audiences. In the early 2000s, production costs for Korean drama series were 36.5 million won per episode; however, this soared to 700 million won (US$615,000) in the early 2020s (Conran, 2021). So-called tent pole dramas, requiring huge production costs due to soaring actor fees, writing fees, staff labor costs to improve the working environment, and post-production costs due to the strengthening of computer graphics (CG), have become the new normal (H. K. Kim, 2021; Yang, 2022).

As Seoul-based critic Pierce Conran (2021) aptly noted, Korean TV's landscape, which used to be characterized by "romantic dramas, family dramas and a few more expensive period dramas dominating schedules" has become far more complicated; "stars command a higher percentage of overall production budgets, series have grown more ambitious, with foreign shoots and visual effects demands, and the wider range of distribution channels has increased both the variety of Korean shows and their international audience."

While competition among local broadcasting corporations has led to big spending, the intrusion of Netflix in the local cultural market has changed the landscape. As pop culture critic Jeong Deok-hyeon analyzed, the increasing production cost is largely due to the influence of Netflix, as shown by popular Netflix shows such as *Kingdom* and *Sweet Home*; these shows are different from previous K-dramas in terms of scale and genre.

Local cultural creators have to create big-budget cultural programs in order to attract OTT platform-saturated global audiences (H. K. Kim, 2021). In fact, Netflix's first original drama *Kingdom* cost over 2.2 billion won per episode, showing how serious the international streaming giant was about breaking into the Korean market and using Korean content as leverage to enhance the streaming platform's global catalogs. Internationally expanding and competitive streaming markets may have raised the content's production value, and accordingly the consumers' expectation for quality content (Conran, 2021). The Netflix model has undoubtedly influenced this current trend.

Indeed, the production costs in the Korean cultural industries have soared. In contrast to previous dramas like *My Love from the Star* (132 billion won, 2013–2014) and *Descendants of the Sun* (130 billion won, 2016), recent cultural content used much higher production costs, as exemplified in *Arthdal Chronicles* (540 billion won, 2019), *Mr. Sunshine* (450 billion won, 2018), and *Vagabond* (250 billion won, 2019). In order to produce cultural products that appeal to global audiences who enjoy Netflix originals, local broadcasters and film companies have to secure funds, and they work with OTT service providers, including Netflix (S. M. Lee, 2019; J. H. Kim, 2020). In fact, "Netflix covered at least 65 percent of the 43 billion won ($36 million) production cost for tvN's 2018 blockbuster series *Mr. Sunshine*. SBS's *Vagabond* collected about half its 25 billion won ($21 million) budget from Netflix while MBC's *Rookie Historian Goo Hae-ryung* received its entire 13 billion won ($11 m.) budget from the company last year" (G. L. Lee, 2020). Netflix has transformed the local broadcasting industry, which used to rely on advertising as its primary revenue source, to focus on the content-centered market (S. M. You, 2019). During the interview process, one network producer (male, mid-50s) who has worked for two decades to produce dramas stated the significance of production costs, which differentiates global OTT platforms and local cultural industries:

> it is challenging for the local OTTs and broadcasters to produce and create blockbusters that Netflix creates because the high amount of investment couldn't be accessible realistically in the Korean cultural industries. Although local OTT services are competitive, they cannot win the global ones due to the lack of global distribution networks and necessary funds. In the case of France, local OTT platforms are integrated, backboned by local broadcasting companies against Netflix's monopolized distribution power. France has a

> unique culture, which shows the power of capital, and the integration of local OTT platforms has been somewhat successful. Korea needs to integrate local OTTs, but the scale of investment is another task that local OTT platforms resolve to compete against global OTT platforms.

Last but not least, the production schedule has also changed, which shows one of the major characteristics of the platformization process. Korean dramas traditionally do not have a seasonal scheme; however, the situation has dramatically changed as people get used to this new system after watching a multitude of American dramas on OTT platforms. For example, Korean dramas are delivered in two one-hour-long weekly episodes, each of which usually ends with cliffhangers, and completed in one season without follow-ups. However, popular K-dramas not only on Netflix but also on network TV channels have gradually included successive seasons (Silva, 2022). Indeed, over the past several years, numerous Korean dramas, such as *Kingdom*, *Love Alarm*, *Voice*, *The Penthouse*, and *Yumi's Cells* have presented subsequent seasons (MacDonald, 2023). *The Glory*, *Taxi Driver*, *D.P.*, and *Vagabond* have also had subsequent seasons. According to Studio Dragon, not only global viewers but also Korean viewers prefer to watch additional seasons of their favorite shows. For cultural producers, a subsequent season also offers a second chance to appeal to viewers who regularly watch television programs with multiple seasons (MacDonald, 2023).

Overall, global OTT platforms have on a large scale transformed local traditions and identities. Unlike in the 1980s and the 1990s, when Western cultural industries dominated the global cultural markets with their popular culture, in the early 21st century, global OTT platforms have played a key role as they are equipped with capital, AI, and cultural content. This level of dominance is far more profound than that of the previous decades (Jin, 2021c). As discussed in chapter 1, the infrastructural control of platforms has reshaped the format of cultural products, such as genre, length, and style. Cultural producers become "increasingly platform-dependent and [this] shifts governance in the market" (Park, Jo, and Kim, 2023, p. 2425). Netflix has transformed both the industrial structure and cultural content. As Galperin (1999) already pointed out with the case of new television channels, the international market in cultural production has undergone dramatic transformations since the mid-2000s, mainly because innovations in distribution have increased the number of media outlets, including Netflix and Disney+, available for cultural products, thus exponentially increasing the demand for cultural content to fill these distribution channels. This mushrooming of channels through OTT platforms has shifted the cultural market. Most of all, resources for new cultural productions have become relatively scarcer in non-Western countries, mainly due to the lack of funds and severe competition. This shift has by and large worked in favor of US-based platforms because they not only are better positioned "to undertake new content productions (due to the economies of scale in their own domestic market) but also own vast libraries of readily available products marketable at relatively low costs" (Galperin, 1999, pp. 629–630). As local digital platforms cannot compete with mega global platform giants, the degree of control by global digital platforms has increased, and the subordination of Korean cultural industries to global OTT platforms has been worrisome.

Conclusion

This chapter has examined the platformization of cultural production in the Korean Wave context. It analyzed the ways in which global OTT platforms transformed the local cultural industries, in particular the broadcasting industry. OTT platforms have deeply changed the media ecology surrounding the Korean broadcasting industry and, eventually, the Korean Wave (Stangarone, 2019; Choi and Raley, 2023). From the production of popular culture to the circulation of cultural content and to the consumption of these locally created cultural programs, global OTT platforms have influenced the Korean cultural industries. Netflix has especially reshaped the Korean cultural industries by testing and incorporating new business models into the local and transnational contexts of Hallyu. After utilizing cost-effective Korea-produced original content or licensing Korean content for global markets, Netflix has tactically advanced another new business model—the subcontractualization of the local cultural industries, which increases the global platform's control over local cultural industries.

In the Korean context, local cultural creators, including network broadcasters and independent cultural production companies, have developed cultural programs targeting both local and global audiences via various OTT platforms, whether local or global. These local cultural industries firms and cultural creators are eager to work with or for global OTT platforms mainly due to their massive distribution channels. As Jennifer Kang (2024, p. 41) aptly puts it, "the Korean video landscape continues to be dynamic, with domestic services and platforms experimenting to best cater to their audiences." However, as local cultural firms have turned themselves into subcontractors of global OTT platforms, they have lost their power to negotiate with these global forces. While Netflix-driven platformization has opened a new door for local content industries to some extent, its growing power has also increased the risk for local content industries and local OTT platforms.

Netflix has controlled the entire circle of cultural industries to actualize its status as a global platform empire, transforming the Korean cultural industries. As global audiences have increasingly relied on global digital platforms to enjoy cultural content, it is essential for local audio-visual industries to work with these platforms, and the structural shift is expected to continue. Netflix is not only shifting people's consumption habits but also destroying the traditional standard of the local cultural industries (Jin, 2021d). In terms of content diversity, for example, global OTT platforms like Netflix have emphasized a handful of commercial genres. They have not paid attention to locally produced genres focusing on culture, history, and people's struggles (Jin, 2021c). In other words, the recent platformization of the local cultural industries has resulted in the lack of diverse voices. The Korean Wave in the digital platform era has experienced a fundamental shift as only a few global OTT platforms churn the entire broadcasting system, and in general, cultural industries.

In sum, cultural production in the Korean Wave has to develop new strategies. It is not avoidable for cultural creators to continue working with OTT platforms; however, they may need strategic negotiations with platforms for a sustainably creative wave of Hallyu, which keeps engaging with local identities in their cultural products. Local creators and industries, separately and together, may explore antidotes to the rapid platformization as a cultural and economic imperialist process. While global OTT platforms have benefited Hallyu creators and industries by accelerating their global reach, the rapid platformization of Hallyu reveals precarious aspects that may ghettoize and restrict the creativity and sustainability of local cultural production.

8

Conclusion: Sustainability of Korean Cultural Production

Introduction

Over the past three decades, Korea has greatly advanced its various local cultural industries and developed numerous forms of popular culture, which are globally popular. Cultural production in Korea has shown a unique trend that differs from other countries. In other countries in the Global South, when they developed local popular culture, they usually advanced a particular cultural form, as can be seen in Telenovelas in Mexico and Brazil, as well as Bollywood movies in India. Japan has developed various forms of popular culture, but television dramas and Japanese popular music (J-pop) are mainly regionally popular, while anime has been globally recognized. In contrast to these countries, Korea has continued to develop all major cultural areas, both popular culture and digital culture, and these different cultural forms work together to establish the current boom of the Korean Wave in the global cultural sphere. The Korean Wave as a local cultural power based in the Global South has shown a great potential to change the status quo in the global cultural markets.

Korea originally targeted the East Asian region in the early stage of the Korean Wave; however, Korean popular culture has expanded its reach beyond Asian boundaries to become an arguably, but truly global phenomenon, fueled by the advent of digital technologies, in the early 21st century. As numerous interviewees correctly observe, COVID-19 has ironically and partially provided great opportunities for the Korean cultural industries to advance their cultural content because local cultural programs are penetrated through digital platforms, both social media (e.g., YouTube and TikTok) and OTT platforms (e.g., Netflix and Disney+). Many Korean cultural industries firms developed their strategies in utilizing social media and OTT platforms in cultural production. One female interviewee in her thirties stated, "younger generations can't ignore TikTok Short Release, a video medium that combines multiple cultures," and therefore, "K-culture has been a big part of various social media platforms."

While there are various elements, the Korean Wave has experienced a fundamental transformation with the growth of digital platforms. In our contemporary cultural production, digital platforms have played major roles in the vicious circle of the Korean Wave, and its influence is expected to continue in the future. Digital platforms used to work as content distributors. However, they now act as producers, while they provide necessary tools for global audiences to consume various cultural content. The advent of digital platforms simultaneously offers opportunities and crises to the Korean cultural industries. The Korean cultural industries may increase their roles if they strategically work with global platforms well; if not, the surge of global platforms in local cultural production will be a severe blow to local cultural industries firms. Global OTT platforms continue to work as a double-edged sword in the Korean cultural sphere.

Local cultural industries firms, and therefore, the Korean Wave, have always been in crisis. Many media critics and media outlets always asked, "how long Hallyu would last," and many believed that it would fizzle out like the fad for Hong Kong films and Japanese anime that once gripped the world, although many global audiences still like Japanese anime. They assumed the Korean Wave boom would subside soon (Bae, 2013). The Korean Wave was viewed as a temporary trend, and many people did not expect Hallyu would stay, much less grow (J. L. Lee, 2022). According to a report released by the Bank of Korea in 2012, many people believed that Hallyu could disappear by the late 2010s mainly because of two major reasons: the extreme commercialization of Korean cultural content and the lack of power to sustain Hallyu as a mainstream culture (*The Korea Times*, 2012). Some people I interviewed also said, "current years are the heyday of Korean culture." They believe this is a time when cultural content can be enjoyed at its peak stage in terms of global popularity.

Unlike some people's expectations and survey outcomes, the surge of the Korean Wave has continued to grow in recent years. Media critics' claims are somewhat misleading, and the survey is not correct because they do not understand a few important issues, such as the globalization of Hallyu beyond Asia, the increasing role of digital platforms like Netflix and YouTube as new growth engines, and the continuous development of different cultural programs, not only dramas, films, and online games, but also K-pop, reality shows, mobile games, and webtoons, which are closely connected to create synergy effects in cultural production. Instead of subsiding, the Korean Wave has advanced its power by integrating a variety of key elements in the New Korean Wave era, mainly starting in the late 2000s. This does not mean that cultural creators and performers are always walking the rose garden. There are several crises and concerns, but they continuously overcome these critical issues to strengthen the current boon in the global cultural sphere.

A variety of crucial dimensions have certainly driven the growth of the Korean Wave, both internally and externally, such as the competitiveness of Korean popular culture, the enthusiastic global fans, talented cultural creators in the local cultural industries, governmental support, and the growth of digital technologies, including social media (see J. S. Kim, 2016). People in different fields undoubtedly emphasize diverse focuses. People in the cultural industries, including cultural creators and planners, attribute the phenomenal success of the Korean Wave to its well-structured production system, including planning, training, and management, as the most significant element in local cultural production. The early adoption of a social media-oriented marketing strategy, as can be seen in PSY's *Gangnam Style* (2011–2012), which made a global sensation based on its utilization of social media, also gave the Korean entertainment system an edge since its counterparts in the U.S., Japan, and Europe were slow to use social media. YouTube has been "a useful gateway for Korean pop stars to present their content without the help of traditional media outlets and to approach a broader range of fans directly" (Bae, 2013). As John Hirai, head of music partnerships at YouTube Japan and Korea, discussed, "YouTube and K-pop groups benefited each other and became a very successful model" (Bae, 2013). Governmental support also provides the necessary infrastructure that the Korean cultural industries rely on during their production and circulation of cultural content, although it is not the only element for the growth of the Korean Wave. Likewise, Korea may persist in its cultural power as long as the Korean Wave world strategically develops new growth engines, while effectively utilizing digital platforms and AI technology.

What is significant, though, is that there are a variety of elements that the Korean cultural industries and cultural creators have to develop in the future. These new tasks, which will be discussed later in this chapter, are not separated from the past practices, because the future of the Korean Wave will rely on what the local cultural industries have done thus far, although they need to advance new strategies and scopes. The past practice is always becoming a foundation for future growth in popular culture, and therefore, it is vital to understand past experiences and relevant lessons.

This chapter summarizes the major characteristics of the new phase of Korea's cultural production in the digital platform era. This concluding chapter also proposes how local digital platforms can be theorized and how the growth of local platforms contributes to this theorization. It delves into the future direction of the local cultural industries and the Korean Wave in the digital platform era based on what cultural creators and cultural consumers alike expect in the post-pandemic era. As the current Korean Wave opens the door toward the Western cultural markets, it addresses whether the Korean Wave will become one of the most significant local-based global cultures that global audiences, not fans only, enjoy. It, then, articulates the Korean Wave as part of an ongoing cultural globalization and explains how Hallyu can be a sustainable global popular culture in terms of the continuing growth of local culture beyond a fan-based regional cultural phenomenon. As the major scope of the book is industry perspectives, this final part of the book especially emphasizes the ways in which the Korean cultural industries advance their unique trends, while the Korean government and cultural industries firms develop necessary industrial elements.

Summary of the Book

As one of the first scholarly books on cultural production in tandem with the Korean Wave, this book talked about why the Korean cultural industries matter in the digital platform era. While emphasizing the increasing role of the cultural industries and cultural industries policy in the Korean Wave, it attempted to show that Korean cultural industries can be compared with other transnational cultural industries in overseas markets. Due to the recent surge of digital platforms, both social media and OTT platforms, in Korean cultural production, this study especially emphasized the ways in which global digital platforms influenced the continuity and change in the Hallyu ecosystem, which is one of the most significant transnational cultural industries in the Global South.

By employing a new industry study termed "critical cultural industries studies," which is a meso-approach, this book examined a few new trends as the primary components, including the increasing role of digital platforms and intellectual property as a significant economic and cultural element. This book's major focus is the advent of digital platforms in local cultural production, and therefore, it articulated power struggles between global and local forces in the realm of digital platforms to determine the power relationships between various actors, including platforms, cultural creators, and platform users. It concluded that local cultural industries have advanced their positions as meaningful forces in the global cultural markets; however, they still face challenges from different forces, including global digital platforms that are rapidly becoming part of Korea's cultural production. Overall, three major pillars sustain cultural production discourses from the industry perspective in this book.

Cultural Industries and Cultural Industries Policy

The growth of local cultural industries mainly started in the early 1990s, which became one of the major backgrounds of the growth of the Korean Wave. Some media scholars and media outlets have mainly focused on global fandom as the major element for the global popularity of Korean cultural content. Admitting the significant role of global fans and audiences exists; however, it is essential to understand that local cultural industries firms and cultural creators have driven the production of quality cultural content. The production of popular culture and the consumption of cultural content should be understood not as a separate, but a connected whole in the Korean Wave context.

In the middle of democratization between the late 1980s and the early 1990s, Korea began to expand its cultural industries, which means that the Korean government gradually ceased severe censorship under the military regime and allowed to establish new cultural industries firms, such as new network broadcasters, cable broadcasters, independent production companies, and new film production companies. The sudden growth of various audio-visual corporations could be made possible because the civilian government, starting in 1993, developed new cultural industries policy measures, differentiating from the existing cultural policy. The Korean government started to build its national infrastructure in both audio-visual and telecommunication sectors, which triggered the growth of the digital media era as well as the initial stage of the Korean Wave. As Kim Jang-ho, director of the Korean Culture and Information Service (KOCIS), stated:

> the roles played by Korean artists, performers, and content producers themselves have been the most significant force behind the

> nation's transformation into an entertainment juggernaut. Their originality and imagination, which in part take cues from the country's unique history and tradition, have come to define Korea's 'creative DNA' and form the foundation of its cultural sector. Such creative output has then been able to cleverly ride on the back of the expanding digital environment since the late 1990s, helping them gain visibility and prominence on the local and global stage simultaneously (H. S. Park, 2023).

According to him, while the Korean government has played a role in terms of policy implementation and financial assistance since the early 1990s, the popularity of Korean cultural content is being organized independently by the private sector in general, which means that "Korea's pop culture is mainly getting its due recognition by players in the private sector" (H. S. Park, 2023). In Korea, quite a few major cultural industries, such as broadcasting, film, music, gaming, animation, and webtoon industries, as well as local digital platforms, have produced popular culture and digital culture.

Therefore, this book analyzed how the local cultural industries have cultivated cultural content. It attempted to map out the crucial role of the local cultural industries in cultural production and discussed various measures that were categorized within cultural industries policy discourses to address the nexus of the cultural industries and the Korean Wave. As the cultural industries played a pivotal role in the Korean Wave, it examined the cultural industries policy that the Korean government developed, and therefore, it delved into the differences between cultural policy and cultural industries policy. Finally, it analyzed the process of platformization to determine how the cultural industries have developed new forms of cultural content.

Increasing Role of Digital Platforms in the Korean Wave

As one of the recent Hallyu trends, digital platforms, both OTT platforms like Netflix and social media platforms, including YouTube, have fundamentally influenced cultural production in the Korean cultural system. Netflix has played a crucial role in expanding the global reach of Korean dramas and films, which are screened in 190 countries. By producing, circulating, and providing a tool to consume Korean cultural content, Netflix has rapidly become a big part of the Korean Wave (Choon, 2023). Since Netflix entered Korea in 2016, it has funded a series of cultural programs to produce

Netflix originals produced in Korea while licensing a variety of existing cultural content. Netflix originally had the role of a global distributor of cultural content; however, when it started its business in Korea, it immediately worked as a global producer of Korean popular culture, which greatly transformed the Korean cultural industries and cultural production.

In the realm of music, there are two different trajectories in relation to digital platforms. On the one hand, K-pop musicians heavily rely on global social media platforms, particularly YouTube, to disseminate their new songs. On the other hand, local entertainment powerhouses have developed fan service platforms, including Weverse, to communicate with global fans. While local OTT platforms in the field of broadcasting and film are struggling due to the increasing role of Netflix and Disney+, local fan service platforms have established their strong footsteps in the global cultural markets, as well as the local music market.

This book thus discussed how Netflix and YouTube influenced the local cultural industries in terms of the shift of the industry structure and cultural content in terms of genres and themes. By examining Korean cultural production in transforming global media environments, it mapped out how Korean cultural industries and creators negotiate global media industries and digitalization. It also discussed the significance of YouTube in the K-pop world. In the early 21st century, K-pop has become one of the most enjoyable local popular cultures emerging from Korea, partially because of social media platforms.

Again, unlike broadcasting and films, in the K-pop world, although Korean idol groups and artists utilize global social media platforms like YouTube, some entertainment houses also use local social fan platforms, such as Hybe-developed Weverse, which play a pivotal role in developing a new form of fandom activities, including participatory fan culture. It discussed how local entertainment houses utilized social media and streaming service platforms to determine the role of digital platforms in the Korean music industry, and found that local fan service platforms are functioning as meaningful platforms, unlike the OTT platform field which global platforms are leading local cultural production. Therefore, it is possible for the readers of the book to easily identify the potential of local-based digital platforms in the global cultural sphere.

Platformization of the Korean Wave

This cultural phenomenon in the global sphere has especially flourished in the 2020s due to the increasing role of digital platforms; therefore, the book focused on the platformization of Korean cultural production and the Korean Wave. Several cultural programs, such as *Kingdom* (2019), *The Glory* (2022–2023), *Gyeongseong Creature* (2023–2024), and *Culinary Class Wars* (2024) have been globally popular on Netflix. Disney+ has also developed many local programs in Korea, including *Moving* (2023), *Han River Police* (2023), and *Worst of Evil* (2023). Among these, *Moving*, the Korean spy series, which was adapted from Kang Full's webtoon and released in August 2023, became Disney+ and Hulu's most-watched K-drama ever globally, including the U.S. within just seven days of release. Viewers in Asia have already watched *Moving* more than Disney's core franchise series like *The Mandalorian* (Brzeski, 2023).

Although Disney+ was a latecomer in the Korean cultural industries and failed to make a tangible force itself in Korea for a while, it aggressively invested in local cultural production to catch up with Netflix. The Korean Wave was represented by made-in-Korean cultural content; however, in the 2020s, Netflix was involved in local cultural production. Consequently, Korean cultural industries have been incorporated into overseas media industries; in particular, they have to partner with global OTT platforms and social media platforms.

This book analyzed the transition of Korean cultural industries to the platform-driven phase of Hallyu by discussing the highly platformized Korean Wave. It discussed how global OTT platforms, including Netflix, platformized the Korean cultural industries. It concluded that Korean cultural industries firms have become subordinated to and rely on global OTT platforms. The implications of the platformization of cultural production for the transnational cultural flows of Hallyu can be applicable in many non-Western countries. A handful of non-Western countries have vehemently developed their cultural industries to become the second Korean cultural industries in the future, and the Korean example offers lessons to these countries.

This book also found that the K-pop industry has developed a bit different trajectory. Although the K-pop world has highly relied on various social media platforms, particularly YouTube, many local entertainment houses have established fan service platforms like Weverse to become globally acceptable. While local OTT platforms, including Wavve, have struggled to survive due to global OTT platforms, local fan service platforms have become tangible forces among global K-pop fans. This certainly implies that local digital platforms can make their platform powerful in the global cultural sphere as long as they develop unique features that appeal to global users and local customers. Admitting that the differences between OTT platforms and music fan service platforms exist, Korea has developed a somewhat different new platform ecology, at least in the music sector.

Creating the Sustainable Cultural Production in the Korean Wave

The future of cultural production concerning the Korean Wave has been a hot issue in the global cultural sphere. Hallyu has greatly changed "the flow of cultural content, not only from West to East but also from East to West, [although] it does not imply that it has eradicated the status quo, but (only) proves potential" (Choon, 2023). As the Korean Wave has symbolized the growth of non-Western cultural power, many media scholars and media outlets are keenly interested in whether Korea will be able to maintain or increase its local cultural force. There are a multitude of different observations and scenarios. However, based on the discussions in this book, as well as other information, it is evident that Korea will continue to develop its cultural supremacy, at least in the near future, because global audiences are increasingly enjoying various Korean cultural programs. Once they start to enjoy dramas, they naturally move to adore K-pop and films, for instance. Global youth who read Korean webtoons have turned their attention to webtoon-based dramas and films. Digital game players who play Korean online and mobile games now enjoy K-pop as part of game music.

There are a couple of warning signals as well. Korean cultural creators, cultural industries firms, and policymakers face various challenges to overcome to level up the current boom of the Korean Wave in the global cultural sphere. They are especially confronted with the increasing role of digital platforms that are supported by AI and big data.

With the consumption of content based on OTT platforms, the genre distinction between movies and dramas is blurring, and the boundaries between countries in content distribution are disappearing. Digital technologies related to cultural content, such as AI, AR (augmented reality), VR (virtual reality), and the metaverse, are giving birth to new forms of cultural products. In the audiovisual sector, along with series content, short-form content, including web dramas and web entertainment is also very popular. The Korean Wave also faces various challenges, including competition from neighboring countries like Japan and China, as well as global OTT platforms.

The Korean Wave has survived the battleground of the global cultural markets, overcoming a multitude of challenges mentioned above, and has reached its current good standing. However, the future of the Korean Wave is not smooth sailing. The environment of the global cultural industries surrounding the Korean Wave is rapidly shifting day by day, which asks local cultural creators to develop strategic plans. The Korean cultural industries have advanced various unique strategies to continue the boom of Hallyu; however, it is time to change its basis strategies according to the rapidly shifting media ecology surrounding the Korean Wave.

The Hallyu world, including the cultural industries, cultural creators, and the government, as well as audiences, has to consider the sustainability of the Korean Wave. They need to create a variety of foreseeable strategies to develop high-quality content in order to sustain Hallyu as a long-lasting cultural phenomenon while reducing or eliminating potentially harmful elements in the Korean Wave tradition. Therefore, making the Korean Wave sustainable will be one of the most significant issues in local cultural production in the digital platform era.

Here sustainability implies that the Hallyu world is not only thinking of the sense of maintaining the status quo of the Korean Wave but also developing new cultural forms and values at the same time. Unlike the concept of sustainable development, which "is often criticized of being in favor of growth," sustainability in Korea's cultural production "can be understood not only as a universal goal to be achieved but as a procedure or continuously evolving" cultural scene (Soini & Dessein, 2016, p. 2). As Throsby (1997, p. 8) pointed out, "the notion of sustainability, wherever it has been applied, has had something to do with the long-term viability of systems, programs and policies," therefore, the longer-term feasibility is a key issue. It is also certain that the Korean Wave needs to emphasize the importance of global audiences as primary actors in cultural production, and therefore, it is essential to advance the ways in which the Hallyu world engages with global audiences.

Developing a sustainable popular culture and digital culture related to the Korean Wave is an essential steppingstone for the local cultural industries to thrive, not only achieving economic goals but also engaging with people, in general, and society. Local cultural creators, cultural performers, and policymakers also have to realize that "Hallyu is more than a product—it boosts the nation's brand and other industries" (Bae, 2013). This implies that they also need to consider the importance of cultural products themselves as they are parts of people's daily cultural activities. The sustainability of the Korean Wave does not only rely on commercial imperatives but also cultural dimensions because popular culture certainly plays a pivotal role in the digital economy and nation-building. A few immediate strategies from the cultural industries studies perspective will be as follows.

To begin with, it is always necessary to prioritize consumers as one of the most significant elements in the Korean Wave. Since this book's scope limits its discourse in the cultural industries as part of cultural production, it does not discuss audiences, who are also very important elements in cultural production. However, as a meso-approach emphasizes the convergence of the production and the consumption of cultural content on digital platforms, it at least addressed the meaningful role of cultural consumers related to Netflix, as can be seen in chapters 2 and 6. As a variety of digital platforms, both social media and OTT platforms, prove, they are not only working as distributors but also as producers and consumers. Without understanding the increasing role of consumers, who play a key role as the sources of big data, it is critical to analyze the entire value change in cultural production. We have to understand the ways in which digital platforms rely on audiences to advance their production based on data learning from consumers' tastes. We cannot disregard the significant role of cultural text and global audiences.

Cultural production cannot be developed by only cultural industries themselves and relevant policy issues. The quality of the content and the important role of global fans and audiences are the other two major pillars that facilitated the growth of the Korean Wave. In particular, these days, cultural consumption by global fans implies that they are working as part of the production system, as these fans and audiences provide meaningful feedback and suggestions when they post their feelings and emotions on various social media. The construction of a new ecosystem, which connects production, distribution, and consumption, is not new, but how to reflect and utilize audiences' involvement in cultural production is vital for the sustainability of the Korean Wave. As Hawkes (2006) argued, the growth of the cultural industries could not be done by top-down and expert-driven dimensions, but it could come within the ground where general people are engaged in various cultural activities that eventually perpetuate cultural practices. The sustainability of the Korean Wave, which continuously develops cultural content that drives cultural consumption among global audiences, can be made when cultural creators fully understand what audiences consume and play.

Second, it is essential to develop relevant digital technologies and culture to develop high-quality cultural content in the digital platform era.

As the Korean Wave has increased its reliance on various OTT platforms, both domestic and global, it is required to develop the necessary technologies and policy measures. Global digital platforms have shifted local cultural production on a large scale because they are key players in the entire value change of cultural production, including the production of popular culture, the circulation of cultural content, and the consumption of cultural programs. Previously, they primarily played as the circulation tools; however, they are now mega cultural producers, and they directly compete with local cultural industries firms. Under these circumstances, the development of necessary technological infrastructure and quality programs is mandatory. Due to the recent advent and growth of AI technologies, including ChatGPT, local cultural creators must develop new strategies to utilize AI in cultural production.

More importantly, the Korean Wave needs to continue developing the convergence of popular culture and digital technologies. This strategy is especially vital with the increasing role of digital platforms and AI. Since digital platforms themselves are producers, distributors, and essential tools for consumption supported by AI and big data, the contemporary production of local popular culture has no choice but to work with digital platforms. Local cultural industries ought to adapt to the rapidly changing global industrial environment, and, to do this, support the advancement of the cultural industries to drive change in the digital platform era (Chae, 2021). Simply, content is the priority, of course. Since the quality of content will be the most significant matter in the future, it is essential to diversify cultural forms supported by AI and digital platforms, which will be one of the major dimensions of the sustainable Korean Wave. The local cultural industries have to advance new forms of cultural products, of course, high-quality content, cultural policies, and necessary digital technologies.

The convergence of high-quality cultural content and new digital platforms is necessary for cultural creators as well; therefore, "how to lead this trend will be one of the most significant agendas to build another form of legend for the Korean Wave in the future" (Jin, 2021a, p. 4160). The crucial point is that digital platforms "do not operate in isolation, but are inextricably entangled with each other within a larger corporate ecosystem. Within this ecosystem, the platform company sets and continuously changes the conditions under which content and services can be distributed and monetized" (Poell, 2020, p. 651), which means that digital platforms act as mediators rather than simply intermediaries.

Contrary to its global appearance, Korea's cultural industries are relatively small in scale and less stable than mega global OTT platforms and

American cultural industries firms. Analyzing how corporate power sets the conditions for cultural production, we cannot simply focus on the platforms themselves but must examine the techno-economic configuration of the larger corporate ecosystem in which these platforms are embedded (Van Dijck et al. 2019).

> This also applies when we consider the alternatives open to creators to distribute and monetize their videos beyond YouTube. Examining the platform in isolation, there appear to be lots of competing video-sharing services, which allow creators to reach audiences and generate revenue. Yet, these services have a hard time competing with YouTube, as its dominance in the online video industry is enabled and sustained by Alphabet's larger platform ecosystem through which it successfully aggregates large numbers of users, creators, and advertisers (Poell, 2020, p. 652).

Given the nature of multisided markets, this, in turn, generates powerful network effects that further consolidate global digital platforms' dominant position (Evans & Schmalensee, 2016; Rochet & Tirole, 2003; Poell, 2020). This situation asks us to consider that the platformization process forces us to ponder "media concentration in terms of corporate ecosystems" (Poell, 2020, p. 652).

In conjunction with the development of digital technologies and cultural content, the Korean government and cultural industries firms need to strengthen the Hallyu industrial base. One particular area at the policy level is intellectual property. As can be seen in *Squid Game* (2021), local cultural creators did not make tangible financial gains with the success of this particular cultural program, mainly because Netflix as the provider of cultural content enjoys monopolized economic benefits, including IPs. Local cultural industries firms have to secure IP rights, although they must work with global OTT platforms. For local cultural creators, it is unavoidable to work with global OTTs because they have to secure production money and circulation channels. However, if they do not secure IP rights, financial benefits will go to these global digital platforms.

Third, local cultural industries firms also need to develop transmedia storytelling as one of the major production strategies. As Ram (2016) points out, "transmedia storytelling is the technique of telling a single story across multiple platforms and formats using current digital technologies. From a production standpoint, transmedia storytelling involves creating content that engages an audience using various techniques to permeate their daily lives." The cultural industries have rapidly changed, and therefore, "the current configuration of the entertainment industry makes transmedia expansion an economic imperative, yet the most gifted transmedia artists also surf these marketplace pressures to create a more expansive and immersive story than would have been possible otherwise" (Jenkins, 2011).

The Korean cultural industries and global OTT platforms have increased their transmedia storytelling practices as they develop big screen culture like films, television dramas, and animation based on famous webtoons. Some of the successful dramas, such as *Kingdom* (2019), *Itaewon Class* (2020), *All of Us Are Dead* (2021), *Extraordinary Attorney Woo* (2022), *Moving* (2023) and *The Trauma Code: Heroes on Call* (2025) are webtoon-based big screen culture. As many cultural creators rely on webtoons as sources for their production, webtoon-based transmedia storytelling will continue its pivotal role in cultural production. Advancing the Korean style of transmedia storytelling, which is a new form of media convergence as well, will be one of the major elements for the success of the Korean Wave in the future. Unlike other cultural genres like television dramas and films, webtoons play as independent cultural genres and sources for big screen culture, not only for local cultural industries firms but also for global OTT platforms. In order to develop these two relevant areas, the government, webtoon platforms, and cultural industries firms must create fair and reliable working environments where webtoonists create their webtoons, which are the treasure troves of the Korean Wave.

Last but not least, cultural creators have to consider both global and regional cultural markets at the same time. In many cases, the majority of cultural creators attempt to focus on the killer content, which made a huge success based on low cultural discount,[1] globalization, or glocalization. However, highly sustainable genres shall be identified and nurtured in the New Korean Wave era where Hallyu is being diversified. It is necessary to pay attention to organic links established in the production, distribution, and consumption of cultural content. During the interviews, a female college student (22) in Vancouver clearly stated:

1. Cultural discount implies that people like other countries' cultural content based on the same background, linguistic competence, and other forms of cultural capital, such as ethnicity and cultural affinity. Differences in cultural values and social norms between countries may lower the appeal of foreign cultural products to local audiences (F. Lee, 2008, p. 119).

> In terms of content diversity, since Netflix, there are fewer romance genres and more epics or action genres with female protagonists. There are more neoliberal feminist narratives, but they still end with women falling in love with men from a heterosexual perspective. Korean dramas are also less sexualized, and I've heard that people from cultures that restrict sexualization, such as fans from Islamic cultures, feel more comfortable with this.

While it is essential to create new cultural forms for global audiences who are familiar with Netflix-scale blockbusters, Korean cultural creators need to target diverse ethnic groups as well. Global OTT platforms are not only targeting global audiences but also local audiences, which means that they need cultural products that appeal to global audiences in general, but they need some cultural programs that mostly appeal to local or regional audiences. The niche market should be considered by local cultural creators. Netflix has indeed pursued local-specific cultural content. For example, Don Kang, Vice President of Korean Content, said, "While *Squid Game* resonated with viewers worldwide, Netflix's approach towards the greenlighting of Korean series and their development remains focused on the local audience. . . . What I genuinely believe is that a story has to be locally relevant first [before wanting to expand it to an international audience]," so "our primary focus is always local." He explained, "if a local story translates internationally, it's proof that we share something universal" (S. Kim, 2023). As such, the construction of an ecosystem in the local culture industries, underlying continuous enjoyment, consumption, participatory immersion, and the materialization of cultural glocalization would be necessary. The development of growth engines of Hallyu, emphasizing the features and success patterns of steady-selling content resulting from the previous Hallyu trend, needs to be concentrated (Park & Lee, 2018).

Cultural production in the Korean Wave context in the digital platform era asks cultural practitioners to deeply think about the shifting role of the local cultural industries. Digital platforms have already become some of the major cultural industries. As they continue to utilize cutting-edge technologies, AI algorithms, and big data gathered from user activities, their dominant roles cannot be easily overcome. In particular, cultural producers have migrated from traditional media outlets to digital platforms, including Netflix, Disney+, and YouTube, and therefore, its implications for creative freedom and intellectual property rights are significant, as can be seen in *Squid Game* (2021, drama) and *Physical:100* (2023, variety show). Therefore, local cultural production must include digital platforms, both national and global, as part of cultural production—the value chain of production, distribution, and consumption. The strategic use of digital platforms will offer new opportunities to cultural creators; however, if they cannot fully utilize digital platforms, local cultural production will face severe challenges.

One caution in our understanding of cultural production in relation to the Korean Wave is that government intervention in the cultural market should be minimized. While the government needs to be proactive in building the infrastructure that is the foundation of the cultural industries, it cannot be directly involved in the cultural production process, which might hurt cultural creativity. As evidenced by the blacklist scandal that happened during the conservative regimes between 2008 and 2017, which consequently resulted in Park Geun-hye's impeachment, cultural industries policies that regulate the cultural industries while controlling cultural creators' freedom and creativity cannot provide positive outcomes in most cases. The blacklist scandal is a good lesson that the government has to remember in their practices. In the digital platform era, the government needs to support the corporate integration of local platforms; however, it supports the process rather than initiating and intervening in the process itself.

Overall, critical cultural industries studies utilized in this book certainly may enhance our understanding of the Korean Wave, as Hallyu has been studied in both social sciences, focusing on cultural industries policy, Hallyu marketing, and systems, and humanities, analyzing fandom and cultural text, although they overlap in some cases. Since we cannot put the Korean Wave only within any specific academic discipline, in both theory and method, Hallyu studies should be interdisciplinary in both academic fields and methodological approaches. Hallyu's scope cannot be limited to only a specific cultural industry, as it does not represent the entire Hallyu phenomenon. The Korean Wave cannot be comprehended by studying either cultural policy or audience studies. The convergence of macro and micro approaches to create a meso-approach is not only ideal but also practical. More importantly, digital platforms—which were not part of the Korean Wave and cultural production—have been some of the most important cultural industries, including in the Korean Wave tradition; therefore, critical cultural industries studies and practices can advance comprehensive and systematic Hallyu studies and practices.

References

ABC News. (2022). 'Dynamite' video from K-pop group BTS sets new YouTube record. 30 August. Retrieved from https://abcnews.go.com/GMA/Culture/dynamite-video-pop-group-bts-sets-youtube-record/story?id=72567086

Ahn, J. H., Oh, S. W., & Kim, H. J. (2013). Korean pop takes off! Social media strategy of Korean entertainment industry. *IEEE Xplore*. 10th International Conference on Service Systems and Service Management, 774–777.

allkpop. (2023). Psy's "Gangnam Style" becomes the first K-pop MV to hit 5 Billion views on YouTube. 31 December. Retrieved from https://www.allkpop.com/article/2023/12/psys-gangnam-style-becomes-the-first-k-pop-mv-to-hit-5-billion-views-on-youtube

Amazon. (n.d.). What is OTT? Retrieved from https://advertising.amazon.com/en-ca/library/guides/what-is-ott

Anderson, T. J. (2014). *Popular music in a digital music economy: Problems and practices for an emerging service industry*. Routledge.

Audley, P. (1994). Cultural industries policy: Objectives, formulation, and evaluation. *Canadian Journal of Communication, 19*(3–4), 317–352.

Bae, J. S. (2013). Hallyu seeks sustainability. *The Korea Herald*. 12 February. Retrieved from https://www.koreaherald.com/view.php?ud=20130212001037

BBC. (2021). K-wave: How fans are supporting their favourite idols. 21 June. Retrieved from https://www.bbc.com/news/world-57489720

Bilton, C. (2017). *The disappearing product: Marketing and markets in the creative industries*. Edward Elgar.

Boccella, N., & Salerno, I. (2016). Creative economy, cultural industries and local development. *Procedia—Social and Behavioral Sciences 223*, 291–296.

Bohdan, K. (2023a). Ride the 'Korean Wave': The best shows to stream on Netflix. *Aljazeera*. 28 April. Retrieved from https://www.aljazeera.com/features/2023/4/28/ride-the-korean-wave-the-best-shows-to-stream-on-netflix

Bohdan, K. (2023b). What's the secret behind the K-drama wave—and will it crash? *Aljazeera*. 23 May. Retrieved from https://www.aljazeera.com/features/2023/5/23/will-the-korean-drama-wave-rise-higher

Bolin, G. (2017). *Media generations: Experience, identity and mediatised social change*. Routledge.

Bouquillion, P., Ithurbide, C., & Mattelart, T. (2024). Introduction. In P. Bouquillion, C. Ithurbide, & T. Mattelart (Eds.), *Digital platforms and the global south: Reconfiguring power relations in the cultural industries* (pp. 1–17). Routledge.

Bourdieu, P. (1983). The field of cultural production, or: The economic world reversed. *Poetics, 12(4–5)*, 311–356. https://doi.org/10.1016/0304-422X(83)90012-8

Bourdieu, P. (1993). *The field of cultural production: Essays on art and literature*. Columbia University Press.

Bruner, R. (2022). HYBE and Bang Si-hyuk are transforming the music business—With a little help from BTS. *Time*. 30 March. Retrieved from https://time.com/collection-post/6159410/hybe-bang-si-hyuk-bts-interview/

Brzeski, P. (2019). Netflix bolsters K-drama lineup in multiyear deal with South Korea's JTBC. *The Hollywood Reporter*. 25 November. Retrieved from https://www.hollywoodreporter.com/tv/tv-news/netflix-bolsters-k-drama-lineup-deal-south-koreas-jtbc-1257822/

Brzeski, P. (2021a). South Korea and Japan emerge as key battlegrounds in the streaming wars. *The Hollywood Reporter*. 16 April. Retrieved from https://www.hollywoodreporter.com/business/business-news/south-korea-and-japan-emerge-as-key-battlegrounds-in-the-streaming-wars-4165483/

Brzeski, P. (2021b). Netflix to spend nearly $500 million on Korean content this year. *The Hollywood Reporter*. 24 February. Retrieved from https://www.hollywoodreporter.com/business/business-news/netflix-to-spend-nearly-500-million-on-korean-content-this-year-4138235/

Brzeski, P. (2023). 'Moving' becomes Disney's most watched Korean drama ever in just 7 days. *The Hollywood Reporter*. 25 August. Retrieved from https://www.hollywoodreporter.com/tv/tv-news/moving-disney-most-watched-korean-drama-ever-1235574770/

Buchanan, K. (2017). Cannes: Despite French boos, *Okja* proved it deserves to be Netflix's first big film. *Vulture*. 19 May. Retrieved from https://www.vulture.com/2017/05/okja-proved-why-it-might-be-netflixs-first-big-film.html

Burgess, J. (2021). Platform Studies. In S. Cunningham & D. Craig (Eds.), *Creator culture: An introduction to global social media entertainment* (pp. 21–38). New York University Press.

Caldwell, J. (2008). *Production culture: Industrial reflexivity and critical practice in film and television*. Duke University Press.

Carr, G. (1991). Trade liberalization and the political economy of culture: An international perspective on FTA. *Canadian-American Public Policy, 6*, 1–56.

Chae, J. Y. (2021). Special feature: Korean Wave and Asia (1): 20 years of Korean Wave, achievements and future strategies. *Asia Brief, 1*(10), 1–5.

Chalaby, J. (2023). *Television in the streaming era: The global shift*. Cambridge University Press.

Chang, H. J. (1996). *The political economy of industrial policy*. Macmillan.

Cho, Y. J. (2023a). Weverse reaches 100 million downloads worldwide. *Korea JoongAng Daily*. 13 July. Retrieved from https://koreajoongangdaily.joins.com/2023/07/13/entertainment/kpop/HYBE-Weverse/20230713173215698.html

Cho, Y. J. (2023b). 'The Glory' becomes most popular show on Netflix globally. *Korea JoongAng Daily*. 14 March. Retrieved from https://koreajoongangdaily.joins.com/2023/03/14/entertainment/television/Korea-The-Glory-Theglory/20230314171532795.html

Choi, E. J., & Raley, R. (2023). K-streams: Global Korea and the OTT era. *Post 45*. Retrieved from https://post45.org/2023/02/k-streams-global-korea-and-the-ott-era/

Choi, J. S. (2021). Global TV markets and digital distribution. In P. McDonald, C. Donoghue, and T. Havens (Eds.), *Digital media distribution: Portals, platforms, pipelines* (pp. 202–221). New York University Press.

Choi, J. Y. (2009). Rethinking economic development and the financial crisis in South Korea and the state in an era of globalization. *Journal of Third World Studies, 26*(2), 203–226.

Choi, S. J. (2011). New apps connect smart devices to TV channels. *Hankyoreh*. 21 October. Retrieved from https://www.hani.co.kr/arti/english_edition/e_entertainment/501823.html

Choi, Y. H. (2013). The Korean Wave policy as a corporate-state project of Lee government: The analysis of structures and strategies based on the strategic-relational approach. *Economy and Society, 97*(3), 252–285.

Choon, C. M. (2023). What's next after the Korean Wave? *The Straits Times*. 4 October. Retrieved from https://asianews.network/whats-next-after-the-korean-wave/

Chua, B. H., & Iwabuchi, K. (Eds.). (2008). *East Asian pop culture: Analysing the Korean wave*. Hong Kong University Press.

Chun, Y. S., & Yang, H. (2022). As K-pop goes global, Koreans fall behind when it comes to consumption. *Korea JoongAng Daily*. 5 April. Retrieved from https://koreajoongangdaily.joins.com/2022/04/05/entertainment/kpop/kpop-bts-kpop/20220405172102571.html

Chung, J. E. (2012). From developmental to neo-developmental cultural industries policy: The Korean experience of the "creative turn". Ph.D. Thesis. University of Glasgow.

Chung, J. E. (2019). The *neo-developmental* cultural industries policy of Korea: Rationales and implications of an eclectic policy. *International Journal of Cultural Policy, 25*(1), 63–74. https://doi.org/10.1080/10286632.2018.1557646

Circle Chart. (2023). *2023 Annual Chart Review*. Circle Chart.

Clarkson, S. (2002). *Uncle Sam and us: Globalization, neoconservatism, and the Canadian state*. University of Toronto Press.

Colbjørnsen, T. (2021). The streaming network: Conceptualizing distribution economy, technology, and power in streaming media services. *Convergence: The International Journal of Research into New Media Technologies, 27*(5), 1264–1287.

Colombo, F. (2018). Reviewing the cultural industry: From creative industries to digital platforms. Mass *Communication and Society, 31*(4), 135–146.

Conran, P. (2021). How much do K-dramas cost to make? Budgets keep growing, hastened by Netflix's entry with Kingdom and Sweet Home. *South China Morning Post*. 26 June. Retrieved from https://www.scmp.com/lifestyle/k-pop/k-drama/article/3138546/how-much-do-k-dramas-cost-make-budgets-keep-growing

Crawford, G., & Rutter, J. (2006). Digital games and cultural studies. In J. Rutter & J. Bryce (Eds.), *Understanding digital games* (pp. 148–165). Sage.

Crotty, J., & Lee, K-K. (2005). From East Asian "miracle" to neoliberal "mediocrity": The effects of liberalization and financial opening on the post-crisis Korean economy. *Global Economic Review, 34*(4), 415–434.

Cummings, M. (2003). *Cultural diplomacy and the United States government: A survey*. Center for Arts and Culture.

Cunningham, S., & Silver, J. (2013). *Screen distribution and the new King Kongs of the online world*. Palgrave.

Cunningham, S., & Craig, D. (2019). *Social media entertainment: The new intersection of Hollywood and Silicon Valley*. New York University Press.

Cunningham, S., & Scarlata, A. (2020). New forms of internationalisation? The impact of Netflix in Australia. *Media International Australia, 177*(1),149–164.

Cunningham, S., Craig, D., & Lv, J. (2019). China's livestreaming industry: Platforms, politics, and precarity. *International Journal of Cultural Studies, 22*(6), 719–736.

Davis, S. (2021). What is Netflix imperialism? Interrogating the monopoly aspirations of the 'World's largest television network.' *Information, Communication & Society, 26(6), 1143–1158*. https://doi.org/10.1080/1369118X.2021.1993955

Davis, W. (2022). Streaming outperforms both cable and broadcast TV for the first time ever. *NPR*. 18 August. Retrieved from https://www.npr.org/2022/08/18/1118203023/streaming-cable-broadcast-tv

Dehnart, A. (2023). Physical: 100 is a visually spectacular but bulky strength competition. *Reality Blurred*. 24 January. Retrieved from https://www.realityblurred.com/realitytv/2023/01/netflix-physical-100-review

Deloumeaux, L. (2018). "Persisting imbalances in the flow of cultural goods and services." In UNESCO, *Re-shaping cultural policies: Advancing creativity for development*. Paris: UNESCO, 125–142.

de Luna, E. (2023). The fandom business is booming. Can Weverse capture its growth? *Mashable*. 25 April. Retrieved from https://mashable.com/article/weverse-app-president-joon-choi-interview

Devoe, N. (2019). Here's everything to know about Weverse, and how it's changing. *Elite Daily*. 1 July. Retrieved from https://www.elitedaily.com/entertainment/weverse-app-explained

Dong, S. H. (2022). YouTube Music emerges as leading streaming platform in Korea. *The Korea Times*. 17 January. Retrieved from https://www.koreatimes.co.kr/www/art/2023/09/398_322406.html

Dong, S. H. (2023). Is K-pop's popularity waning after reaching its peak? *The Korea Times*. 2 March. https://www.koreatimes.co.kr/www/art/2024/01/398_346351.html

Druick, Z., & Deveau, D. (2015). Guest editorial: Cultural production in Canada. *Canadian Journal of Communication, 40*(2), 157–163.

du Gay, P. (Ed.). (1997). *Production of culture: Cultures of production*. Sage.

Duffy, B. (2017). *(Not) getting paid to do what you love: Gender, social media, and aspirational work*. Yale University Press.

Duffy, B., Poell, T., & Nieborg, D. (2019). Platform practices in the cultural industries: Creativity, labor, and citizenship. *Social Media + Society*, 1–8.

Dunleavy, T. (2020). Transnational co-production, multiplatform television and *My Brilliant Friend*. *Critical Studies in Television, 15*(4), 336–356.

Dwyer, T., & Hutchinson, J. (2019). Through the looking glass: The role of portals in South Korea's online news media ecology. *Journal of Contemporary Eastern Asia, 18*(2), 16–32.

Dwyer, T., Shim, Y. W., Lee, H. J., & Hutchinson, J. (2018). Comparing digital media industries in South Korea and Australia: The case of Netflix take-up. *International Journal of Communication, 12*, 4553–4572.

The Economic Times. (2021). Netflix's 'Squid Game' success sparks debate in South Korea over IP rights. 1 November. Retrieved from https://economictimes.indiatimes.com/tech/technology/netflixs-squid-game-success-sparks-debate-in-south-korea-over-ip-rights/articleshow/87452562.cms

The Economist. (2006). The king, the clown and the quota. 16 February. Retrieved from https://www.economist.com/asia/2006/02/16/the-king-the-clown-and-the-quota

The Economist. (2024). 'The wall for the first place was high' . . . In the end, native OTT failed to surpass Netflix. 22 January. Retrieved from https://economist.co.kr/article/view/ecn202401080001

European Commission DG For Competition. (2006). Strengthening the European creative industries in the light of the i2010 strategy. 2 March. European Union, Brussels. Retrieved from https://ec.europa.eu/commission/presscorner/detail/en/SPEECH_06_140

Evans, D. S., & Schmalensee, R. (2016). *Matchmakers: The new economics of multisided platforms*. Harvard Business Review Press.

Farley, A. (2022). How the BTS ARMY turned their fandom into the future of entertainment. *Fast Company*, 8 March. Retrieved from https://www.fastcompany.com/90721903/bts-hybe-korean-record-label-weverse

Ferchaud, A., & Proffitt, J. (Eds.). (2023). *Television's streaming wars*. Routledge.

Flew, T. (2012a). Michel Foucault's *The Birth of Biopolitics* and contemporary neoliberalism debates. *Thesis Eleven*, *108*(1), 44–65.

Flew, T. (2012b). *The creative industries: Culture and policy*. Sage.

Flew, T. (2021). *Regulating platforms*. Polity.

FlixPatrol. (2023). Top TV shows on Netflix on March 15, 2023. Retrieved from https://flixpatrol.com/top10/netflix/

Forbes. (2013). Korea's S.M. Entertainment: The company that created K-Pop. 31 July. Retrieved from https://www.forbes.com/sites/forbesasia/2013/07/31/koreas-s-m-entertainment-the-company-that-created-k-pop/?sh=239cde0407dd

Friedman, M. (1951, February 17). Neo-Liberalism and its prospects. *Farmand*, 89–93.

Fung, A. (2016). Comparative cultural economy and game industries in Asia. *Media International Australia*, *159*(1), 43–52. https://doi.org/10.1177/1329878X16638940

Galperin, H. (1999). Cultural industries policy in regional trade agreements: the cases of NAFTA, the European Union and MERCOSUR. *Media, Culture & Society*, *21*(5), 627–648.

Gandy, O. (1992). The political economy approach: A critical challenge. *Journal of Media Economics* *5*(2): 23-42.

Garnham, N. (2005a). A personal intellectual memoir. *Media, Culture & Society*, *27*(4), 469–493.

Garnham, N. (2005b). From cultural to creative industries. *International Journal of Cultural Policy*, *11*(1), 15–29.

Gillespie, T. (2010). The politics of platforms. *New Media & Society* *12* (3): 347–364.

Gillespie, T. (2018). *Custodians of the Internet: Platforms, Content Moderation, and the Hidden Decisions that Shape Social Media*. New Haven, CT: Yale University Press.

Gómez, R., & Larroa, A. M. (2023). Netflix in Mexico: An example of the tech giant's transnational business strategies. *Television & New Media* *24*(1), 88–105.

Gray, J., & Lotz, A. (2019). *Short introductions: Television studies*. Polity.

Gruger, W. (2012, December 21). PSY's "Gangnam Style" video hits 1 billion views, unprecedented milestone. *Billboard.com*. Retrieved from https://www.billboard.com/music/music-news/psys-gangnam-style-video-hits-1-billion-views-unprecedented-milestone-1483733/

Guillem, S. M. (2013). Rethinking power relations in critical/ cultural studies: A dialectical (re)proposal. *Review of Communication*, *13*(3), 184–204.

Gunaratne, S. A. (Ed.). (2000). *Handbook of the media in Asia*. Sage.

Ha, S. (2022). YouTube Music surpasses Melon Music as the most used streaming platform on Android in South Korea. *Allkpop*. 16 November. Retrieved from https://www.allkpop.com/article/2022/11/youtube-music-surpasses-melon-music-as-the-most-used-streaming-platform-on-android-in-south-korea

Hall, S. (1986). Gramsci's relevance for the study of race and ethnicity. *Journal of Communication Inquiry*, 5, 2–24.

Hamilton, G., & Biggart, N. W. (1988). Market, culture, and authority: A comparative analysis of management and organization in the Far East. *American Journal of Sociology, 94(1)*, S52–S94.

Han, B. (2023). Netflix Korea and Platform Creativity. *International Journal of Communication* 17: 6934-6951.

Havens, T., Lotz, A., & Tinic, S. (2009). Critical media industry studies: A research approach. *Communication, Culture & Critique*, 2(2), 234–253.

Hawkes, J. (2006). *The fourth pillar of sustainability: Culture's essential role in public planning*. Cultural Development Network.

Helmond, A. (2015). The platformization of the Web: Making Web data platform ready. *Social Media + Society, 1(2)*. https://doi.org/10.1177/2056305115603080

Hennessey, K. (2012). 'Hallyu' back: Obama catches the 'Korean Wave.' *Los Angeles Times*. 26 March. Retrieved from https://www.latimes.com/archives/blogs/world-now/story/2012-03-26/hallyu-back-obama-catches-the-korean-wave

Herbert, D., Lotz, A., & Punathambekar, A. (2020). *Media industry studies*. Polity.

Herman, E., & McChesney, R. (1997). The global media: The new missionaries of global capitalism. Bloomsbury.

Hesmondhalgh, D. (2012). *The cultural industries* (3rd ed.). Sage.

Hesmondhalgh, D., & Lotz, A. (2020). Video screen interfaces as new sites of media circulation power. *International Journal of Communication, 14*, 386–409.

Hesmondhalgh, D., & Pratt, A. C. (2005). Cultural industries and cultural policy. *International Journal of Cultural Policy, 11*(1), 1–13.

Hesmondhalgh, D., & Saha, A. (2013). Race, ethnicity, and cultural production. *Popular Communication, 11*(3), 179–195. https://doi.org/10.1080/15405702.2013.810068

Hofmeyr, I. (2007). The Black Atlantic Meets the Indian Ocean: Forging New Paradigms of Transnationalism for the Global South – Literary and Cultural Perspectives. *Social Dynamics* 33(2), 3–32.

Horkheimer, M., & Adorno, T. ([1947]1979). *Dialectic of enlightenment*. Verso.

Horkheimer, M., & Adorno, T. (1972). *Dialectic of enlightenment* (John Cumming, Trans.). Verso.

Howard, K. (2014). Mapping K-pop past and present: Shifting the modes of exchange. *Korea Observer, 45*(3), 389–414.

Huijgh, E. (2007). Diversity united? Towards a European cultural industries policy. *Policy Studies, 28*(3), 209–224.

Hutchinson, J. (2017). *Cultural intermediaries: Audience participation in media organisations*. Palgrave Macmillan.

Hutchinson, J. (2023). Digital intermediation: Unseen infrastructure for cultural production. *New Media & Society*, 25(12), 3289–3307.

International Federation of the Phonographic Industry. (2023). *Global Music Report 2023*. IFPI.

Iqani, M., and Resende, F. (2019). Theorizing media in and across the global south: narrative as territory, culture as flow. In Iqani, M., and Resende. F. (eds.). *Media and the Global South. Narrative territorialities, cross-cultural currents*, 1-16. London: Routledge.

Jenkins, H. (2011). Transmedia 202: Further reflections. Retrieved from http://henryjenkins.org/2011/08/defining_transmedia_further_re.html

Jenner, M. (2018). *Netflix and the re-invention of television*. Springer.

Jeon, H., & Limb, J. U. (2014). President Park announces three-year plan for economic innovation. Korea.net. 27 February. Retrieved from https://www.korea.net/NewsFocus/policies/view?articleId=117839

Ji, S.H.(2024). Min Hee-jin's words are right? . . . Seventeen albums were dumped in bulk in Shibuya, Japan. *Maeil Economic Daily*. 3 May. https://www.mk.co.kr/news/world/11006567

Ji, S. W. (2008). Enactment of the basic act on broadcasting and communications development. *Journalists Association of Korea*. 19 November.

Jin, D. Y. (2006). Cultural politics in Korea's contemporary films under neoliberal globalization. *Media, Culture & Society, 28*(1), 5–23.

Jin, D.Y. (2011). *Hands on/Hands off: The Korean state and the market liberalization of the communication industry*. Hampton Press.

Jin, D. Y. (2015). *Digital platforms, imperialism and political culture*. Routledge.

Jin, D. Y. (2016). *New Korean Wave: Transnational cultural power in the age of social media*. University of Illinois Press.

Jin, D. Y. (2019). *Globalization and media in the digital platform age*. Routledge.

Jin, D. Y. (2020). Comparative discourse on J-pop and K-pop: Hybridity in contemporary local music. *Korea Journal, 60*(1), 40–70. https://doi.org/10.25024/kj.2020.60.1.40

Jin, D. Y. (2021a). Ten myths about the Korean Wave in the global cultural sphere. *International Journal of Communication, 15*, 4147–4164.

Jin, D. Y. (2021b). Cultural production in transnational culture: An analysis of cultural creators in the Korean Wave. *International Journal of Communication, 15*, 1810–1835.

Jin, D. Y. (2021c). *Artificial intelligence in cultural production: Critical perspectives on digital platforms*. Routledge.

Jin, D. Y. (2021d). Netflix's corporate sphere in the digital platform era in Asia. In D. Y. Jin (Ed.), *The Routledge handbook of digital media and globalization* (pp. 167–175). Routledge.

Jin, D. Y. (2022). *Global South Discourse in East Asian Media Studies*. London: Routledge.

Jin, D. Y. (2023). *Understanding the Korean Wave: Transnational Korean pop culture and digital technologies*. Routledge.

Jin, D. Y. (2024). Historiography of the Korean Wave: Cultural shifts in genres and themes in the screen industry. *European Journal of Korean Studies 23*(2): 349-373.

Jin, D. Y. and Chee, F. (2008). Age of New Media Empire: A Critical Interpretation of the Korean Online Game Industry. *Games and Culture: A Journal of Interactive Media 3*(1): 38-58.

Jin, D. Y., Yoon, K., & Min, W. J. (2021). *Transnational Hallyu: The globalization of Korean digital and popular culture*. Rowman & Littlefield.

Jin, D. Y., Han, X., & Bizberge, A. (2024). Online video services markets in the Asia-

Pacific Region and Latin America. A Panel Proposal to the International Communication Association Conference. ICA.

Johnson, D. (2014). After the industry turn: can production studies make an audience turn? *Creative Industries Journal*, *7*(1), 50–53.

Ju, H. J. (2020). Korean TV drama viewership on Netflix: Transcultural affection, romance, and identities. *Journal of International and Intercultural Communication*, *13*(1), 32–48, https://doi.org/10.1080/17513057.2019.1606269

Ju, H. J. (2021). K-dramas Meet Netflix: New Models of Collaboration with the Digital West. In Y. A. Kim (Ed.), *The Soft Power of the Korean Wave* (pp. 171–183). London: Routledge.

Ju, H., & Lee, S. (2015). The Korean Wave and Asian Americans: The ethnic meanings of transnational Korean pop culture in the USA. *Continuum: Journal of Media & Cultural Studies*, *29*(3), 323–338. https://doi.org/10.1080/10304312.2014.986059

Jun, Y. J. (2021). DearU: A K-pop fan engagement platform success story. *The Korea Economic Daily*. 18 October. Retrieved from https://www.kedglobal.com/entertainment/newsView/ked202110180002

Jung, S. K., & Li, H. M. (2014). Global production, circulation, and consumption of Gangnam Style. *International Journal of Communication*, *8*, 2790–2810.

Kang, J. M. (2024). Not just Netflix: Interventions of Korea's domestic streamers. *International Journal of Cultural Studies*, *27*(1), 28–46.

Kang, J. S. (2017). Okja, Netflix, and the future of film. *Culture Science*, *9*, 248–268.

Kang, S. G. (2022). Fandom platform and the shift of the digital-based entertainment industry. *Media Issue and Trends*, *50*, 1–18.

Kassing, J. W., & Sanderson, J. (2009). "You're the kind of guy that we all want for a drinking buddy": Expressions of parasocial interaction on Floydlandis.com. *Western Journal of Communication*, *73*(2), 182–203.

Keane, M. (2006). Once were peripheral: Creating media capacity in East Asia. *Media, Culture, & Society*, *28*(6), 835–855.

Kil, S. (2019). Korean OTT Players, SK Telecom join forces to compete against Netflix. *Variety*. 17 January. https://variety.com/2019/biz/asia/korea-broadcasters-sk-telecom-compete-against-netflix-1203110343/

Kim, B. K.. (2022). The upheaval of the domestic *OTT market . . . 2nd and 3rd place overturned, the number of new rate plans and services. Chosun Ilbo*. 5 December. Retrieved from https://www.chosun.com/economy/tech_it/2022/12/04/KIZQP5MB3BCNTN3AN2BQKIX2OA/

Kim, C. Y., & Cha, J. H. (2022). Kakao closes in on $800 mn deal to buy SM Entertainment stake. *The Korea Economic Daily*. 11 March. Retrieved from https://www.kedglobal.com/mergers_acquisitions/newsView/ked202203110002

Kim, D. K., Jang, M. K., & Baek, H. M. (2021). How does the global audience watch Korean TV show on Netflix? *Korean Journal of Broadcasting and Telecommunication Studies*, *35*(6), 5–33.

Kim, E. J. (2019). SK Telecom, 3 broadcasters to launch OTT platform next month. *Yonhap News*. 20 August. Retrieved from https://en.yna.co.kr/view/AEN20190820009300320

Kim, G. Y. (2018). *From factory girls to K-pop idol girls: Cultural politics of developmentalism, patriarchy, and neoliberalism in South Korea's popular music industry*. Rowman & Littlefield.

Kim, H., Chan-Olmsted, S., Hwang, K. H., & Chang, B. H. (2021). Examining the use, perception, and motivation of cord-cutting: A consumer segment approach. *Journalism & Mass Communication Quarterly, 98*(1), 126–147.

Kim, H. H. (2023). Current status of Korean OTT platform and how to secure competitiveness—Focusing on the OTT policy. *Journal of Digital Contents Society, 24*(3), 497–505.

Kim, H. J. (2006). A history of Korean film policies. In M. H. Kim (Ed.), *Korean cinema: From origins to renaissance* (pp. 351–355). Seoul: Korean Film Council.

Kim, H. K. (2021). Hundreds of billions of production costs for luxurious casting . . . Tentpole drama war. *Hankyung*. 31 January. Retrieved from https://www.hankyung.com/life/article/2021013116561

Kim, H. Y. (2004). [Assertion] "How great were the dramas of the 80s?" *OhmyNews*. 12 August. Retrieved from http://www.ohmynews.com/NWS_Web/View/at_pg.aspx?CNTN_CD=A0001025106

Kim, J. H. (2020). K-drama adds Netflix's wings- captures Asia against the walls of production cost and subjects. *Dong-A Ilbo*. 1 July. Retrieved from https://www.donga.com/news/Opinion/article/all/20200701/101761296/1?ref=main

Kim, J. O. (2016). Establishing an imagined SM town: How Korea's leading music company has produced a global cultural phenomenon. *The Journal of Popular Culture, 49*(5), 1042–1058.

Kim, J. S. (2016). Success without design: Hallyu (Korean Wave) and its implications for cultural policy. *The Korean Journal of Policy Studies, 31*(3), 101–118.

Kim, J. S. (2018). Reinterpretation of Hallyu policy. In KOFICE (Ed.), *Hallyu and cultural policy* (pp. 63–69). Seoul: KOFICE.

Kim, K. (2024). Corporate clashes in K-pop: The HYBE vs. Ador controversy. *The Korea Times*. 1 May. Retrieved from https://www.koreatimes.co.kr/www/opinion/2024/10/638_373803.html#:~:text=The%20genesis%20of%20the%20conflict&text=The%20conflict%20began%20to%20surface,promotional%20strategies%20and%20artistic%20directions

Kim, K.A., Park, J.H., Yoon, S., Wang, Y., Bae, H., and Lue, K.T. (2023). Duality of K-Content in the Era of Netflix: An Investigation of Korean "Netflix Original" Characteristics. *International Journal of Communication* 17, 7015–7039.

Kim, K. C. (2013). The characteristics and achievements of Korean government's content industry policy: A longitudinal study on the cultural budget between 1974 and 2011. *Journal of Communication Research, 50*(1), 276–308.

Kim, K. C. (2023). Platform Hallyu: Definition and meaning. Paper presented at the 2023 Korean Society for Journalism & Communication Studies Conference. Seoul, Korea. 14 October.

Kim, M. Y. (2021). Minyoung Kim. VP of Content for Korea, Southeast Asia, Australia & New Zealand. Netflix. 24 February. Press Release.

Kim, N. Y. (2023). Operators of Tving, Wavve sign MOU for platform merger. *Yonhap News* Agency. 5 December. Retrieved from https://en.yna.co.kr/view/AEN20231205006300320

Kim, R. (Ed.). (2022). *Hallyu! The Korean Wave*. Victoria and Albert Museum.

Kim, S. (2023). How Netflix aims to deliver the next 'Squid Game.' *Newsweek*. February 4. Retrieved from https://www.newsweek.com/netflix-korea-slate-next-squid-game-hit-kdrama-1778957

Kim, S. C., & Jin, D. Y. (2024). *Korea's platform empire: An emerging power in the global platform sphere*. London: Routledge.

Kim, S. C., Hwang, S. Y., & Kim, J. H. (2021). Factors influencing K-pop artists' success on V live online video platform. *Telecommunications Policy, 45(3)*, 1–13.

Kim, S. Y. (2019). Wavve, Oksusu +Pooq New Local OTT Started Today. *Star Today*. September 18. Retrieved from https://www.mk.co.kr/star/hot-issues/view/2019/09/742015/

Kim, Y. A. (Ed.). (2013). *The Korean Wave: Korean media go global*. Routledge.

Kim, Y. H. (2022). OTT services use data by household. *KISDI Stat Report, 22*(7), 1–7.

Kim, Y. J. (2014). A possibility of the Korean Wave renaissance construction through K-Pop: Sustainable development of the Korean Wave as a cultural industry. Hastings Comm. & Ent. L. J. 59, 36(1), 59–88.

Knoche, M. (2021). Capitalisation of the media industry from a political economy perspective. *tripleC, 19*(2), 325–342.

Korea Communications Commission. (2023). 2023 Foreign OTT Market Survey. 22 December. Press Release.

Korea Creative Content Agency. (2011). *Music industry white paper*. Seoul: KOCCA.

Korea Creative Content Agency. (2018). *Music industry white paper of 2017*. Naju: KOCCA.

Korea Creative Content Agency. (2020). *Broadcasting industry white paper*. Naju: KOCCA.

Korea Creative Content Agency. (2021). *2021 outsource production transaction status report*. Naju: KOCCA.

Korea Creative Content Agency. (2022). *The first half of the content industry trend report*. Naju: KOCCA.

Korea Creative Content Agency. (2023). *2022 second half and annual content industry trend report*. Naju: KOCCA.

The Korea Foundation. (2010). *2010 Annual Report*. Seoul: KF.

The Korea Times. (2012). Will 'Hallyu' last long? 10 August. Retrieved from https://www.koreatimes.co.kr/www/opinion/2023/10/137_117143.html

The Korea Times. (2021). Netflix to invest $500 million in Korea in 2021. 25 February. Retrieved from https://www.koreatimes.co.kr/www/art/2023/03/398_304600.html?utm_source=RD

Koreaboo. (2023). MelOn is no longer the most used streaming service in South Korea . . . But who took its place? Retrieved from https://www.koreaboo.com/news/melon-no-longer-used-streaming-service-in-south-korea/

Korean Broadcasters Association. (2018). LG U+ and Netflix's partnership is the starting point of the destruction of the media industry ecosystem. 17 May. Press Release.

Korean Film Council. (2008). *2007 Korean film industry report*. Seoul: KOFIC.

Korean Film Council. (2019). *2018 Korean film industry report*. Busan: KOFIC.

Korean Film Council. (2022). *2021 Korean film industry report*. Busan: KOFIC.

Korean Foundation for International Cultural Exchange (KOFICE). (2023). *2023 overseas Hallyu survey*. Seoul: KOFICE.

Korean Movie Database. (2023). Database. https://www.kmdb.or.kr/db/main

Kowalczyk, I., & Cichoń, J. (2021). The significance of cultural policy—Case study of South Korea. *Sustainability, 13(24)*, 1–15.

Kraidy, M. (2010). *Reality television and Arab politics: contention in public life*. Cambridge University Press.

Kwak, K. T., Oh, C. J., & Lee, S. W. (2021). Who uses paid over-the-top services and why? Cross-national comparisons of consumer demographics and values. *Telecommunications Policy, 45*(7), 102–168.

Kwak, Y. S. (2023). Korea aims to become one of world's top four cultural powerhouses. *The Korea Times*. 23 February. Retrieved from https://www.koreatimes.co.kr/www/art/2023/10/398_346008.html

Kwon, H. Y. (2023). K-contents should become a 'global production base' rather than a 'Netflix subcontract base.' *Digital Daily*. 9 May. Retrieved from http://m.ddaily.co.kr/page/view/2023050912122804324

Kwon, S. H., & Kim, J. (2013). From censorship to active support: The Korean state and Korea's cultural industries. *The Economic and Labour Relations Review, 24*(4), 517–532.

Kwon, S. H., & Kim, J. (2014). The cultural industry policies of the Korean government and the Korean Wave. *International Journal of Cultural Policy, 20*(4), 422–439.

La Monica, P. (2020). Take that, Disney! Goldman Sachs is super bullish on Netflix. *CNN*. 10 July. Retrieved from www.cnn.com/2020/07/10/investing/netflix-stock-goldman-sachs/index.html

Lee, D. (2012). The ethics of insecurity: Risk, individualization and value in British independent television production. *Television & New Media, 13*(6), 480–497.

Lee, D. J. (2022). A paradigm shift for Hallyu policy: Revisiting 2020 (new) Hallyu policy discourse. *The Korean Society of Culture and Convergence, 44*(3), 725–748.

Lee, F. (2008). Hollywood movies in East Asia: examining cultural discount and performance predictability at the box office. *Asian Journal of Communication, 18*(2), 117–136. https://doi.org/10.1080/01292980802021855

Lee, J. (2024). Disney+ Korea focuses on keeping the K in kuality kontent. *Korea JoongAng Daily*. 12 March. Retrieved from https://koreajoongangdaily.joins.com/news/2024-03-12/entertainment/television/Disney-Korea-focuses-on-keeping-the-K-in-kuality-kontent/2000341

Lee, G. L. (2020). See what's next: Netflix reshapes Korean TV industry trends. *The Korea Times*. 31 July. Retrieved from https://www.koreatimes.co.kr/www/art/2020/07/688_293689.html

Lee, G. T. (2016). *K-pop's era: From cassette tape to streaming*. Hanul.

Lee, H. K. (2013). Cultural policy and the Korean Wave: From national culture to transnational consumerism. In Y. N. Kim (Ed.), *The Korean Wave: Korean Media Go Global* (pp. 185–198). Routledge.

Lee, H. K. (2020). Making creative industries policy in the real world: Differing configurations of the culture-market-state nexus in the UK and South Korea. *International Journal of Cultural Policy, 26*(4), 544–560.

Lee, H.K. (2024, online first). Reflecting on cultural labor in the time of AI. *Media, Culture & Society*. 1–12.

Lee, H. J., & Jin, D. Y. (2019). *K-pop idols: Popular culture and the emergence of the Korean music industry*. Lexington.

Lee, H. K. (2019). *Cultural policy in South Korea: Making a new patron state*. Routledge.

Lee, H. K., & Zhang, X. (2021). The Korean Wave as a source of implicit cultural policy: Making of a neoliberal subjectivity in a Korean style. *International Journal of Cultural Studies, 24*(3), 521–537.

Lee, H. W. (2018). Netflix acquires rights to South Korean TV drama 'Mr. Sunshine.' *The*

Hollywood Reporter. 25 June. Retrieved from https://www.hollywoodreporter.com/tv/tv-news/netflix-acquires-rights-south-korean-tv-drama-mr-sunshine-1122996/

Lee, H. W. (2017). Netflix inks multi-title licensing deal with South Korea's JTBC. *The Hollywood Reporter*. 24 April. Retrieved from https://www.hollywoodreporter.com/tv/tv-news/netflix-inks-multi-title-licensing-deal-south-koreas-jtbc-997072/

Lee, J. (2022). BTS fandom tech firm Weverse reaches beyond K-Pop. *Reuters*, 22 December. Retrieved from https://www.reuters.com/article/bts-hybe-weverse-idCAKBN2T61JB

Lee, J. I. (2023). The Wugong Isan myth still persists in K-pop, which only focuses on idol training. *Pressian*. 25 August. Retrieved from https://v.daum.net/v/20230825143833224?f=p

Lee, J. K. (2011). *Animating globalization and development: The South Korean animation industry in historical-comparative perspective*. Dissertation at Duke University.

Lee, J. L. (2022). The Hallyu Korean wave is not just here to stay—it's gaining momentum. *Korea JoongAng Daily*. 23 October. Retrieved from https://koreajoongangdaily.joins.com/2022/10/23/culture/features/Hallyu-Hallyu-30-Squid-Game/20221023161627136.html

Lee, J. L. (2023). K-pop fan service Universe to shut down, transfer to Dear U Bubble. *Korea JoongAng Daily*. 11 January. Retrieved from https://koreajoongangdaily.joins.com/2023/01/11/entertainment/kpop/Universe-NCSoft/20230111105854122.html

Lee, J. Y. (2009). Contesting digital economy and culture: Digital technologies and the transformation of popular music in Korea. *Inter-Asia Cultural Studies, 10*(4), 489–506.

Lee, K. B. (2009). Select 17 new growth engines. *The Science Times*. 14 January.

Lee, S. H. (2019). JTBC decided to work with Netflix: Providing dramas for 3 years. *Seoul Economic Daily*. 25 November. Retrieved from https://www.sedaily.com/NewsView/1VQXNPRBBX

Lee, S. J. (2021). Kim Tae-ho makes Netflix debut with 'The Hungry and the Hairy.' *The Korea Herald*. 11 August. Retrieved from https://www.koreaherald.com/view.php?ud=20210811000734

Lee, S. J., & Nornes, A. M. (Eds.). (2015). *Hallyu 2.0: The Korean Wave in the age of social media*. Ann Arbor: University of Michigan Press.

Lee, S. M. (2019). Networks are riding Netflix: Platforms become partners for survival. *Newspaper and Broadcasting*, 583, 45–49.

Lee, S. M. (2023). Platform Hallyu and Cultural Diversity. Paper presented at the 2023 Korean Society for Journalism & Communication Studies Conference. Seoul, Korea. 14 October.

Levander, C., and Mignolo, W. (2011). Introduction: The Global South and World Dis/Order. *The Global South, 5*(1), 1–11.

Li, K., & Yang, H. K. (2021). South Korea's pop culture machine boosts Netflix's international growth–source. *Reuters*. 21 October. Retrieved from https://www.reuters.com/article/netflix-results-southkorea-idUSKBN27607G

Liang, A., & Hoskins, P. (2023). Netflix to invest $2.5bn in new South Korea films and TV shows. *BBC News*. 25 April.

Lie, J. (2012). What is the K in K-pop? South Korean popular music, the culture industry, and national identity. *Korea Observer, 43*(3), 339–363.

Lim, H. C., & Jang, J. H. (2006). Neo-liberalism in post-crisis South Korea: Social conditions and outcomes. *Journal of Contemporary Asia, 36*(4), 442–463.

Littleton, C., & Layne, S. (2022). K dramas can't be denied: Global streaming spurs demand for Asian content platforms. *Variety*. 18 August. Retrieved from https://variety.com/2022/streaming/news/korean-dramas-kocowa-viki-asiancrush-kcon-1235344275/

Lobato, R. (2018). Rethinking international TV flows research in the age of Netflix. *Television & New Media, 19*(3), 241–256.

Lobato, R. (2019). *Netflix nations. The geography of digital distribution*. New York University Press.

Lotz, A. (2022). *Netflix and streaming video: The business of subscriber-funded video on demand*. Polity.

Lotz, A., & Eklund, O. (2024). Beyond Netflix: Ownership and content strategies among non-US-based video streaming services. *International Journal of Cultural Studies, 27*(1), 119–140.

Lotz, A., Lobato, R., & Thomas, J. (2018). Internet-distributed television research: A provocation. *Media Industries, 5*(2). Retrieved from https://quod.lib.umich.edu/m/mij/15031809.0005.203/--internet-distributed-television-research-a-provocation?rgn=main;view=fulltext;q1=lobato

Lyan, I. (2023). Shock and surprise: Theorizing the Korean Wave through mediatized emotions. *International Journal of Communication, 17*, 29–51.

MacDonald, J. (2019). Netflix expands Korean programming with romance, thrillers and espionage. *Forbes*. 14 June. Retrieved from https://www.forbes.com/sites/joanmacdonald/2019/06/14/netflix-expands-korean-programming-with-romance-thrillers-and-espionage/?sh=64f3599b4b50

MacDonald, J. (2023). More Korean dramas aim for a second—and even a third season. *Forbes*. 12 January. Retrieved from https://www.forbes.com/sites/joanmacdonald/2023/01/12/more-korean-dramas-aim-for-a-second-and-even-a-third-season/?sh=721320e56a76

Mark, S. (2009). A greater role for cultural diplomacy. A discussion papers in diplomacy. Retrieved from https://www.clingendael.org/sites/default/files/pdfs/20090616_cdsp_discussion_paper_114_mark.pdf

Masuda, H. (2007). *Anime bijinesu ga wakaru = Understanding animation business*. Tokyo: NTT Shuppan.

Mattelart, T. (2024). US digital platforms in the global south: A critical review of an emerging research field. In P. Bouquillion, C. Ithurbide, & T. Mattelart (Eds.), *Digital platforms and the global south: Reconfiguring power relations in the cultural industries* (pp. 19–36). Routledge.

Maxwell, R. (1995). *The spectacle of democracy: Spanish television, nationalism, and political transition*. University of Minnesota Press.

Mayer, V. (2011). *Below the line: Producers and production studies in the new television economy*. Duke University Press.

Mayer, V., Banks, M., & Caldwell, J. (2009). Introduction: Production studies: Roots and routes. In V. Mayer, M. Banks, & J. Caldwell (Eds.), *Production studies: Cultural studies of media industries* (pp. 1–12). Routledge.

McChesney, R. (1999). *Rich media, poor democracy: Communication politics in dubious times*. University of Illinois Press.

McChesney, R. (2001). Global media, neoliberalism, and imperialism. *Monthly Review, 52*(10), 1–19.

McDonald, P. (2021). *The Routledge companion to media industries*. Routledge.

McDonald, P., Donoghue, C., and Havens, T. (2021). *Digital media distribution: Portals, platforms, pipelines*. New York University Press.

Meimaridis, M., Mazur, D., & Rios, D. (2021). From São Paulo to Seoul: Netflix's strategies in peripheral markets. *Comunicación y Sociedad*, e8038, 1–25. https://doi.org/10.32870/cys.v2021.8038

Messerlin, P., & Shin, W. K. (2017). The success of K-pop: How big and why so fast? *Asian Journal of Social Science, 45*(4/5), 409–439.

Messina, M. (2022). Exploring vertical integration in the supply chain. *Forbes*. 29 December. Retrieved from https://www.forbes.com/sites/forbestechcouncil/2022/12/29/exploring-vertical-integration-in-the-supply-chain/?sh=645c35123c5b

Miège, B. (1987). The logics at work in the new cultural industries. *Media, Culture & Society, 9(3)*, 273–289.

Miège, B. (2011). Theorizing the cultural industries: Persistent specificities and reconsiderations. In J. Wasko, G. Murdock, & H. Sousa (Eds.), *The handbook of political economy of communications* (pp. 83–108). Blackwell.

Miller, T. (2006). Gaming for beginners. *Games and culture, 1*(1), 5–12.

Milne, B. (2013). *The history and theory of children's citizenship in contemporary societies*. Springer.

Ministry of Culture and Tourism. (2006). *2006 cultural industry white paper*. Seoul: MCT.

Ministry of Culture and Tourism (2008). *MCT 2008 Plan Report to the President*. 3 March.

Ministry of Culture and Tourism (MCT). (2002). *Munhwa Sanup Backsuh* [Culture Industry White Paper 2002]. Seoul: Ministry of Culture and Tourism.

Ministry of Culture, Sports and Tourism. (2007). *2006 content industry whitepaper*. Seoul: MCST.

Ministry of Culture, Sports and Tourism. (2011). *Summary of 2011 content industries*. Seoul: MCST.

Ministry of Culture, Sports and Tourism. (2013). *2013 content industry statistical analysis: 2012 basis*. Seoul: MCST.

Ministry of Culture, Sports and Tourism. (2017). *2016 content industry whitepaper*. Seoul: MCST.

Ministry of Culture, Sports and Tourism. (2022). *2021 content industry whitepaper*. Seoul: MCST.

Ministry of Culture, Sports and Tourism. (2023). *2022 content industry whitepaper*. Seoul: MCST.

Ministry of Culture, Sports and Tourism (MCST). (2010). *Digital yoonhap sidae contents sanop mirae jungchaek yonkoo* [Research on the future policy of contents industry in the era of digital convergence]. Seoul: Ministry of Culture, Science and Technology.

Ministry of Government Legislation. (2008). *Enactment of the framework act on broadcasting communications development*. 31 October. Seoul: MGL.

Money Today. (2021). Korean content is always working . . . Invest $550 million this year alone. 24 September. Retrieved from https://news.mt.co.kr/mtview.php?no=2021092320231286650

Moore, K. (2023). Netflix Originals Now Make Up 55% of US Library. What's on Netflix. 13 July. Retrieved from https://www.whats-on-netflix.com/news/netflix-originals-now-make-up-55-of-us-library/

Morris, J. (2020). Music platforms and the optimization of culture. *Social Media + Society, 6*(3), 1–10.

Mosco, V. (2009). *The political economy of communication*. Sage.

Mulcahy, K. (2006). Cultural policy: Definitions and theoretical approaches. *The Journal of Arts Management, Law, and Society, 35*(4), 319–330.

Mulligan, M. (2013). The curious case of the South Korean music market. *Music Industry Blog*, 8 May. Retrieved from https://musicindustryblog.wordpress.com/2013/05/08/the-curious-case-of-the-south-korean-music-market/

Murdock, G., & Golding, P. (2005). Culture, communications and political economy. In J. Curran and M. Gurevitch (Eds.), *Mass media and society*, 4th ed. (pp. 60–83). Arnold.

Negus, K. (2015). The South Korean music industry: A literature review. CREATe Working Paper, 1–19.

Netflix. (2017). Netflix simulcasts new Korean original series MAN x Man by JTBC in over 20 languages globally. 7 April. Press Release.

Netflix. (2018). UBS's 2018 global media and communications conference in New York. 3 December. Press Release.

Netflix. (2019). CJ ENM/Studio Dragon-Netflix announce a long-term partnership. Press Release. 21 November.

Netflix. (2019). Machine learning: Learning how to entertain the world. Retrieved from https://research.netflix.com/research-area/machine-learning

Netflix. (2021a). Letter to shareholders. 19 October. Retrieved from https://s22.q4cdn.com/959853165/files/doc_financials/2021/q3/FINAL-Q3-21-Shareholder-Letter.pdf

Netflix. (2021b). Q3 results and Q4 forecast. 19 October. Press Release.

Netflix. (2021c). What's on Netflix. 1 November. Retrieved from https://www.whats-on-netflix.com/library/list-of-korean-movies-tv-series-on-netflix/

Netflix. (2021d). What's Next Korea 2021. 24 February. Retrieved from https://www.youtube.com/watch?v=-5PqVaIIxSE

Netflix. (2022). Letter to shareholders. 20 January. Retrieved from https://s22.q4cdn.com/959853165/files/doc_financials/2021/q4/FINAL-Q4-21-Shareholder-Letter.pdf

Netflix. (2023a). Annual report/ Form-10K. Las Gatos, CA: Netflix.

Netflix. (2023b). New series and returning favorites. Press Release. 16 July.

Netflix. (2024a). Letter to shareholders. Las Gatos, CA: Netflix.

Netflix (2024b). What's on Netflix. 11 November. Retrieved from https://www.whats-on-netflix.com/library/list-of-korean-movies-tv-series-on-netflix/

Nichols, R., & Martinez, G. (2019) (Eds.), *Political economy of media industries: Global transformations and challenges*. Routledge.

Nieborg, D., Poell, T., & Duffy, B. (2021). Analyzing platform power in the cultural industries. Paper presented at AoIR2021: The 22nd annual conference of the Association of Internet Researchers. Virtual Event: AoIR. Retrieved from https://spir.aoir.org/ojs/index.php/spir/article/view/12219

Nieborg, D. B., & Poell, T. (2018). The platformization of cultural production: Theorizing the contingent cultural commodity. *New Media & Society, 20*(11): 4275–4292. https://doi.org/10.1177/1461444818769694

Noh, J. M. (2022). What is the answer to the criticism that the domestic production company has become a Netflix 'subcontractor'?. *Media Today*. 22 January. Retrieved from http://www.mediatoday.co.kr/news/articleView.html?idxno=301882

Nye, J. (2004a). The benefits of soft power. *Harvard Business School*. 2 August. Retrieved from https://hbswk.hbs.edu/archive/the-benefits-of-soft-power

Nye, J. (2004b). Soft power and American foreign policy. *Political Science Quarterly, 119*(2), 255–270.

Nye, J., & Kim, Y. (2013). Soft power and the Korean Wave. In Y. Kim (Ed.), *The Korean Wave: Korean media go global* (pp. 31–42). Routledge.

OECD. (2020). General government spending. Paris: OECD. Retrieved from https://data.oecd.org/gga/general-government-spending.htm

OECD. (2021). 12 ways Korea is changing the world: Sustaining the Miracle on the Han River. 25 October. Retrieved from https://www.oecd.org/country/korea/thematic-focus/sustaining-the-miracle-on-the-han-river-103653fa/

Oh, C. Y. (2021). More K-pop fans go online for intimate fan-star interactions. *ABC News*. 18 September. Retrieved from https://abcnews.go.com/Entertainment/pop-fans-online-intimate-fan-star-interactions/story?id=80073722

Oh, I. G., & Lee, H. J. (2014). K-pop in Korea: How the pop music industry is changing a post-developmental society. *Cross-Currents: East Asian History and Culture Review, 3*(1), 72–93.

Oh, Y. K., & Choeh, J. Y. (2022). Social media engagements of music videos on YouTube's official artist channels. *Convergence: The International Journal of Research into New Media Technologies, 28*(3), 804–821.

Oi, M. (2016). The dark side of Asia's pop music industry. *BBC News*. 26 January. Retrieved from http://www.bbc.com/news/world-asia-35368705

Okimoto, D. (1989). *Between MITI and the market: Japanese industrial policy for high technology*. Stanford University Press.

Osur, L. (2016). *Netflix and the development of the internet television network*. Dissertation. Syracuse University.

Otmazgin, N. (2021). Cultural industries and the state in East Asia. In S K. Hong & D. Y. Jin (Eds.), *Transnational convergence of East Asian pop culture* (pp. 207–229). Routledge.

Oxford Reference. (2019). *Cultural production*. Oxford University Press.

Park, E. J. (2016). SK Broadband starts mobile video streaming. *Korea JoongAng Daily*. 26 January. Retrieved from https://koreajoongangdaily.joins.com/2016/01/26/industry/SK-Broadband-starts-mobile-video-streaming/3014419.html

Park, H. S. (2023). KOCIS aims to promote 'sustainable hallyu' via Korean cultural centers worldwide. *The Korea Times*. 16 February. Retrieved from https://www.koreatimes.co.kr/www/culture/2023/10/135_345534.html

Park, J. C., & Lee, J. S. (2018). Some strategies for sustainable Korean Wave with cultural contents—In the case of K-comics. *Korean Studies, 36*, 549–588.

Park, J. H., Kim, K., & Lee, Y. S. (2023). Netflix and platform imperialism: How Netflix alters the ecology of the Korean TV drama industry. *International Journal of Communication, 17*(2023), 72–91.

Park, S. H. (2022). Catch Netflix: TVing and Seezn mergered: 5.6 million users to become No 1 local OTT. *ChosunBiZ*. 14 July. Retrieved from https://biz.chosun.com/it-science/ict/2022/07/15/ER35GPEIVRAUPENXYC2Z5PHFZI/

Park, S. J. (2023). Facebook. 23 January.

Park, S. Y. (2023). MBC, the reason why Netflix invested and produced 'Physical 100.' *Media Today*. 3 February. Retrieved from http://www.mediatoday.co.kr/news/articleView.html?idxno=308324

Park, S. Y., Jo, H. J., & Kim, T. Y. (2023). Platformization in local cultural production: Korean platform companies and the K-Pop industry. *International Journal of Communication, 17*, 2422–2443.

Peterson, R., & Anand, N. (2004). The production of culture perspective. *Annual Review of Sociology, 30*(1), 311–334.

Plantin, J. C., & Punathambekar, A. (2019). Digital media infrastructures: Pipes, platforms, and politics. *Media, Culture & Society,* 41(2), 163–174 https://doi.org/10.1177/0163443718818376

Poell, T. (2020). Three challenges for media studies in the age of platforms. *Television & New Media, 21*(6), 650–657.

Poell, T., Nieborg, D., & Duffy, B. E. (2022). *Platforms and cultural production*. London: John Wiley & Sons.

Poell, T., Nieborg, D., & van Dijck, J. (2019). Platformisation. *Internet Policy Review, 8*(4), 1–13. https://doi.org/10.14763/2019.4.1425

Prashad, V. (2014). *The Poorer Nations: A Possible History of the Global South.*London and New York: Verso.

Pratt, A. (2005). Cultural industries and public policy: An oxymoron? *International Journal of Cultural Policy, 11*(1), 31–44.

Prey, R. (2020). Locating power in platformization: Music streaming playlists and curatorial power. *Social Media + Society*, *6*(2), 1–11. https://doi.org/2056305120933291

PricewaterhouseCoopers. (2023). *Global Entertainment & Media Outlook 2023–2027*. PwC.

Pyo, K.M. (2024).Dispute between HYBE, Ador CEO highlights challenges in multi-label system. *The Korea Times*. 23 April. Received from https://www.koreatimes.co.kr/www/art/2024/10/398_373281.html

Radošinská, J. (2017). New trends in production and distribution of episodic television drama: Brand Marvel-Netflix in the post-television era. *Communication Theory, 8*(1), 4–29.

Raessens, J. (2005). Computer games as participatory media culture. In J. Raessens & J. Goldstein (Eds.), *Handbook of computer game studies* (pp. 373–388). Cambridge, MA: MIT Press.

Ram, A. (2016, November 8). Asia to be a major player in transmedia content. *Digital News Asia*. Retrieved from https://www.digitalnewsasia.com/personal-tech/asia-be-major-player-transmedia-content

Rapir, J. (2019). Lee Seung Gi & Suzy's new K-drama 'Vagabond' premiere date pushed back to September. *Korea Portal*. 2 April. Retrieved from http://en.koreaportal.com/articles/46791/20190402/lee-seung-gi-suzys-new-k-drama-vagabond-premiere-date-pushed-back-to-september.htm

Reality Tidbit. (2023). The Physical 100 prize is 300 million won but how much is that in US dollars? 25 January. Retrieved from https://www.realitytitbit.com/netflix-reality-shows/the-physical-100-prize-is-300-million-won-but-how-much-is-that-in-us-dollars

Rimkutė, A., (2009a). Kultūra kaip politikos objektas. From Svičiulienė, J., 2009. *Kultūros vadyba*, 1 t. Vilnius: VU leidykla, 17–46.

Rimkutė, A. (2009b). Kultūros politika ir kultūros industrija: tradicinis santykis ir nauji iššūkiai, *Respectus Philologicus, 15*(20), 62–75.

Robinson, M. J. (2017). *Television on demand: Curatorial culture and the transformation of TV*. Bloomsbury.

Rochet, J. C., & Tirole, J. (2003). Platform competition in two-sided markets. *Journal of the European Economic Association, 1*(4), 990–1029.

Rousse-Marquet, J. (2012). K-pop: The story of the well-oiled industry of standardized catchy tunes. *Ina: The Review of Creative Industries and Media*. 29 November.

Roxborough, S., & Szalai, G. (2011, Oct. 12). Can Netflix sell U.S. users on foreign shows? *The Hollywood Reporter*. Retrieved from https://www.hollywoodreporter.com/tv/tv-news/can-netflix-sell-us-users-246003/

Ryall, J. (2023). Why is Netflix pouring billions into South Korean shows? *DW*. 1 May.

Ryoo, W. J. (2008). The political economy of the global mediascape: the case of the South Korean film industry. *Media, Culture & Society, 30*(6), 873–889.

Ryoo, W. J., & Jin, D. Y. (2020). Cultural politics in the South Korean cultural industries: Confrontations between state-developmentalism and neoliberalism. *The International Journal of Cultural Policy, 26*(1), 31–45.

Sarandos, T. (2014, Oct. 14). Keynote. MIPCOM 2014. Retrieved from https://www.youtube.com/watch?v=4QRI8wIum00

Schiller, D. (1999). *Digital capitalism*. MIT Press.

Schiller, H. (1975). Genesis of the free flow of information principles: The imposition of communications domination. *Instant Research on Peace and Violence, 5*(2), 75–86.

Schiller, H. (1989). *Culture, Inc.* Oxford University Press.

Schiller, H. (1992). *Mass communications and American empire*, 2nd ed. Westview Press.

Seabrook, J. (2012). Factory girls. *The NewYorker*. 1 October. Retrieved from http://www.newyorker.com/reporting/2012/10/08/121008fa_fact_seabrook

Shan, S. L. (2014). Chinese cultural policy and the cultural industries. *City, Culture and Society, 5*(3), 115–121.

Shaw, L. (2021). Netflix estimates 'Squid Game' will be worth almost $900 million. *Bloomberg*. 16 October. Retrieved from https://www.bloomberg.com/news/articles/2021-10-17/squid-game-season-2-series-worth-900-million-to-netflix-so-far#

Shim, D. (2008). The growth of Korean cultural industries and the Korean Wave. In C. B. Huat & K. Iwabuchi (Eds.), *East Asian pop culture: Analysing the Korean Wave* (pp. 15–31). Hong Kong University Press.

Shin, C. O., & Lee, E. J. (2019). S. Korea's mega OTT platform Wavve readies for launch next month. *Pulse*. 21 August. Retrieved from https://pulsenews.co.kr/view.php?year=2019&no=646827

Shin, N. H. (2022). Merger of streaming services Tving and Seezn finished. *Korea JoongAng Daily*. 1 December. Retrieved from https://koreajoongangdaily.joins.com/2022/12/01/business/industry/Korea-Tving-Seezn/20221201153912713.html

Shin, S. L., & Kim, L. (2013). Organizing K-pop: Emergence and market making of large Korean entertainment houses, 1980–2010. *East Asia, 30*, 255–272.

Silva, G. (2022). The 15 best K-dramas with more than one season, ranked. *Screen Rant*. 3 August. Retrieved from https://screenrant.com/best-k-dramas-more-than-one-season/

Silverstone, R. (Ed.). (2005). *Media, technology and everyday life in Europe: From information to communication*. Ashgate Publishing.

Sim, Y. H. (2016). Commentary: Behind the Korean Wave. *Jakarta Globe*. 25 February. Retrieved from https://jakartaglobe.id/opinion/behind-korean-wave

SM Entertainment. (2023). *Company introduction*. SME.

Sohn, J. Y. (2018). Netflix to push boundaries of Korean media content. *The Korea Her-*

ald. 25 January. Retrieved from http://www.koreaherald.com/view.php?ud=20180125000871

Soini, K., & Dessein, J. (2016). Culture-sustainability relation: Towards a conceptual framework. *Sustainability, 8(2)*, 1–12.

Song, S. H. (2019). KT enters global OTT competition with AI-equipped Seezn. *The Korea Herald*. 28 November. Retrieved from https://www.koreaherald.com/view.php?ud=20191128000622

Spangler, T. (2019). Netflix ranked as No. 1 fastest-growing U.S. brand in 2019. *Variety*. 28 March. Retrieved from https://variety.com/2019/digital/news/netflix-brand-value-ranking-2019-1203175244/

Stangarone, T. (2019). How Netflix is reshaping South Korean entertainment: The streaming giant is reshaping Korean entertainment, even while boosting its popularity around the world. *The Diplomat*. 29 April. Retrieved from https://thediplomat.com/2019/04/how-netflix-is-reshaping-south-korean-entertainment/

Statista. (2022). Most frequently used music streaming or download services in South Korea as of August 2022. Retrieved from https://www.statista.com/statistics/943272/south-korea-most-frequently-used-music-streaming-download-services/

Steemers, J. (2004). *Selling television: British television in the global marketplace*. British Film Institute.

Stitch. (2021). K-pop's fandom platforms are changing what it means to be an idol. 31 July. Retrieved from https://www.theverge.com/22589460/kpop-fan-cafe-weverse-universe-lysn-bts-idol-fandom-group

Sundet, V. S., & Colbjørnsen, T. (2021). Streaming across industries: Streaming logics and streaming lore across the music, film, television, and book industries. *MedieKultur: Journal of media and communication research*, 37(70), 12–31. https://doi.org/10.7146/mediekultur.v37i70.122425

Sundet, V.S., & Lüders, M. (2023). Young people are on YouTube: industry notions on streaming and youth as a new media generation. *Journal of Media Business Studies, 20*(3), 223–240. https://doi.org/10.1080/16522354.2022.2125262

Sung, Y.J. (2024). MLB hits and transfer romance receives; native OTT's counterattacks. 26 April. *Chosun Ilbo*. Received from https://www.chosun.com/economy/industry-company/2024/04/26/LTZHAYPSOJCXDLOGRAA3DVM4HU/

Sunio, P. (2020). From BTS to Blackpink–what it takes to become a K-pop idol in South Korea. *South China Morning Post*. 30 January. Retrieved from https://www.scmp.com/magazines/style/news-trends/article/3048154/bts-blackpink-what-it-takes-become-k-pop-idol-south

Surber, J. P. (1998). *Culture and critique: An introduction to the critical discourses of cultural studies*. Westview Press.

Tamera, M. (2021). A look back on 2021—How streaming changed the music industry during the pandemic + what next? In June 2023, tell us what you think! *Medium*. 14 October.

Tefertiller, A. (2020). Cable cord-cutting and streaming adoption: Advertising avoidance and technology acceptance in television innovation. *Telematics and Informatics, 51*, 1–9.

Throsby, D. (1997). Sustainability and culture: Some theoretical issues. *Cultural Policy, 4*(1), 7–20.

Throsby, D. (2001). *Economics and culture*. Cambridge University Press.

Toh, M. (2023). Netflix plans its biggest-ever slate of Korean content. *CNN*. 16 January. Retrieved from https://www.cnn.com/2023/01/16/business/netflix-korean-content-expansion-2023-intl-hnk/index.html

UNESCO Institute for Statistics. (2016). *The globalisation of cultural trade: a shift in consumption; international flows of cultural goods and services 2004–2013*. UNESCO-UIS.

van Dijck, J. (2013). *The culture of connectivity: A critical history of social media*. Oxford University Press.

van Dijck, J., & Poell, T. (2013). Understanding social media logic. *Media and Communication, 1*(1), 2–14.

van Dijck, J., Nieborg, D., & Poell, T. (2019). Reframing platform power. *Internet Policy Review, 8*(2), 1–18.

Velkova, J., & Jakobsson, P. (2017). At the intersection of commons and market: Negotiations of value in open-sourced cultural production. *International Journal of Cultural Studies, 20*(1), 14–30.

Verdegem, P. (2021). Social media industries and the rise of the platform. In P. McDonald (Ed.), *The Routledge Companion to media industries*. Routledge.

Vitkauskaitė, I. (2015). Cultural industries in public policy. *Journal of International Studies, 8*(1), 208–222.

Vlassis, A. (2019). Cultural policies, digital platforms and global cultural economy: European Union in the American imperium (still)? Eucross. Working Paper, 1–26.

Weiss, L. (1992). The politics of industrial organisation: A comparative View. In J. Marceau (Ed.), *Reworking the world: Organisations, technologies, and cultures in comparative perspective* (pp. 95–124). Walter De Gruyter.

Williams, R. (1974). *Television: Technology and cultural form*. Fontana.

Winseck, D. (2011). The political economies of media and the transformation of the global media industries. In D. Winseck & D. Y. Jin (Eds.), *The political economies of media: The transformation of the global media industries* (pp. 3–48). Bloomsbury.

Wolf, M. J. P., & Perron, B. (Eds.). (2003). *The video game theory reader*. Routledge.

Won, Y. J. (2012). Evaluation of cultural contents policies of Lee Myung-bak government. Paper presented at the Cultural Policy Forum, Seoul, 27 April.

Yang, H. (2021). In a digital age, why are CD sales flourishing in Korea? *Korea JoongAng Daily*. 10 August. Retrieved from https://koreajoongangdaily.joins.com/2021/08/10/entertainment/kpop/kpop-albums-kpop-albums-photo-card-Hanteo-Global-KPop-Report/20210810170500503.html

Yang, S. H. (2015). The birth of cable TV . . . In 1995, the Korean Wave exploded. *JoongAng Ilbo*. 16 March. Retrieved from https://www.joongang.co.kr/article/17367730#home

Yang, S. J. (2022). 'Woo Young-woo' is also a 'silver spoon' . . . Drama production costs skyrocketing. *Hankook Ilbo*. 19 August. Retrieved from https://www.hankookilbo.com/News/Read/A2022081808480003524

Yeo, S. J. (2023). Behind the search box: Google and the global internet industry. Urbana: University of Illinois Press.

Yim, H. S. (2002). Cultural identity and cultural policy in South Korea. *International Journal of Cultural Policy, 8*(1), 37–48.

Yim, H. S. (2021). FTC gives go ahead for merger deal between V Live and Weverse. *The Korea Herald*. 13 May. Retrieved from https://www.koreaherald.com/view.php?ud=20210513000792

Yonhap News. (2019). Netflix breaks the wall of networks . . . airs Vagabond and One Spring Night simultaneously. 23 April. Retrieved from https://www.yna.co.kr/view/AKR20190423082900005

Yoon, S. W. (2016). Kakao acquires Loen. *The Korea Times*. 11 January. Retrieved from http://www.koreatimes.co.kr/www/news/tech/2016/01/133_195188.html

Yoon, S. W. (2016). CJ E&M pushing to revitalize internet-based broadcast platform. *The Korea Times*. 30 November. Retrieved from https://www.koreatimes.co.kr/www/tech/2021/04/133_219259.html

Yoon, T. J., & Kang, B. R. (2017). Emergence, evolution, and extension of "*Hallyu* studies": What have scholars found from Korean pop culture in the last twenty years? In T. J. Yoon & D. Y. Jin (Eds.), *The Korean Wave: Evolution, fandom, and transnationality* (pp. 31–56). Lexington Books.

You, G. S. (2019). *Netflixonomics: Netflix and Korean Broadcasting Media*. Hanul Plus.

You, K. S. (2021). *How Netflix transformed the Korean drama market*. Hanul M Plus.

You, S. M. (2019). OTT-analysis of Korean drama's storytelling: A case study of Netflix drama kingdom. Proceeding of the Korean Association for Broadcasting & Telecommunication Conference, 211–213.

YouTube Trends. (2012, December 1). Gangnam Style crosses one billion view mark. Retrieved from http://youtube-trends.blogspot.com/search?q=gangnam+style

YouTube Trends. (2013, July 15). A year since Gangnam Style, K-pop keeps getting bigger [Web log post]. Retrieved from https://youtube-trends.blogspot.com/2013/07/a-year-since-gangnam-style-k-pop-keeps.html

Yu, G. S. (2023). Physical:100–Reasons why its success is not welcoming. *PD Journal*. 13 February. Retrieved from https://www.pdjournal.com/news/articleView.html?idxno=74655

Yuniya, K., & Marc de Jong, J. W. (2021). *Cultural appropriation in fashion and entertainment*. Bloomsbury.

Zeng, W., & Sparks, C. (2019). Production and politics in Chinese television. *Media, Culture & Society, 41*(1), 54–69.

Zhang, Z. (2021). Infrastructuralization of Tik Tok: Transformation, power relationships, and platformization of video entertainment in China. *Media, Culture & Society*, 43(2), 219–236.

Yonhap News. (2016). Netflix breaks the wall of networks . . . airs Vagabond and One Spring Night [illegible]. Retrieved from https://www.yonhapnews.co.kr/[illegible]

Yoon, S. W. (2016). [illegible]. *The Korea Times*. Retrieved from http://www.koreatimes.co.kr/www/[illegible].html

Yoon, S. W. (2016). [illegible] *The Korea Times*. Retrieved from http://www.koreatimes.co.kr/www/[illegible]

Yoon, T.-J., & Kang, B. R. (2019). [illegible] "What have schemas [illegible] from Korean pop culture in the [illegible]" In T.-J. Yoon & D. Y. Jin (Eds.), *The Korean Wave: Evolution, fandom, and transnationality* (pp. [illegible]). Lexington Books.

[illegible]

[illegible]

Yun, K. S. [illegible]

Yoon, S. M. (2010). [illegible] analysis of Korean dramas [illegible]

[illegible]

YouTube [illegible]

[illegible]

Yu, [illegible] [illegible]

Zeng, W. [illegible]

Zhang, [illegible]

Index